CW00797334

The Tories and Ireland 1910–1914

Conservative Party Politics and the Home Rule Crisis

JEREMY SMITH

IRISH ACADEMIC PRESS
DUBLIN • PORTLAND, OR

First published in 2000 by
IRISH ACADEMIC PRESS
44, Northumberland Road,
Dublin 4, Ireland

and in the United States of America by
IRISH ACADEMIC PRESS
c/o ISBS, 5824 NE Hassalo Street,
Portland, OR 97213-3644

Website: www.iap.ie

Copyright © 2000 Jeremy Smith

British Library Cataloguing in Publication Data

Smith, Jeremy
The Tories and Ireland : Conservative Party politics and the home rule crisis, 1910–1914
1. Conservative Party – History 2. Great Britain – Politics and government – 1910–1936 3. Ireland – Politics and government – 1910–1921
I. Title
324.2'4104'09041

ISBN 0-7165-2696-4 (cloth)

Library of Congress Cataloging-in-Publication Data

Smith, Jeremy, 1965–
The Tories and Ireland : conservative party politics and the home rule crisis, 1910–1914 /Jeremy Smith.
p. cm.
Includes bibliographical references
ISBN 0-7165-2696-4 (hb)
1. Ireland–Politics and government–1910–1921. 2. Great Britain–Politics and government–1910–1936. 3. Conservatism–Great Britain–History–19th century. 4. Unionism (Irish politics)–History–20th century. 5. Tories, English–History–20th century. 6. Home rule–Ireland. 7. Irish question. I. Title.

DA960.S66.2000
320.9415'09'041–dc21 00-059808

All rights reserved. Without limiting the rights under copyright reserved alone, no part of this publication may be reproduced, stored in or introduced into a retrieval system, or transmitted, in any form or by any means (electronic, mechanical, photocopying, recording or otherwise), without the prior written permission of both the copyright owner and the above publisher of this book.

Typeset by Vitaset, Paddock Wood, Kent
Printed by
Creative Print and Design (Wales), Ebbw Vale

Contents

Acknowledgements

FOR ACCESS to various manuscript sources and permission to quote from them I would like to thank the following; the Earl of Balfour, Birmingham University Library, the Bodleian Library, the British Library, Churchill College Cambridge, the Earl of Crawford and Balcarres, the Earl of Derby, Durham Record Office, the Clerk of Records, House of Lords Record Office and the Beaverbrook Foundation, the Imperial War Museum and the National Army Museum, trustees of the National Library of Scotland, the Marquess of Londonderry, the Marquess of Lansdowne, the PRO of Northern Ireland, the Marquess of Salisbury, the Scottish Record Office and Lord Long of Wraxell.

I should like to thank Linda Longmore of Irish Academic Press for all her efficiency, help and indeed patience over a number of years and in the face of my technological ineptitude. I am also most grateful to several readers at IAP and elsewhere for their invaluable advice and encouragement. Friends and colleagues at a variety of teaching establishments have been (whether they know it or not) invaluable both to the success of this venture and to my own peace of mind. In particular, Felix Aubel, Quincy Adams, John Barnes, Peter Borsay, Tim Boyle, Bruce Coleman, Ian and Kate Davenport, David Dean, Pat Finney, Richard and Julie Greed, Alvin Jackson, Michael Kandiah, John Kirk, Peter Mandler, Malcolm Smith, Nev and Joan Stace, Andrew Thorpe and Graeme White. To Stuart Ball I owe a great debt for all his unswerving support over many years. And to my supervisor Alan Beattie the debt is perhaps too big to ever repay. His combination of deep knowledge, shrewd insight and playful cynicism has been stimulating. Though he will shudder at the traces of 'ideas' I have let into the account, this work owes a great deal to his inspiration. Finally, let me thank my parents for all their love and support. To Pud and Fred this work is dedicated as an inadequate recompense for all they have given me.

Jeremy Smith
University College Chester
July 2000

Introduction

DURING the thirty-seven years from the beginnings of the first Home Rule struggle in 1885 to the creation of the Irish Free State in 1921, the fortunes of the Conservative party have been intimately tied to the issue of Ireland. This association was one of high drama and intense politics, but no part of this long connection was more sensational than the period of the third Home Rule bill between 1912 and 1914. For it was during this struggle that the Tory Party – rather than see Ireland achieve self-governing status along similar lines to that of Canada, Australia and, since 1910, South Africa – appeared willing to eschew constitutional precedents, de-stabilise the British state, encourage civil disobedience, succour army mutiny and tolerate Ireland's slide into civil war with the very real danger of it spreading to mainland Britain. Sir Ian Gilmour has written of this period that the 'opposition was fractious, inflamed and under Arthur Balfour's successor, Andrew Bonar Law, unconstitutional. From 1905 to 1914 the Conservative Party in opposition betrayed itself and came close to betraying its country.'[1] The purpose of this work is to explain how and why these extraordinary events occurred. What was the thinking of the Tories? How did they justify their actions and what were they trying to achieve? Why, ultimately, did they pursue such extreme ends that were to have such momentous consequences for the future of Ireland?

The need for such a text, in an area already crowded with much excellent research, rests upon four justifications: to fill a gap in the existing literature, to offer a fresh understanding of the nature of the party in the period 1910 to 1914, to present a more rounded account of the various Unionist reactions to the introduction of Home Rule and to make a contribution to the increasingly popular notion of a crisis of conservatism. The first concerns the nature and structure of existing studies. What work there has been on the pre-war Tory struggle against Home Rule has tended to be short, taking the form of an academic article or as part of a wider general history of the party, or as an episode in a biographical sketch.[2] The limited extent of such studies, combined with the sheer complexity and intricacy of the crisis, have, necessarily, limited the depth of analysis and insight that is possible. Only, then, from a close detailed narrative of the Tory reaction to Home Rule can a full, deep comprehension of events be grasped, with all the shifting contours of individual competition and internal party bargaining. And only a detailed analysis can reconstruct the full multiplicity of tactical options pondered by the Unionist leaders at specific moments and the clear chain of action that flowed from these conclusions.

A second justification is that the current work seeks to offer fresh understandings about the nature of the Tory party and its ideological outlook between the election of January 1910 and Britain's entry into the war in August 1914. A problem with many of the existing studies is their tendency to reproduce certain assumptions concerning the actions and motivations of the party during the crisis over Home Rule. This was the result of a moderate, consensual political culture that impregnated much of mid-twentieth century Conservatism[3] and which translated itself into the historical research of the 1960s and 1970s. Within this consensual paradigm two views predominate. First, that the push by the Tory leadership towards extreme methods over Ireland came from intense pressure on them by Sir Edward Carson, leader of the Ulstermen, in alliance with certain die-hard individuals on the Tory backbenches. Such an understanding served to exonerate the vast majority of the party and leadership from having truly held an extreme stance against Home Rule, being instead simply deluded, beguiled or browbeaten by Sir Edward Carson, rather than fully committed to an unconstitutional stance. Or the party and leadership were casualties of poor direction from a necessarily weak, vacillating Bonar Law,[4] who failed to impose his own essentially moderate course upon them (despite his public rhetoric, Bonar Law is widely regarded as an adherent of partition), and instead was forced to pander to the extremists on his right wing.[5] 'I am their leader', Bonar Law reportedly told Asquith, 'I must follow them.' On both counts, the Conservative party was out of control and prey to dynamic sections. Second, what the bulk of the party and Bonar Law were *actually* engaged in was a pragmatic or theatrical extremism,[6] designed to elicit better terms from the Liberal government in the eventual compromise, those terms being the exclusion of all or part of Ulster. It was a form of scaremongering to improve the party's position when it came to the moment to make a deal. In other words beneath all the intemperate language and dire warnings generated by the struggle against Home Rule, much of the Conservative leadership and party operated on the basis of a normal party political contest, corresponding to the established (if slightly threadbare) rules of engagement as determined by parliamentary convention. Underneath all the sanguinary froth a fairly typical political game was still being played.

These two assumptions concerning the Tory reaction to Home Rule were entrenched by R. Blake's influential 1955 biography of Bonar Law and replicated in subsequent studies, particularly J. Ramsden's history of the party and J.D. Fair's study of inter-party conferences.[7] But as the post-war political consensus shattered by the 1980s, so new perspectives on the party's history emerged. Bruce Coleman, for example, has re-injected Toryism into the nineteenth-century party where the likes of Peel, Derby and Disraeli (never Salisbury) had begun to appear but pale imitations of Macmillanite Conservatives of the 1950s and 60s.[8] The essence of this work is also that the Conservative Party, in its struggle over Home Rule, was much more 'Tory' than 'conservative' in attitude and deed, and where the die-hard spirit was mainstream to their political outlook rather than marginal to it. The years after 1911 witnessed a Tory renaissance, a re-assertion of Salisburian negativism and a move against the modernising, reformist Chamberlainite tendencies, that had dominated the party since 1903, under the unlikely leadership of Bonar Law and Lord Lansdowne.

The Tory renaissance centred upon a defence of the Constitution, a cause that had animated Lord Salisbury during the 1880s and 1890s, in response to the growing power of the Executive over the Parliamentary system.[9] Salisbury argued the need for some type of check upon executive control of parliament, in the face of its remorseless growth in strength with the rise of mass parties, greater party discipline inside the House and government's increased control of the parliamentary timetable. Given the irreversible decline of the Crown, Salisbury looked to the House of Lords to perform such a 'checking' role, most spectacularly in rejecting Gladstone's second Home Rule bill by 419 votes to 41. Under Salisbury's successor, Arthur Balfour, the Lords were used to check a series of Liberal bills, between 1906 and 1909, despite a government majority in the Commons. A course of action that backfired disastrously in 1909 when the Lords rejected a government budget, opening the door to the removal of their veto powers with the Parliament Act of 1911.

Bonar Law absorbed these constitutional anxieties about an over-powerful executive and employed them in his resistance to Home Rule. Unfortunately, without the Lords' power of veto, Tories were denied all constitutional means of *guaranteeing* the government were checked; they could, of course, still protest, table amendments, scrutinise bills, delay and disrupt, but with no certainty of success. To replace the Lords, Bonar Law now looked to the concept of a popular mandate as a checking mechanism and demanded that Extraordinary legislation (bills, such as Home Rule, that altered the constitution) receive the people's blessing before passage.[10] The notion of a popular mandate was not a new development and to some extent emerged from a wide-ranging discussion within Tory circles about the merits of a referendum, during 1910–11. In short, Bonar Law sought to obstruct an over-powerful executive, by requesting Home Rule be first put before the people in the form of a general election and if the government refused, having the justification to indulge in all manner of behaviour to resist it, even unconstitutional methods.

At a broader level we might make several observations. Bonar Law and the Tory leadership's resistance to Home Rule was located in a unique moment in the constitutional history of this country, a point when a bi-cameral parliamentary system gave way to a uni-cameral[11] one, and before the type of widespread governmental powers, controls and influence, that would characterise the twentieth century, became established and accepted.[12] In addition, these concerns about checks upon a government were, in the long run, to prove correct, but given the Tory dominance of the executive throughout much of the twentieth century, they found few champions within the party. Not until Lord Hailsham's famous speech in 1976 warning of an elective dictatorship was this issue revived, against the backdrop of another unchecked 'socialist' ministry endangering national interests; although again this was quickly subsumed by eighteen years of strong, centralising government under Margaret Thatcher and John Major.

Apart from constitutional arguments the Tory renaissance was also evident in a certain political resolution and hardness whereby many Unionists were willing to resist Home Rule in extreme terms and to see the struggle through to the bitter end, even if this entailed civil war in Ireland. This militancy kept the Conservative Party and their Irish Unionist allies together notwithstanding their differences of opinion and the degree to which it pushed the British Constitution and state to the brink of collapse. This, what we might term, 'move to the right' was the product of miscellany of determinants. These included an awareness of the party's continuing electoral weakness, with three election defeats on the trot, scant future prospects for exciting policy initiatives, the growth of grass-roots disenchantment within the party, rising Imperial tensions, radical

Liberal legislation over finance and the government's subversion of the Constitution with the Parliament Act of 1911. But a key influence was the leader of the party in the Commons after 1911, Bonar Law.

Emphasis on the importance of Bonar Law is an attempt to reverse the historiographical neglect of a politician who still resides under Asquith's tart sobriquet as the 'unknown Prime Minister'.[13] During the Ulster crisis Bonar Law was a more resolute and determined Tory leader than he is often characterised as. He was a leader who was able to impose an extreme and dangerous strategy towards Home Rule onto the party, nullifying alternative causes from acquiring ascendancy within the party, such as land issues or social policy. Yet, unlike other interpretations, this work argues that Bonar Law sponsored an extreme course over Home Rule less because of his Presbyterian background or family connections to Ulster or as a tactic to incorporate some form of exclusion for Ulster in the final settlement, but in order to thrust the Liberal government to an election and, hopefully remove them from office. Bonar Law was never an exclusionist. His professed sympathy for it, at certain moments, was to maintain a public image of responsibility. Exclusion was also something he might well be forced to accept if the Ulstermen reached an agreement with the government and even as a technique for maintaining Ulster Unionist support during a tense phase of the crisis. But he was never an enthusiast for it. We might also include here Lord Lansdowne, the leader in the Lords, who despite his image as a reasonable Whig (the man who called for peace in 1917) pursued a hard-line and far from consensual approach to Ireland. In particular, it was Lansdowne who helped scupper attempts to reach a compromise upon the basis of the partition of Ireland, in the autumn of 1913 and again in February / March 1914.

A third justification for this work is that it presents a more rounded and 'total' picture of the Unionist reaction to Home Rule than previous studies. Much excellent research has already been done on individual parts of the Unionist alliance. A.T.Q. Stewart, A. Jackson and P. Bew, have all explored developments within Ulster Unionism,[14] revealing the period 1912–14 as one central to the construction of a modern Ulster identity and a fully independent political organisation. P. Buckland has investigated the development of Irish Unionism and the relations (often discordant) between its Ulster and Southern Unionist wings.[15] Amongst Tories, while the moderates – that silent majority that followed fashion and the leadership – remain the unresearched backbone of the Tory party, other component parts have received attention. The die-hard sections have had extensive historical treatment, far in excess of their numbers and importance.[16] Federalism, both in the Tory party and as a wider movement has also found its historians.[17] Less attention, however, has been focused on the totality of all the Unionist groups and the complex interplay and cross currents that embraced southern Irish Unionists and Ulster Unionists alongside Tory die-hards, federalists or devolutionists and moderates. Unionism was, after all, a wide coalition of diverse opinions, values and strategies. As with any coalition forward motion could only come as the result of internal mediation between the various strands. It is this mediation, and how it conditioned the direction and policy of the Unionist leadership, that the study will re-construct, and from which a more complete understanding of Unionist resistance in the years 1910 to 1914 will emerge. Such an integrative analysis can reveal many things. For example the bitter points of friction between Conservative federalists and the Ulstermen, despite a common desire, by 1914, to reach a political solution. Also the subtle differences between Bonar Law's position and that of the Ulstermen, and how they influenced both their rhetoric and tactics. The growing co-operation of Tory die-hards and Southern Unionists, by early 1914, that helped obstruct eleventh-hour attempts to partition Ireland. The process of estrangement between Southern and Ulster Unionism and the increasingly precarious position of Sir Edward Carson perched between them. And, ultimately, how all of these strands impacted upon each other to shape the Unionist response to Home Rule.

Two important conclusions stand out from such an examination of the relations between the various parts of the Unionist coalition. First, that the Ulster crisis was, to a greater extent than previously thought, manufactured by the Conservative leadership. Conservative leaders chose to make the issue of Ulster an acute political problem, after 1912, for English domestic electoral reasons. The intention was to force the government into an election upon an issue with which Tories believed they could sweep the country and so return them to office. To achieve this their leaders engaged in extreme rhetoric, personal abuse, they legitimated and sanctioned recourse to armed resistance, and attempted all manner of parliamentary trickery. They also encouraged King George V to enter the political game, interfered with the loyalty of the army and raised funds to help build a paramilitary force in Ireland. More dramatically, they actively thwarted any settlement of the Irish issue, either along federal lines or around the exclusion of Ulster, sponsored by Carson and the Ulstermen from 1913 onwards, that could well have formed the basis of an agreement with Asquith. In other words, the Tory leadership resisted *closure* to the Home Rule crisis, deliberately perpetuating the imbroglio until the government caved in and granted an election. Indeed, Bonar Law's choice to fight Home Rule on constitutional grounds and demand an election, made a settlement more difficult because it shifted attention from the specific details of the bill, where a compromise could be brokered, onto more open-ended and abstract questions about the legality of the bill itself.

Secondly, drawing upon the assumptions underlying recent work on the nature of popular political mobilisation and the importance to it of linguistic, rhetorical strategies,[18] it is implicit here that the rhetoric and political posturing of Conservative leaders, particularly Bonar Law, played an important role in activating and sustaining the Ulster rebellion. Taken in conjunction with the expertly orchestrated street theatre and theatricality of leading Ulster Unionists, revolving around the construction of a saviour-figure of Sir Edward Carson,[19] the Ulster crisis emerges as more the contingent result of Unionist rhetoric and thus electoral and domestic political calculation, than of more structural determinants, such as religious, sectarian and economic differences. In this sense Ulster as a block to Irish Home Rule was *constructed* and *invented* by the politicians, rather than springing naturally or inevitably, according to Marxist perspectives, from the cultural and economic differences of the north eastern counties of Ireland. These assumptions challenge an emphasis in much historiography that connects the inexorable onward march of Ulster to inbedded, deep-rooted structural factors, a representation that derives sustenance from an image of Ulster Protestants as strong, dominant and able to 'set the agenda' in British politics, whether it be the 1973–75 strike or resistance to the Anglo-Irish Agreement in 1985. They also draw upon recent re-workings of Ulster Unionism, concerning its nature and relative strength and unity. A highly suggestive article by A. Jackson indicates certain difficulties and dilemmas confronting Ulster's campaign to resist Home Rule before 1914, views endorsed by M. Foy in a valuable study of the Ulster Volunteer Force.[20] From a different direction, A. Jackson and A. Gailey have shown the degree to which Carson was a manufactured leader, emphasising the importance of propaganda, rhetoric and image in an age of growing political democratisation.[21] They also suggest Carson was a neurotic character, desperately keen to reach a political settlement and acutely aware of the fissures within the Ulster movement. And P. Bew's excellent recent study of the Home Rule struggle has suggested a more heterogeneous movement, comprised of temperate even consensual opinions while displaying a strong sense of insecurity and self-doubt.

Lastly, this work seeks to make a contribution within an unfurling debate about the predicament in which the Edwardian Unionist party found itself in. Several outstanding studies have addressed themselves to the general difficulties the party encountered adjusting to the advance of democracy early in the twentieth century.[22] Finding a fresh and appealing voice in an increasingly open political system was no easy matter and the pains encountered in this operation have led some to conceive of a general crisis of Conservatism.[23] This was a crisis that revolved around party disunity, parliamentary weakness, ideological confusion, threats to the Empire, a shrinking socio-economic power base, an inability to formulate popular policies and a powerlessness to break the Liberal–Labour electoral stranglehold. This combination of factors left the Unionist alliance prone to fragmentation and facing the prospect of collapse, if not permanent opposition; a return to the party's self imposed mid-Victorian minority status. This study has relevance for the idea of a crisis of conservatism by suggesting that at the core of the Conservative leaderships' hard-line resistance to Home Rule lay a response to the prospect of permanent opposition. With the failure of other 'regenerative' strategies by 1911–12, such as Tariff Reform, naval scares, government corruption and reform of the second chamber, the struggle over Home Rule was a course of action that could offer the possibility of a revival of the Unionist party's electoral fortunes. Only by viewing the struggle over Home Rule as a method to revitalise the party can we understand the degree of extremism Bonar Law was willing to contemplate on an issue which, frankly, many Tories regarded as 'a dead quarrel for which neither the country nor the party cares a damn'.[24] After all, Ireland by 1912 was a very different place to 1886 or 1893, much of it at the hands of Unionists themselves, and reflected in the willingness of some Unionists in 1903 to contemplate a form of devolved government. In addition, few of the younger Tories, who entered the Commons for the first time in 1910, had either recollections of, or interest in, repeating the struggles of the 1880s. A passivity that echoed the acute lack of public concern with the issue; indeed for much of the period 1911–14, National Insurance was a question of far more vitality than Home Rule. In light of these observations the need for a close, detailed study of the Tory campaign against Home Rule becomes even more pressing.

METHOD

This book has been organised into seven chapters, running from January 1910 through until the suspension of normal party-political conflict, in August 1914, as a result of the outbreak of war. Each chapter starts with a short survey of affairs in order to set the examination upon a firm chronological bed. To make the analysis more accessible, events have been interpreted through the imposition of several categories; these conform to the various strands of the Unionist coalition and to the categories frequently used in much of the existing historiography. These include Tory die-hards, Southern Irish Unionists, Ulster Unionists, Federalists or devolutionists and moderates.[25] Sometimes more general labels will be used where circumstances demand. Conservative or Tory will denote non-Irish Unionists while Irish Unionism will refer to both Southern and Ulster (but not British) Unionists. The 'right' or 'traditionalist' will signal a die-hard trait whether from the Conservative, Ulster or Southern Unionist quarter whereas 'constructive' will designate a general proclivity towards devolutionary solutions from any section of the Unionist alliance. And though federalists and devolutionists will be analysed in the same section of each chapter they represent slightly differing views of a similarly constructive outlook.

Like all such impositions the labels used here never entirely capture the variety of political shades that make up a party nor the shifting concerns of politicians. They are always artificial, imposed by the historian onto an otherwise chaotic situation, in pursuit of 'meaningful totalities' or cognitive order.[26] Carson, for example, clearly found support from the die-hard and Irish Unionist wings, yet by late 1913 was recognised as a possible federalist and even won the sympathy of moderate sections, when he advocated exclusion. Similarly Lansdowne, was seen by some as a force for moderation, yet was amongst the more zealous defenders of Southern Unionist interests and a keen devolutionist. Classifications never calibrate with any degree of precision and should be perceived as fluid; within themselves they contain a spectrum of varying grades and definitions; whilst individuals may float from one to the other or may span several at any one moment.

However, interpreting the Unionist party as a coalition of groups, each one centred around a specific agenda, a set of ideas or even just a particular mentality, raises serious methodological implications. It implies that politicians are simply reflections of the ideological substratums from which they emerge, draw the support of or believe to be their particular niche. Politicians, in other words, are merely the embodiments of the various ideological or personal baggage they bring with them or are seen to inhabit in politics, be they group loyalties, friendship, personal dislikes, filial inheritances, reputations, felt rules and assumptions or even genuine social concerns. Yet this denies them more human qualities around which a high-political methodology is positioned, namely ambition and the pursuit of power for its own sake. Personal baggage also denies politicians independence and width, the protean quality which is the politicians' essence in such a parliamentary setting that requires them to demonstrate the ability to adjust, change, re-orientate, mutate, adopt and discard. These qualities are inevitable in a political setting that is continuously fluctuating and even the most narrow of politicians (in the sense of one who is ideological or sincere and who enters this setting with a single professed aim) still has to play by the established rules; and will therefore have to compromise, react and alter.[27] There is, then, a tension between what the politician is and what the politician does; between the private and the public.

Different historians have approached this dialectic in different ways, from M. Cowling, doyen of the high-political school, who would deny the role of such baggage completely through to political biographers who show baggage as all-important.[28] The present study, though clearly high-political, has sought a degree of balance, to bridge what a politician *is* to what they *do*, combining an appreciation of the prejudices of high politics with a recognition that politics might be more than simply the sum of various tactical options. It fuses the mobilising and motivating potential of ideas, within a parliamentary setting guided by high political presuppositions. Nor does this work claim to be the last word; it merely presents one representation of events without denying that those same events will and should dance to other tunes.

TORIES, UNIONISTS AND IRELAND BEFORE 1910

Toryism, as it evolved during the late eighteenth and early nineteenth centuries, stood for law and order, upholding the Anglican church, the inviolability of private property, a defence of the existing social order, the authority of the Crown and an obsession with national security. Ireland challenged (and in so doing helped to clarify) these strongly held principles and emotional attachments. Tories perceived it as a deeply backward society, where lawlessness was rife, where rural crime at the hands of secret societies was endemic, where the population was torn apart by religious and class differences and where the majority of the ordinary people were held under clerical sway. Moreover, they believed the Irish were a 'naturally' disloyal people, born of the survival of Catholicism amongst three-quarters of her population which connected her to Britain's traditional enemy, France, and so, for Tories, was a constant threat to national security and her imperial possessions. This was all the more worrying since those same 'disloyal' Irish people represented about a third of the total population of the United Kingdom.[29]

Events in Ireland during the 1790s reinforced these Tory prejudices. Here against a backdrop of Britain's war with France rebellion broke out across Ireland. As a result thousands died in sectarian bloodshed, the Anglican Church was endangered, landowners were attacked, republican revolutionaries threatened the connection with Britain, and French troops landed in Ireland in 1796 and again in 1798, hoping to drum up local support against the British. It was clear, or so it appeared to Tories, that Ireland was too unreliable to ignore and geographically too close to remain unconnected. And since her semi-independent Parliament, instituted in 1782, could not guarantee Britain's territorial security, Ireland had to be controlled from the mainland. To this end William Pitt passed the Act of Union in 1801, integrating Ireland into the British parliamentary system.

The Act of Union was the constitutional structure by which stability for Ireland could be maintained, for only a stable Ireland would guarantee the security of the United Kingdom. For Tories, stabilising Ireland under the Union meant the fortification and protection of those institutions deemed essential to an ordered society. Accordingly, the Anglican Church in Ireland was strengthened by combining it with the Church in Britain, creating a wider British 'Pan-Protestant alliance'; an alliance which even the dissenting Presbyterians of north-east Ulster could participate in. The status and economic position of the Protestant landowning élite was maintained via entry into the British economic and parliamentary systems. And private property was vigorously upheld by reinforcing the forces of law and order, against agrarian crime and in a country 'thick' with secret societies and banditry. Under the chief secretary Robert Peel (1812–18), a system of coercive instruments and legal innovations were introduced into Irish law. Certain pragmatic Tories also believed that stabilisation could be achieved by reform under the Union, whether from economic investment or the gradual abolition of 'abuses', particularly if those abuses continued to alienate certain groups from British rule. Peel went far to appease Irish Catholic sentiment. In 1829 he steered Catholic Emancipation through the House of Commons, against much of his party and his own predilections. Later, during his 1841–46 ministry, he introduced the Charitable Bequests Act and increased the state grant to the Catholic seminary of Maynooth. Clearly, then, a strain of Toryism believed Union carried a Christian obligation to bring justice as well as order to Ireland, and to alleviate legitimate grievances. But all Tories, whether of a defensive or 'accomodationist' outlook, regarded Union as a vital mechanism by which stable government and social discipline were to be entrenched in Ireland. And attacks on the Union during the nineteenth century, whether from the Repeal politics of Daniel O'Connell, or from the separatist Young Ireland movement or from the Fenians with their commitment to physical force, were seen as attacks on the very basis of civilisation.

By the last quarter of the nineteenth century, the Act of Union began to take on broader, representative qualities for many Tories. This was partly the result of Disraeli sharpening the ideological basis of Toryism by firmly attaching the party to 'Nation and Empire', the latter overlapping with an admiration for the Union. A broadening appeal for Union also emerged from the growing strains in the British economy and society. Strains that included the 'rediscovery' of poverty, the growth of long-term unemployment, the rise of working-class politics with the expansion of trades unions, and an agricultural depression with the concomitant spread of radical ideas for land redistribution. The last development was most evident in Ireland with the outbreak of the Land War in 1879. Furthermore, it was an environment where Britain faced mounting imperial competition from the Great Powers and rising colonial nationalism, not least in Ireland with the emergence of the Home Government Association in 1870. In such a menacing atmosphere the Union became an emblem for the wider defence of traditional society across the whole of the United Kingdom. With multiple threats to established authority and pressures upon the existing social order, Union provided an attractive symbol of fixity and permanence. This was a representation that also resonated with the instincts and priorities of Lord Salisbury, the emerging leader of the Tories who would dominate the party during the last two decades of the nineteenth century. But the broadening definition of the Union owed most to the transformation in the party political struggle following Gladstone's conversion to Home

Rule late in 1885, and the domestic electoral advantages Tories perceived in raising the banner of Unionism.

Unionism, as both an ideological construct and a practical coalition of various political groups, emerged as a powerful political force in the period between the election of November 1885 and the election of July 1886, which returned for the first time a 'Unionist' majority. As a political alliance, it was Gladstone's conversion to Home Rule, late in 1885, and his subsequent introduction of a bill on 8 April 1886, that brought together a varied mix of politicians dedicated to the preservation of the Act of Union in its existing form.[30] In addition to British Tories, the mix comprised of two further groups. Firstly, there was a sizeable Liberal faction (Liberal Unionists) led by Lord Hartington and Joseph Chamberlain, whose hostility to Home Rule led to a split with Gladstone early in 1886. Secondly there were the Irish Unionists who had emerged out of Irish Toryism during the late 1870s as a parliamentary ginger group to monitor specifically Irish issues, particularly Church ones, and to prevent backsliding or compromises by the Tory leadership.[31] It was also as a response to the enhanced position of Parnellite Nationalism from 1880 onwards and especially after the 1885 election. Yet under the banner of Irish Unionism, different regional and cultural identities existed that would become more distinct in the future. These included a southern, Protestant land-owning section, who, although weak in terms of parliamentary representation, remained economically powerful and were well represented in the House of Lords and organised at a constituency level through the Irish Loyal and Patriotic Union. Finally, there was an Ulster Unionist strain, which was increasingly well marshalled behind the leadership of Colonel Edward Saunderson and groups such as the Ulster Loyal Union and Orange Order, which organised support amongst the Presbyterians of north east Ulster.[32]

This unwieldy Unionist alliance was cemented, on 8 June 1886, when it combined to defeat Gladstone's Home Rule bill on second reading, and at the general election that followed in July when the various groups formed an electoral pact to successfully challenge Gladstonian Liberals and Parnellite Home Rulers. The results, with 394 Unionist MPs elected (298 Tories, 19 Irish Unionists and 77 Liberal Unionists) against 276 Home Rulers (191 Gladstonians plus 85 Parnellites), brought to power a Unionist ministry under Lord Salisbury (though only Tories served in cabinet) which would dominate British government for the next twenty years.

Electoral success established the Union as an appeal that could mobilise a broad and diverse range of voters (although a closer look at the Tory election victory of 1886 would suggest Liberal abstention was a more significant factor than any popular swing behind Unionism). The effectiveness of that appeal owed much to the combination of representations that had been associated with cause of the Union since the 1870s. Namely, the preservation of imperial unity, national security, upholding private property and the existing social order, protection of the established Church, and a defence of traditional society. And in a political environment shaped by trades union militancy, socialist activity, radical Chamberlainite policies, imperial conflict (even weakness after the recent murder of General Gordon), rising republicanism and religious decline, the Union was a powerful totem for stability and tradition. As such, Unionists were able to repeat their electoral success in the 1895 and 1900 elections (though not in the 1892 election, while it is important to remember the election of 1900 turned as much upon recent events in South Africa). Ironically, perhaps, the appeal of Unionism was less successful in Ireland where from a pool of 103 Irish seats, Unionists never won more than 23 (at the 1892 election), the overwhelming majority of which were centred in north-east Ulster. Clearly, then, the defence of the Union was heavily reliant upon British Unionism and the political state of affairs on the mainland.

However, relying upon British Unionism was never straightforward. For although British Tories professed loyalty to the cause and had constructed a powerful political appeal in the Union, Irish Unionists were well aware that tactical and electoral calculations remained a priority for Tories. Tories had already shown a willingness to 'desert' their Irish comrades and 'endanger' the Union. Salisbury's agreement with Gladstone over the Franchise and Redistribution Acts of 1884–85, in strengthening Parnellite Nationalism at the expense of Irish Tories, was seen as a betrayal of Loyalism in Ireland.[33] Similarly, during Salisbury's minority government (June 1885 to January 1886), the quest for a secure Commons majority had led the Tory Viceroy, the Earl of Carnarvon, to open negotiations with Parnell, along the lines of local government or 'attenuated Home Rule'.[34] Even Lord Randolph Churchill, before 'playing the Orange card', in February 1886, when he declared that 'Ulster will fight and Ulster will be right', had earlier in 1885 struggled hard to appease Irish Nationalists in parliament.[35] The potential for Tory treachery (Liberals were already guilty by their commitment to Home Rule in 1885) was never far from the mind of Irish Unionists and bred suspicion between them. This distrust perhaps explains why Irish Unionists established a variety of associations in Ireland dedicated to winning popular support for the Union.

Nor were relations helped by the obvious dissimilarities between the various components of the Unionist alliance. This was particularly the case with Ulster Unionists, whose religious and cultural roots were very different to the Tory party's. On the other hand, with an average of twenty seats and considerable influence in the House of Lords (greater than their numbers would suggest), Irish Unionists could also be a source of annoyance and embarrassment for any Tory government.[36] Salisbury could not afford to ignore their concerns. Moreover, Tories and Liberal Unionists had little in common apart from an anti-Home Rule stance and were often at loggerheads, as in the period leading up to the 1892 election. Even amongst Liberal Unionists, composed of such different spirits as Chamberlain and Lord Hartington, divisions were a fact of life. Similarly, strains within Irish Unionism were increasingly perceptible, especially as Ulster Unionism grew more assertive, the result of its parliamentary dominance within Irish Unionism and the political strength it drew from a regional concentration of its support. It was clear, then, that the Unionist alliance was an unstable and fractious coalition, which without the 'threat' of Home Rule was always liable to fragment. This became more acute from 1895 onwards, when other 'threats' were removed; these included the retirement of Gladstone in 1894; splits in the Nationalist party as revealed during the 1895 election; and Liberals shelving their pledge to Home Rule. In a twenty-year period when Tories dominated government, only the brief periods of 1885–86 and 1893–94, when Gladstone introduced a second Home Rule bill that was defeated in the Lords, were moments of real strength in the Unionist alliance.

Strains within Unionism became particularly acute when in government, as they were from 1886 to 1892 and again from 1895 to 1905. Office brought with it the responsibility for administering Ireland, an obligation that required something more than just defending the Union. Whereas in opposition a simple commitment to defend the Union was sufficient, in government a 'positive, imaginative, progressive yet respectable approach' was necessary.[37] Union also had to be demonstrably effective and viable, to counter claims by Nationalists and Liberals that it was unworkable and in need of reform.[38] This was particularly true after 1895 when the Liberal commitment to Home Rule was shelved, so changing the context in which Irish questions were considered at Westminster. Thus in Salisbury's Cabinet the initiative shifted away from defensive Unionists towards more progressive ones. While under a series of Tory Irish chief secretaries, Sir Michael Hicks Beach (1886–87), Arthur Balfour (1887–91), his brother

Gerald Balfour (1895–1900), and finally George Wyndham (1900–05), Tory administration in Ireland gravitated towards a more accomodationist line that echoed Peel's earlier administration and even Salisbury's brief ministry of 1885–86. It combined financial investment and economic revitalisation with a firm commitment to upholding law and order. Tory defence of the Union was re-packaged as imaginative administration and economic improvement. This included several Land Acts in 1887, 1888, 1891 and Wyndham's 1903 Act.[39] A Light Railways and Technical Instruction Act in 1889, a Congested Districts Board Act in 1891 and an Agricultural and Technical Instruction Act in 1899. Finally, in 1898, a Local Government Act that brought county councils to Ireland and in the process gave over the local governance of much of Ireland to the Nationalist party. Alongside reform, Balfour strengthened the legal system with the Criminal Law and Procedure Bill in 1887 and pressed magistrates to exert the full rigour of the law against rural crime. This policy amalgam of reform and order, what historians once referred to as 'killing Home Rule with kindness', was in fact a much more pragmatic, even rather chaotic, response to political events than such a rationally crafted description would suggest.[40]

The various reforms, though arguably of great value to Ireland, injected further discordance into the Unionist alliance, to such an extent that by the Chief Secretaryship of George Wyndham the coalition was 'near collapse'.[41] Liberal Unionists, though generally appeased by the positive direction of Irish policy, were angered by the recourse to coercion and incidents such as the Mitchelstown 'massacre' in 1887. For many Irish Unionists, as well as Tories of a more defensive inclination (the traditional or right wing of the party), flexibility and impartiality by a Tory government smacked of gradual retreat and weakness. Ulster Unionists saw killing Home Rule with kindness as misplaced and liable to invigorate Nationalism, not pacify it. As a result they continued to develop their own organisations (always a sign of their suspicion) with the creation of the Ulster Convention in 1892. And in the process they acquired a little more of that independent identity that would be such a feature of the 1910–14 period. Southern Unionists were infuriated by the actual details of legislation rather than just alarmed by what they symbolised. For example, the Irish Local Government Act opened the door to Nationalist control of administration of the countryside and under-cut any residual political power and authority the old landlord class may have possessed. More alarming, the 1903 Land Act which in extending the provisions and resources of previous land purchase schemes, effectively began the final transfer of land from a predominantly Unionist landlord class to the Nationalist inclined Irish tenant farmers. It seemed that outside of Ulster, the economic and political base of Unionism was being destroyed, and at the hands of a Tory government! These changes, in turn, encouraged a general questioning of what Unionism now stood for? If land purchase and the Local Government Act were undermining the central Tory objectives of maintaining private property and social stability in Ireland, what (or who) was Union upholding? If the Protestant landed elite was now being 'wound up' (the Irish Church had already been disestablished in 1869) what was the Union to defend? What did the Union now mean, particularly for Tories? What was it there to protect? And were there now alternatives to Union?

This general questioning of Unionism reflected wider changes in the politics of the period 1900–04 which suggested old style Unionism was a thing of the past. A fresh and positive disposition towards imperial problems had emerged. The successful federation of Australia in 1900 raised the profile of progressive imperial reconstruction. A sentiment reiterated at the 1902 Colonial conference where an emphasis upon imperial co-operation and reciprocal connections replaced an older imperial attitude of power and authority. Amongst Nationalists, a more consensual approach emerged under the leadership of John Redmond and William O'Brien, whose new inclusive brand of nationalism sought self-rule through agreement with all Ireland's peoples.[42] This emphasis upon agreement and consensus found expression in an All-Irish Land Conference, formed in 1902, which sought a compromise to the land question and provided the momentum upon which Wyndham introduced his radical Land Act of 1903. Furthermore, the Irish Reform Association, founded in 1904 to investigate further possible reforms for Ireland, particularly political ones, and composed of Nationalists and progressive Irish Unionists, such as Lord Dunraven. Last, the Liberal party, having sidelined its commitment to Home Rule, was intent upon a more gradual 'step by step' approach to settle Irish differences. It appeared new forces were emerging in politics that looked beyond the 'stale' debates over the Union of the 1880s and towards a new, harmonious and constructive path for Anglo-Irish affairs.

Nowhere were those 'new forces' more in evidence than in the Tory party during the early years of the twentieth century, with the spread of a constructive ideology based around tariff reform. This was a policy that aimed, through a system of duties on foreign trade, to modernise the British economy and to strengthen the Empire through economic integration and preferential tariffs. Its attraction for many Tories, after it was launched by Joseph Chamberlain in May 1903, lay in its ability to respond to the challenges of the new century, particularly electoral ones, in a way that defence of the Union did not. These challenges had become acute following a string of by-election losses during 1902–03, an erosion in the Unionist electoral position that was blamed upon growing public disinterestedness in Irish affairs, mixed with a rise of new political issues, such as welfare provision, the incidence of poverty and levels of taxation. For some Tories, by the early 1900s, the Union had lost its electoral purchase.

Moreover, the constructive and modernising impulse behind Tariff Reform encouraged its enthusiasts to seek a more 'modern' approach to the problem of imperial organisation. From this it was but a small step to embrace a federal system of government as a structure that might marry colonial aspirations for self-rule with a grander imperial vision.[43] Applied to Ireland, constructive Tories saw it the means to transform her into a stable and loyal member of the British Empire, reconstituting the Union into a more balanced relationship based upon good will, co-operation and shared values. Given these developments within the Tory party it was clear, by the early 1900s, that Unionism was a very different creature to that of the mid 1880s. The various defensive representations, that had been projected onto the Union and which had resonated closely with the more menacing atmosphere of the 1880s, were of less purchase in the 'constructive' atmosphere of the new century. Solid defence of Union appeared out of date, if not irrelevant to the electoral and political needs of the Tory party.

All these tensions and re-definitions within Unionism came to a head in 1904–5 with the Devolution affair,[44] a curious episode that implicated the Irish chief secretary, George Wyndham, and his permanent secretary, Sir Antony MacDonnell, in a scheme to introduce devolved government to Ireland. The affair, far from being a plot to introduce Home Rule by the back door, was more the product of poor communication and insufficient checks on an independently minded permanent secretary. However, as we have already seen, the episode occurred against a background of growing disenchantment with the traditional stance on the Union and the spread of devolutionist ideas amongst Tories. In addition, many regarded devolved government as the logical consequence to the Tory economic reforms of the 1890s, and a necessary response to the positive, constructive spirit so evident in Irish political circles, circles that included the Irish Reform Association, with its Southern Unionist leadership and moderate Nationalists such as William O'Brien.

Unfortunately, talk of devolving power to a Catholic-dominated, Dublin-based government shattered the Unionist alliance. Ulstermen, Tory die-hards and the vast majority of Southern Irish Unionists were filled with alarm. For these groups, devolution (or indeed federalism) appeared to be little more than Home Rule by stealth, with its promoters if not openly treacherous then seriously misguided. The Ulstermen reacted hysterically to what appeared to be a Tory government moving towards a devolved, federal structure. Early in 1905 they launched a bitter assault on Wyndham, effectively ending his career in March, and pressured hard for the resignation of his permanent secretary, Sir Antony MacDonnell, who was suspected all along of being a traitor. The affair confirmed what Ulstermen had long suspected, namely that the Tory party was an untrustworthy ally whose commitment to the Union was contingent upon political and electoral considerations. The conclusion they drew was that only constant vigilance by Irish Unionists in the future would keep Tories up to the mark. To this end, and in an effort to raise the profile of the Union amongst the Tory leadership, they elected Walter Long, a well-connected and fervently pro-Union English squire who had replaced Wyndham at the Irish Office, to the chairmanship of their party.[45] Also the Ulstermen, much the most suspicious of Irish Unionists, restructured their local power base by creating the Ulster Unionist Council in 1905. This enabled them to control and mobilise support more effectively, independent of Westminster and against local challenges to their authority.[46] If, then, Home Rule were to come by stealth at some point in the future, it would not catch them unprepared. This dual approach of the Ulstermen in bolstering their political position in Ulster, while strengthening their influence in Tory circles at Westminster prefigured their tactics from 1910 onwards. The Devolution affair also left Tories feeling bruised and bitter, leaving their relations with Ulster Unionists sour for some time. Ruptures in the Unionist alliance played a significant part in further destabilising Balfour's already tottering government, and contributed to their catastrophic defeat in the 1906 general election. The party, many Tories believed, had paid a heavy price for 'Orange' bigotry. Many also assumed that their collapse at the 1906 election was clear proof that the party needed a new, fresh, constructive appeal for the new century, with old dead 'quarrels' pushed to the side.

Several developments kept relations between Irish Unionists and Tories frosty in the period of Liberal government from 1905–10. One source of continuing Unionist friction was the Liberal commitment to a 'step-by-step' approach to satisfying Irish demands for self-rule. By not introducing a Home Rule bill, despite their massive majority at the 1906 election, they gave the Unionist alliance no 'threat' to rally around, in the same way as in 1893–94. Thus the divisions and mistrust of the period 1904–05 lingered just beneath the surface of the Unionist alliance. A second cause of friction was the slump in Tory seats, to just 156, that emptied the party of much of its 'deadwood', which diluted the more traditional, pro-Union sentiment and shifted the party balance in the direction of young, constructive Unionists. Unionists whom the political crisis of the mid-1880s had little meaning and who showed more concern for Tariff Reform and Imperial reorganisation than with the old Salisburian defence of the Union. As such, during 1906–10 Home Rule and the Union were distinctive in British politics only by their absence.

The fall in Unionist representation at the 1906 election, brought other problems for the Tory leadership. With only 156 MPs, Tories could offer very little 'real' opposition, forcing them to fall back upon the veto powers of the House of Lords as the means to resist the legislation of an all-powerful Liberal Executive. But front-line party political service was not a role the Lords were either used to or particularly relished in an age of growing democracy, rendering them vulnerable to attack when forced to act. Yet rather than keep its powder dry for guillotining a future Home Rule Bill, the Lords under Lord Lansdowne's guidance hacked at a larger, if skilfully chosen, quarry of Liberal legislation between 1906–09, so, incrementally, jeopardising their veto powers. This held many dangers. For if the Lords were to lose their power of veto, as Nationalists and Liberals were demanding, then nothing, in terms of institutional blocks, stood in the way of a future Liberal government granting Home Rule to Ireland. Despite these consequences, in 1909 the House of Lords, enraged at what they regarded as unconstitutional behaviour by the chancellor of the exchequer, Lloyd George, rejected the Budget and provoked an election in January 1910 upon the removal of the Lords veto powers. The prospect of this thrust Ireland back to the centre of British politics.

Jeremy Smith
Manorbier
April 1999

CHAPTER ONE

Ireland and Unionist politics, 1910–12

INTRODUCTION

THE GENERAL election of January 1910 thrust Ireland back to the forefront of party political controversy by bestowing upon the returning eighty-two Irish Nationalists the balance of power within the House of Commons, what McNeill saw as 'a wonderful windfall'.[1] The parliamentary arithmetic, of 273 Unionists counterbalancing 275 Liberals (plus forty MPs for Labour), enabled Nationalists to extract from Asquith, the Liberal prime minister, a Common's resolution on 16 April promising to suspend the Lords' power of veto. Ever since the Lords had destroyed the second Home Rule bill in 1893, the removal of their veto powers had been a vital pre-requisite for attaining Home Rule.

Asquith initially sought a less radical solution to the Lords question by inviting Unionist leaders into a conference upon reform of the Constitution. The conference first met in June and held twenty meetings throughout the summer and autumn of 1910, but was unable to reach agreement, principally because of differences over the future for Ireland. These were always likely, given the revived fortunes of the Irish Nationalist party and the likelihood of a third Home Rule bill following on from the removal of the Lords veto. To keep the conference going and overcome this disagreement, Lloyd George proposed its reconstitution as a coalition government,[2] whose first reform would be the federation of the UK, to remove the 'Irish incubus' from British politics once and for all. The proposal attracted support from Tory devolutionists, who pressed their leader, Arthur Balfour, to accept. Unfortunately it outraged traditional Tories and Irish Unionists, alarmed at what they imagined was a betrayal of loyalists in Ireland. Balfour, sensitive to these opinions, drew back from the tantalising offer, so bringing the conference to an end and forcing Asquith to push ahead with removal of the Lords veto. This he did by requesting in November 1910 another general election, in order to provide public sanction for his reform.

Unhappily for the Tories, the outcome of the election simply confirmed the result of January, though with one or two minor differences.[3] Asquith interpreted the result as sufficient mandate to introduce his bill for suspending the Lords' veto powers. This he did in February 1911, accompanied in July by the threat to swamp the Upper House with peers if the Lords rejected it. To prevent such a swamping, the Unionist leadership recommended passage of the bill. However, right-wing elements or 'last ditchers' attempted a sizeable revolt against the decision, believing Asquith was bluffing in his threat to create peers. Their revolt, though loud and hostile, did not attract enough support and on 9 August 1911 the Parliament Act finally received royal assent. For many Unionists this was the last straw for a leadership that had shown little clear direction, had lost three consecutive elections and now had participated in the destruction of the ancient and balanced constitution. As criticism mounted, Balfour decided to retire from the leadership. He passed the baton (or poisoned chalice), after a messy struggle between Walter Long and Austen Chamberlain, to a compromise candidate, Andrew Bonar Law. He faced a most unenviable inheritance, with Unionists demoralised, badly divided and bereft of new ideas or policies. Meanwhile, with no institutional obstacle lying in the path of Home Rule, Irish Unionists, and particularly the Ulstermen grouped around Sir Edward Carson and Sir James Craig, set about organising their own resistance during the autumn of 1911.

THE RISE AND FALL OF FEDERALISM, 1910–12

Federalism evolved as a practical policy during the late nineteenth century,[4] as a structure that might synthesise growing pressures within the Empire for greater self-rule, with the continued direction and control of Imperial policy from Westminster. Applied to Ireland, this meant restructuring the United Kingdom into regional assemblies for Scotland, Wales, Ireland and England, each with control of local affairs, while central command over the key areas of defence, Empire, foreign policy and taxation were kept by parliament. These ideas were touted by supporters as an alternative to Home Rule or the full separation of Ireland, that appeased Irish Nationalist demands but from within the British Empire; a balance that might have lessened the fears of Unionists and especially the northern Protestants. It seemed to offer all things to all men, a panacea that could finally answer the Irish Question. However, federalism was a rather vague term and raised as many problems as it solved. What, for example, would be the balance between local and central power? Would not the division of responsibility between centre and periphery cause innumerable political conflicts? Was there a demand in the other parts of the UK for such an assembly? And were they to be regarded as national Parliaments or a form of devolved local government or little more than town councils.

Despite the lack of clarity (or perhaps because of it) support for devolved government and/or federalism had spread amongst some Unionists during the early years of the new century, and was aided by the clearout of old-styled Tories at the 1906 electoral disaster. Following the January 1910 election, the political situation appeared more receptive to such constructive solutions for Ireland.[5] The influx of fresh, young Unionists into parliament, weaned on a diet of Chamberlainite reformism and more concerned with fiscal reform, land policy, social reform and relations with Industrial labour, lessened their regard for the question of the House of Lords or Ireland. The prospect in early 1910, of a hard, drawn-out parliamentary struggle over the Lords and then Home Rule, filled them with despair, raising the attraction of devolution as a quick and equitable method of removing unwanted controversies. Tory sympathy for federalism was also a consequence of the Round Table Movement, a clique of Empire enthusiasts and reform-minded young thinkers, which included Leo Amery, Phillip Kerr, Edward Grigg, Geoffrey Dawson and Lionel Curtis. They enjoyed close contacts with influential politicians and editors, and along these channels they espoused their ideas for remedying outstanding Imperial problems.[6] More recently, in 1910, they had played a key role in the application of a federal structure to South Africa, which successfully reintegrated the colony back into the Imperial bosom. If federalism pacified South Africa, so the thorny problem of Ireland might also be susceptible to its therapeutic powers.

Interest in federalism amongst some Unionists ripened into pressure on the Unionist leadership to move in that direction, throughout the spring and summer of 1910. Much of this came from the pen of influential editors and publicists, such as J.L. Garvin, editor of *The Observer*,[7] and F.S. Oliver, who wrote in *The Times* under his pseudonym 'Pacificus'. During May and June 1910 both men sought to raise the public profile of federal ideas and urged settlement of the Irish question through United Kingdom devolution.[8] Also to the fore of this early movement were the Imperial pro-consuls Earl Grey, ex-governor of Canada, and Lord Milner, ex-high commissioner of South Africa. The latter wrote directly to Balfour on 17 April, commenting that he did not 'suppose the Unionist party can go in for H.R. in any form, but if it comes in spite of us not much harm would be done by provincial Home Rule'.[9] Milner's rather moderate views at this stage are interesting given his growing influence in Tory circles and his later advocacy of more hardline Tory policies.

Such early pressure on the Tory leadership had little effect. Even the formation of the Conference in June, with its remit to search for a compromise on the constitution, did not immediately kindle interest in federal solutions, although the likes of Garvin, Oliver and F.E. Smith, Unionist MP for Walton, believed it could be manoeuvred in that direction.[10] Indeed it was not until the conference was reportedly deadlocked, by the autumn of 1910 and over the question of Ireland, that federalism grew in popularity. At the heart of this development was an offer made to Balfour by Lloyd George, the chancellor of the exchequer, in the form of a memorandum sent to him on 12 October,[11] for the conference to reconstitute itself into a coalition government, as a sort of 'ad hoc super cabinet'.[12] For Lloyd George, such an arrangement offered both the freedom from the stale conflict of party politics and the capability of addressing the variety of problems facing British society and the Empire at that time. Moreover, they could remove forever the Irish question from British politics by settling it upon federal basis. Balfour, though circumspect and not a little concerned at to what degree the offer had Asquith's agreement, was in no way dismissive of the plan for a coalition or of the proposed devolutionary solution for Ireland.[13] By temperament he was ideally suited to 'governing the country on middle lines acceptable to both parties'.[14] Lloyd George later claimed Balfour had 'by no means (been) hostile',[15] but simply required time to confer with colleagues. It is also important to remember that Balfour had already speculated on how to prevent a return to normal party politics, recommending to Lord Esher, a close confidant of the King, that His Majesty might dismiss Asquith and place the reigns of government in the safer hands of a non-party dignitary, such as Rosebery.[16]

As rumours of the offer seeped out, sections of the Unionist press eagerly took up the scheme. Garvin, amongst the first to learn of the chancellor's plan, spearheaded a broad press campaign of support with a leading article on 16 October entitled 'The Case of A Larger Settlement', recommending a federal solution as the basis for a wider reconstruction of government.[17] Oliver revived Pacificus with a series of letters to *The Times* that echoed the sentiments of Garvin's editorial.[18] More surprisingly, *The Morning Post*, bastion of traditional Unionism, came out in favour of federalism on the 17th, arguing that if certain safeguards were included, such as no separate treatment for Ireland and Ulster to be an autonomous unit, then it 'certainly should be submitted to the consideration of the Unionist party'.[19]

Within the Unionist leadership supporters of the federal option now broke cover. F.E. Smith, who had first learnt of the proposal from Winston Churchill and was subsequently to act as intermediary between Balfour and Lloyd George, urged Balfour to accept the offer. 'I do not think in the history of England such terms have ever been offered to a beaten party and I am confident that in accepting them you would carry with you the country and the party.' This overly optimistic assessment he sweetened with the more partisan calculation that 'if you agreed tomorrow to the terms offered in conference it would smash the Liberal party. The extremists of Labour will never give us concern.'[20] As the self-proclaimed leader of the 'young men' in the party, Smith was active strengthening federalist sympathies in these quarters.[21] He had already, on Balfour's authorisation, canvassed Austen Chamberlain and Bonar Law, a prominent tariff reformer who he found sympathetic,[22] while J.S. Sandars, Balfour's private secretary, reports him trying to win over Sir Edward Carson.[23] Carson was a natural target for such overtures, given his prominence within the Tory leadership and since February 1910 as leader of the Irish Unionists. 'F.E. said', wrote Sandars,

> that Carson frankly admitted that there was much to be said in favour of the policy (federalism) and he quite realised the changed conditions in Ireland; but that he considered in his position in Ireland he was not free to entertain the question at all events, *at the present time*.[24]

We can perhaps detect here the beginnings of that famous partnership during the Home Rule crisis of Carson and his sidekick 'galloper' Smith. More importantly, if this was a fair reflection of Carson's position (and we must be aware of both Smith's and Sandars sympathies for federalism) then it suggests a little more flexibility towards federalism than many historians have credited him with and, like Balfour, his constraint was more from current circumstance than by any ideological impediment.

Far closer to Balfour than either Carson or Smith was Alfred Lyttelton, an ex-colonial secretary, who was stirred by Garvin's article of the 16th and informed Balfour that his own enquiries had found 'a very great sympathy with local federation among our younger intellectuals': in fact 'two of our most important pro-consuls Grey and Milner … (and) … some of our best young men … lean that way'.[25] He also warned Balfour of the political danger of a breakdown in the conference and subsequent election, 'I dread the submission to the electorate of the H of L's question – never an advantageous one for us'.[26] These reflections were reiterated by Sandars, who reported his unofficial soundings amongst the younger Unionists to Balfour. 'He (Amery) thinks a scheme of that kind may well be considered – he would do much to avoid an election now, consequently upon the naked failure of the conference. He says many of the young men of the party are of this opinion.'[27] He reinforced this with the observation, 'we shall hug a delusion if we imagine that Home Rule will alarm the average voter of 1911 as it did in 1886 and 1895'.[28]

Against such an onslaught Balfour remained guarded but not hostile. He informed Lyttelton that 'on the question of devolution or provincialism or Home Rule all round I say nothing at the moment. I doubt whether most of those who talk about it have thought it out. *Certainly I am not prepared to dogmatise on the subject.*'[29] And two days later he told Chamberlain,

> I did not take up a non-possumus attitude upon any of them. I think it quite possible though perhaps improbable, that a modus vivendi might be arrived at on the substance of a common policy, if the enormous initial difficulties of a coalition could be overcome.[30]

There was, however, hesitancy on Balfour's part. It sprang from the need to measure opinion within the party, and especially the opinion of Austen Chamberlain, leader of the constructive Unionists and heir apparent to Balfour. Similarly, Lloyd George perceived that Balfour would only 'jump' if he took Chamberlain with him. He, therefore, made a bid for his support with a moderate speech at the City Temple on 17 October, where he paid handsome tribute to Austen's father, Joe Chamberlain, whom he claimed had given 'outstanding service to the masses'.[31] Garvin also urged the 'larger settlement' on Chamberlain,[32] as did F.E. Smith who warned that 'to refuse this offer at this crisis would almost be a crime against the Empire'. A bargain over Ireland, on the basis of federalism, would secure more significant prizes such as National Service, big Navy, Fiscal reform, closer Colonial ties, social and Poor Law reform.[33] Chamberlain, though ideologically convinced of devolution and able to assure Garvin that 'there is indeed little with which I disagree in what you have written',[34] remained, like Balfour, hesitant of such a bold step. Revealing that innate conservatism that would typify his career, he felt 'all this is very dangerous and we must walk warily'.[35] By mid-October, then, considerable pro-devolution momentum had built up within the Unionist party.

Yet for all the frenzied activity, the federalist initiative appeared to be all smoke without fire. Balfour waited to 'feel' party opinion and by late October it registered as unfavourable. On the 31 October Sandars informed Garvin that 'he's gone back a bit',[36] and by 8 November that 'the game was up'.[37] Such an outcome was always likely. A significant part of the Unionist press, including *The Telegraph*, *The Spectator* and *The Express*, remained sceptical of the plan. More hostile were the Irish Unionists, incensed at what seemed the lapse by the Tory leadership in its Unionism and perceiving in events a sordid replay of their treachery in 1904/5. They pressed Balfour hard to reject the plan and to avoid entanglements with Lloyd George. Ronald McNeill, an Ulstermen sitting for Mid-Kent, announced his 'profound regret' at what appeared little more than a 'new disguise' for Home Rule.[38] His irritation was shared by the standing committee of the Ulster Unionist Council, who passed a resolution 'reaffirm(ing) their uncompromising opposition' to the type of constitutional proposals that were currently being rumoured.[39] And Lord Balcarres, Tory chief whip from 1911, detected similar tremors; 'Ulster members are firing blank cartridges about devolution, banging the orange drum and denouncing in future those of us who may concede something to Nationalism'.[40] Irish Unionist anxieties filtered through to the shadow cabinet where at a meeting on 8 November 1910, traditional Unionism, as represented by Lords Midleton, Londonderry, Salisbury, Curzon and Selborne, Walter Long and Carson, aligned themselves against any flirtation with Lloyd George and his federal scheme.[41]

Of most significance in persuading Balfour against the coalition idea were the views of his inner shadow-cabinet, the 'Unionist Four', comprising Lord Lansdowne, Akers-Douglas, chief-whip under Salisbury, Acland-Hood, the present chief whip and Chamberlain.[42] All had acute doubts about the plan and mistrusted Lloyd George, doubting particularly whether he could actually deliver an agreement on federalism, relying, as it did on his word that Asquith was with them? There was, then, a deep-rooted scepticism about whether, beyond a few 'warm words', the venture was practical given the current state of politics. Balfour could see 'no object in a detailed discussion about the pattern of the wall-papers which are to adorn this new political structure when the foundations have not been laid'.[43] In light of this, many thought Lloyd George was simply contriving a snare to compel the Unionist leadership into displaying its hand on Ireland before the forthcoming election.[44] As H.A. Gwynne told Balfour, 'it is either the most astonishingly generous offer ever made by one political party to another or it means an astute and cunning move towards some gigantic fraud'.[45] And by late October the idea of a fraud seemed more likely. It was clear Lloyd George had misled Smith by insisting the conference was disintegrating over the issue of devolution for Ireland, an issue they knew had never been discussed at the meetings. In addition, Smith, Garvin and Milner had been encouraged to speculate well beyond what was politically realistic, so revealing, in the process, the disunity of the Tory leadership while fuelling tension within the Unionist alliance. Given these suspicions Lloyd George's plan for a coalition government with a federal agreement on Ireland collapsed. Both parties quickly returned to normal partisan politics with a bitter election campaign, during November and December 1910, in which sympathy for federal solutions melted instantly away. All attempts to find a cross-party agreement over Ireland were for the moment curtailed.

They were not curtailed for long. Several events during the latter half of 1911 helped revive interest in federal or devolutionary ideas. The Parliament Act, in leaving the Constitution without a second chamber, or in 'suspension' and in need of repair, raised the profile of various constructive remedies of which a federal structure was the most obvious. A second was Balfour's retirement from the leadership in November 1911. This removed a traditional Unionist block to federal plans, but brought to the leadership Bonar Law, a man who had attended several Roundtable 'moots' during 1910, whose close associates were all key federalists (Goulding, Beaverbrook and Garvin) and who, according to Smith, had been persuaded of the idea in October 1910. 'The advent of a new leader of the Unionist party', Lord Milner was assured by W.B. Johnston, 'appears to be an opportune time for calmly and fearlessly reviving our programme and strengthening the weak places.'[46] But most importantly the revived interest in federalism, late in 1911, came as a reaction against the simmering revolt in Ulster, with its unconstitutional rhetoric and sectarian undertones. These developments worried many moderate Tories, who looked favourably upon any scheme that offered a practical basis for compromise. The Ulster campaign also alarmed those enthusiasts of the 1910 attempt at a cross-party settlement who hoped for another effort in the future. One such hopeful, Earl Grey, was quick to warn the new leader of the dangers in 'tak(ing) up a non-possumus (position) against all forms of Home Rule. The refusal of the Unionist party to even consider H.R. (Home Rule) made it necessary for Redmond ... contrary to his own inclinations to fall back upon the extreme party.'[47] Unionist extremism, for Grey, lessened the chance of a compromise, the only path out of the crisis (it never occurred to him that Bonar Law might actually have intended to polarise politics to prevent a compromise). In place of extremism Grey recommended, 'without any reproof from our conscience, the expediency of granting to the people of Ireland powers of local self-govt, somewhat similar to those enjoyed by the people of Quebec'.[48] Horace Plunkett, ex-vice president of the Department of Agriculture and Technical Instruction, and similarly moved by recent intemperance in Ulster, implored Bonar Law to consider such positive proposals.[49]

Receiving little encouragement from Bonar Law, Grey tried to persuade the Unionist chief whip, Lord Balcarres, that only by federating the UK could Ireland become a loyal member of the Empire. After all 'the Catholic Celt is against socialism, against secularisation and for Tariff Reform'.[50] Grey then threatened revolt, warning that a 'non possumus' stance by the Unionist leadership would 'compel Milner, Plunkett, Oliver and a lot of others and myself to come out into the open against you'.[51] F.S. Oliver was another influential Unionist who at the end of 1911 campaigned against an extreme posture. He cautioned Chamberlain (whom he thought could be pushed into a leading role for the federalist cause) against 'trumpeting all over the country against a Home Rule bill'[52] and petitioning Robinson, editor of *The Times*, to criticise Carson and his 'Ulster shouting and drumbeating and treasonable Tom Foolery'.[53]

Not all federalists reacted to the growth of extremism amongst Unionist leaders in this way. Lord Milner, never one to shy away from extreme methods, believed the unfolding situation in Ulster would actually aid a federal solution to the Irish question, as long as supporters had the stomach for the long game. 'It may be', he advised Oliver, 'that an intransigent attitude on the part of Ulster, if it takes a responsible and not its present untenable form, is a necessary element in the working out of a settlement on our lines.'[54] A violent campaign would demonstrate the impossibility of Home Rule and drive politics to an impasse, an ideal position for federalism to be embraced by one or both political parties. Until that point they had to 'abstain from immediate, direct advocacy of federal Home Rule' until the moment was right.[55] Oliver was convinced and urged Chamberlain and Steel-Maitland, the Tory Party chairman 'against preaching or even hinting at federalism at the present time ... This is not so much for the Unionist party as for federalism ... The time for federalism is not now but later when you have got yourself locked in a constitutional impasse.'[56] Garvin also saw the benefits of the long game: 'it is no good offering terms which Ulster ... would certainly reject ... so they [events] will get worse before they will get better, and we shall come nearer chaos though I hope not into it'.[57] George Wyndham, ex-chief secretary for Ireland, agreed with these sentiments, advocating to Chamberlain, 'ultimately a federal U.K ... in the meanwhile for a line of vigorous criticism and attack'.[58]

By early 1912 it seemed a new consensus had emerged. Tory devolutionists and federalists construed that if the government were unlikely to jump for federalism at the start of a political campaign and with the Ulster revolt carrying all before it, there was little practical use publicly championing a federal solution. Instead, they bedded down their sacred idea until the warm rays of a constitutional impasse, at some future point in time, made it both opportune and suitable. What was also encouraging for the future was the degree of support for such a constructive proposal, in the party, in the press and amongst the leadership.

DIE-HARDS, UNIONISTS AND ULSTERMEN

For those on the right or traditional wing of the Tory party, Union with Ireland remained something inviolable and permanent. It was deeply embedded in their ideological make-up and symbolised many of the most pressing concerns of early twentieth-century Toryism, namely rule by political elites, the preservation of social stability, loyalty to the crown, Constitution and Protestant Church, the maintenance of property rights and the defence of the British Empire. Such ideological baggage made the Union an issue few could (easily) compromise over, and especially for the Irish Unionists whose ideological prejudices were grounded, quite literally, in their ownership of large acres of Irish soil. For traditional Unionists of whatever hue, the various threats of the Edwardian era, albeit Lloyd Georgian taxation, militant trades unions, suffragettes, the emerging Labour Party or external pressures on the Empire, simply reinforced their disposition not to abandon the Union – an anchor, indeed the only one, in a stormy sea.

The formation of the Constitutional Conference of June 1910 naturally filled many with alarm. Lord Willoughby de Broke, a rising star of the die-hard right, complained that the 'people were surfeited with tactics and meaningless debates', desiring instead a 'strong frontal attack pressed home'.[59] *The Morning Post* echoed these concerns, regarding the conference as little more than 'a device for postponing a general election, to a date more convenient to the Liberal party'.[60] Lord Salisbury, on the other hand, mistrusted what the Unionist leadership would do; 'our representatives do not seem to have any clear limits in their minds. They are in search of formulae but without much view as to what they want',[61] a misgiving shared by Leo Maxse, the editor of *The National Review*, who told Goulding that, 'great parties can't play fast and loose with their principles as many Unionists are now doing'.[62] Yet for much of 1910, comment on the Tory right was reasonably muted, such grumbles as these being limited to the more irascible of their members.[63] When, therefore, the conference was rumoured to be at an impasse, by late July 1910, sceptics on the right were heartened.

However, the growth of interest in federalism within the party during the autumn was greeted with dismay and anger. Acland-Hood, Balfour's close political confidant, regarded this 'new form of Home Rule being hinted at', as 'a specious trap'.[64] Less dramatically, Arthur Elliot believed 'federalism for the U.K. … is absolute downright Tom foolery'.[65] Behind the scenes Lords Midleton and Salisbury, along with the latter's brother, Hugh Cecil, moved forcefully against the scheme. Discerning this growing unease, Chamberlain warned Balfour that devolution would 'shock the older ones',[66] as did Sandars, 'I quite agree that federalism will not be popular with the more Conservative section of the party'.[67] Walter Long, another ex-chief secretary of Ireland and traditionalist, responded with characteristic hostility by organising a letter to *The Times*, signed by himself, Carson and Willoughby de Broke, defending a single united parliament at Westminster.[68]

More serious for Balfour was the creation of the Reveille group, early in October 1910, a 'forward movement' of about fifty wealthy Unionist

MPs, led by Willoughby de Broke and Page-Croft.[69] Its intention was to 'steel' the leadership against, what Page-Croft called, 'the new hare of local and Imperial devolution',[70] and to mobilise all the grumblers and hot-heads of the right into a unified organisation.[71] The group focused its fire against federalism, announcing in its manifesto of 5 November, to all 'federalists, federationists, devolutionists, Home Rule all rounders and other constitution mongers, the subjection of Belfast to Dublin is a triviality hardly worthy of consideration'.[72] The leadership had been warned.

It was the Irish Unionists who reacted with most violence to the federalist 'turn'. Since the start of 1910 they had been sufficiently alarmed at the enhanced parliamentary position of the Nationalists to revive Unionist and Orange clubs in Ireland. The outburst of federalist sympathy now threatened them with a political arrangement that compromised the essential basis of the Union. John Lonsdale, MP for Mid-Armagh, declared federalism to be 'absurd and illogical',[73] whilst Ronald McNeill reminded Tories that it 'undermined the central citadel of the Unionist position'.[74] With more fire William Moore, MP for North Armagh, berated Edward Goulding that 'it is monstrous that we who have borne the fight for the Unionist party for years should be thrown to the wolves because your friends wish to pander to disloyalty' (a reference to Smith).[75] Under pressure from the UUC, Carson sent Balfour a forceful rejection of 'the setting up of a Parliament in Dublin, with an executive responsible to it',[76] and more privately he complained to Lady Londonderry that he was 'sick to death of this Home Rule tragedy … It (federalism) will split the party to pieces and should it turn out to be true I earnestly hope the Conservatives will never again be in office during my lifetime.'[77] Of course, in making such statements, it must be remembered that he was writing to Lady Londonderry, Tory hostess and wife of Lord Londonderry, a leading light of Irish Unionism.

One ominous consequence of these developments was the radicalisation of Ulster Unionism. The Ulster Convention of 1892 and the formation of the UUC in 1905, had already shown a predisposition for independent action by the Ulstermen when under threat. Early in 1910 saw a similar, if gradual, movement. Small cachets of arms entered Ulster in the spring.[78] By the autumn, this was taken over by the UUC with the creation of a secret committee to purchase armaments on a larger scale. At its head was F.H. Crawford, who in the summer of 1910 travelled to Germany to purchase some 2,000 weapons, laying what Jackson has called 'the groundwork for civil war'.[79] Late 1910 was an important stage in the rise of militant Ulster Unionism, but its strength should not be overemphasised. As yet there was no force to arm in Ulster and the acquisition of weapons seemed more like a propaganda venture than a serious attempt to provide a viable military defence. Indeed, what they were to defend and against whom were far from clear. Perhaps, Ulster's move towards a paramilitary option also suggests a certain frustration – even desperation – that their voice was not being heard within the wider Unionist alliance.

The election defeat of January 1911 gave momentum to Ulster's preparations and was further encouraged by the introduction of the Parliament bill in February, accompanied by Asquith's threat to create peers to insure its passage. These developments meant a Home Rule Parliament could be just months away. Following the example of Nationalists, who had shown just how pliable a British parliament was to the threat of popular violence, the Ulstermen re-doubled their efforts. Sir James Craig, MP for North Down and chief architect of the Ulster rebellion, reiterated to Crawford the seriousness of the situation: 'I am strongly of the opinion that the fishing rods should be got in as secretly as possible ... My great fear is that the game will be up before anything is done. It is a mere matter of time.'[80] Arming Ulster was predicated upon the rationale that the government could be intimidated into dropping its plans for Home Rule or, although this still remained unsaid, offer a satisfactory compromise to Ulster. Though apparently preparing for civil war, the Ulstermen had an eye on, and deep interest in, the political game at Westminster.

The Ulster rebellion was about convincing the government that they possessed the massed support of Ulster and enjoyed widespread sympathy on the British mainland, not least from the large Non-Conformist communities that were such an important electoral component of popular Liberalism. To the task of arousing an otherwise apathetic British public behind Ulster's cause, the Ulster Unionist clubs were reorganised under the leadership of Lord Templetown, providing a framework for the dissemination of propaganda in Britain.[81] Further clubs were established on the mainland and twinned with an Ulster branch to coordinate publicity. In April 1911 the Unionist Associations of Ireland (UAI) launched its campaign in Britain, sending four full-time agents to organise the distribution of literature, funds and speakers throughout the British Isles.[82] By December over 481 meetings had been held and 734,850 leaflets distributed, at a monthly cost of £2,000.[83] Alongside the UAI's activities, Lady Londonderry's newly formed Women's Ulster Unionist Association, sent platform speakers to various British constituencies.[84] Through these structures British public opinion was to be alerted to the imminent dangers of Home Rule, again highlighting the importance of electoral considerations to their campaign. Yet in private Craig was far from optimistic about the effectiveness of such a campaign. 'Living as they do over here', he moaned to Hugh Cecil, 'the people are accustomed to the cry of "wolf, wolf" (i.e.) no Home Rule and no surrender. It has been cried so often that it takes a bit of doing to persuade them.'[85]

Here, then, were the two mutually reinforcing parts to the Ulster campaign as it unfolded from early 1911, the paramilitary and the political. To harmonise these activities the Ulster Unionist Council appointed an executive committee,[86] at the heart of which lay the organisational expertise of Craig. Tentative planning for a provisional government began from an executive of five, with the intention of assuming control of Ulster (or parts where they had a majority) if or when Home Rule was introduced. In January 1912 offices were acquired in Belfast's old town hall[87] and a defence fund set up under Lord Dunleath.[88] The movement, however, needed a frontman or figurehead, who would not ask too many questions about the military side of things, who was well placed politically and who could capture the public's attention. It also needed someone able to unite the various political and local differences within Ulster and Unionism,[89] behind one movement. Into this role was manoeuvred a hesitant Sir Edward Carson, who in February 1910 became leader of the Irish Unionists.

It seems unlikely that Carson, on assuming the leadership, was intimate with developments on the ground in Ulster. He was an unknown and still erratic character to the Ulstermen, 'not familiar with the psychology of the northern Irish'.[90] He was a little distrusted by them because of his southern origins (audible in his brogue), Dublin constituency, his legal background, his Liberal even Gladstonian past and his close association with the likes of Wyndham, Chamberlain and F.E. Smith. By the summer of 1911 he appeared an unlikely leader of the Ulster revolt.[91] Nor was Carson resolved on the course or role he would play in resisting a future Home Rule bill. He was committed to saving the Union for all-Ireland, but unclear how this could be achieved in the circumstances of 1910–11. This was all the more problematic since Irish Unionism outside of Ulster was a sickly creature, unrepresented except for Dublin University and weakened by reforms to the ownership of land and local government. Moreover, British public opinion remained unmoved by Irish issues and the

House of Lords, who had rescued the Union in 1893, faced the imminent loss of their veto powers. Leadership of the Irish Unionists in the circumstances of 1910–11 looked an impossible brief.

The seeds to Carson's later role as 'generalissimo of Ulster Unionism',[92] though faint, can be traced through his activities during the struggle over the Parliament bill. Carson recognised the tactical implications for Ireland of the loss of the Lords' powers, in removing the last obstacle to Home Rule. This led him into the Ditcher camp, rejecting the leadership's call for abstention, for a dogged resistance to the Bill. These developments made him bitter and determined, but scarcely more clear-sighted about how Home Rule was to be resisted. The passage of the Parliament Act in August brought some clarity to Carson's thinking, persuading him of two important assumptions. Firstly, that he could not trust the existing Tory leadership with the forthcoming fight over Home Rule, as he told Lady Londonderry 'I feel very doubtful about the way our leaders intend to fight Home Rule, but in any event I will lead for myself this time'.[93] To forestall another humiliating reverse he would 'make a big effort ... to stir up some life over this Home Rule fight'.[94] With this in mind Carson set about channelling the outrage and exasperation in the Unionist party caused by events of the summer, into a fresh, tough campaign to 'save' the Union: 'I am sure the whole party in the country is crying out for something more than the "gentlemanly party".'[95] Re-mustering the die-hards into the coming battle over the Union, was initially effected through the Halsbury Club, the institutionalised focus of the revolt against Balfour. By 18 October, the club was already dedicated 'to become a fighting body for the furtherance of Unionist policy' and 'in particular stress is laid upon the necessity of the position in Ulster being made clear to the electorate'.[96] Ulster and the Union were to be the new 'last ditch'. It was also a means for Carson to establish leadership over the forward elements in the party, displacing Chamberlain, the once acknowledged leader of these sections, and his attempt to re-group the right around Tariff Reform. That issue had lost its allure with prosperous conditions and a party compromise few were willing to challenge, and was easily eclipsed by Ulster as the pole-star of the right. No better illustration of this was the shift of F.E. Smith, the once loyal lieutenant to Chamberlain, who emerged as Carson's gallant 'galloper'.

Of help to Carson in marshalling the Tory right behind the Ulster rebellion was Hugh Cecil, youngest son of the former prime minister and the party's most doctrinaire Conservative.[97] In August in the House of

Commons he had sanctioned rebellion by Ulster in defence of their rights. 'The contest about Home Rule', he told the House of Commons in August, 'will not be decided in the city of Westminster. It will rather be decided in the city of Belfast.'[98] For Cecil, a stubborn fight by Ulster would also demonstrate the Parliament Act as unworkable, forcing the government to restore a bicameral parliamentary system. He, therefore, recommended to Craig an Ulster 'Plan of Campaign', and the development of a para-military force to defeat Home Rule. 'Lord Hugh's letter and memorandum', he told Carson, 'were admirable and practically follows a course of action which some of us have had mapped out.'[99] Both Carson and Craig were well aware of the publicity value of the son of a great Tory prime minister sanctioning their deeds, as well as the support he would garner in die-hard circles.

The second conclusion Carson reached in the hiatus following the Parliament Act, was that the resistance of Ulster was the best, and perhaps the only, tactical method for defeating Home Rule. With all its wealth, industry, political organisation and concentration of support, if Ulster eschewed a Dublin-based parliament, then so Carson and others believed, they rendered it inoperable. 'If Ulster succeeded Home Rule is dead. Home Rule for Ireland was impossible without Belfast.'[100] For Home Rule to be defeated 'the Ulstermen must do it themselves'.[101] His concern was:

> to satisfy myself that the people over there mean to resist. I am not for a mere game of bluff … We will … be confronted by many weaklings in our own camp, who talk very loud and mean nothing and will be the first to criticise us when the moment of action comes. For this we must be prepared'.[102]

Of course the logic of Ulster 'doing it herself', though he chose not to address the point, led as easily to her exclusion from a Home Rule parliament and the partition of Ireland, as it did to destroying the bill. Though committed to an all-Ireland solution in the fight against Home Rule, the political stance Carson was beginning to take up pointed towards a narrowing in his Unionism from an Irish to an Ulster perspective.[103]

Craig held few qualms about this; his prime concern was to stamp Ulster at the heart of any discussion on Home Rule for Ireland, so 'making it an Ulster question'.[104] He was, therefore, greatly encouraged by the response and role Carson now set for himself. During August and September 1911, under his tutelage, Carson was brought into the inner sanctum of Ulster Unionism and informed of their innermost preparations and plans. The process began whereby he was manufactured into King Carson, the Prince of Ulster. Instrumental in capturing Carson was a huge popular demonstration of loyalty, organised by Craig at his country estate of Craigavon, on 23 September, and designed to convince Carson that Ulster was not about a mere game of bluff:

> To tender you [Carson] personally as leader in the forthcoming struggle a hearty and generous welcome to the North but also prove in the most emphatic way that we could conceive, that you had at your back in a solid phalanx the very best of all Ulster'.[105]

The rally was also about convincing Ulster that Carson was, after all, the right man to lead them.[106]

But the growing alignment of Carson to Ulster, even if for purely tactical grounds, created unease amongst Unionists from the south and west of Ireland. Aware of their weak position and reliance upon their northern brethren, many feared Carson had 'gone native' and resented talk of a provisional government, with its disregard for the south and implication of independent action by Ulster. The Dublin correspondent of *The Times* observed that 'Ulster and the south attach different values to different parts of the Irish Unionist policy'.[107] Such early divisions within Irish Unionism worried Carson. 'The difficulties have been', he reassured Cecil, 'that the older leaders such as Sinclair fear it may look like an abandonment of the rest of Ireland.'[108] Carson was sufficiently worried to assuage Unionist fears in a speech in Dublin in January, where he declared Ulster's role as the best 'weapon' to defeat a bill, and ideas of a provisional government simply a 'last resort'.[109] Many clearly remained unconvinced, with *The Irish Times* commenting the next day, in rather frosty terms; 'the programme of the UUC may not have the approval of all Unionists even in Ireland'.[110] Such strains would make Carson's position a delicate one, a colossus bestride an ever widening, ever more fractious Irish Unionist movement.

CHAPTER TWO

Bonar Law, leadership and the issue of Home Rule

INTRODUCTION

BONAR LAW took over the leadership in desperate circumstances, after three election defeats and with a dearth of policy initiatives. Moreover, events of 1910–11 had revealed deep strains within the party. To remedy these difficulties Bonar Law turned to engage the Liberal government on the basis of its 'alleged' destruction of the Constitution, with the Parliament Act, that removed the veto powers of the second chamber. Tories argued that until a new second chamber was introduced major legislation could not be presented to parliament. This understanding of parliamentary operations the government chose to ignore when on 11 April 1912 it introduced a bill granting Home Rule for Ireland. Historic Unionist antipathy towards Irish self-government now combined with contemporary arguments about a 'suspended' Constitution, to inaugurate a Tory policy of resistance to Home Rule for Ireland that went way beyond anything contemplated in either 1886 or 1893.

PARTY PROBLEMS AND THE ARRIVAL OF MR BONAR LAW

Balfour was in a difficult situation by the autumn of 1911. Three consecutive election defeats left the party deeply demoralised and exposed his leadership to severe criticism from the right, particularly at his handling of affairs during the parliament bill crisis. This mistrust of Balfour's leadership was evident in the emergence of another die-hard campaign late in 1911 in preparation for another Home Rule bill. This had the express purpose of offering something more than what Carson called Balfour's 'milk and water' leadership.[1] Given these strains, Balfour retired from the leadership on 9 November, forcing a contest between two equally unsuitable candidates. On one side stood Walter Long, the leader of the red-faced Tory squires, on the other Austen Chamberlain, the talentless son of a famous father, who was head of the more constructive Tories. With no love lost between them, the selection of either stood to divide the party, so a third 'unity' candidate, Bonar Law, was chosen to lead the party in the Commons. Bonar Law is closely linked with the fortunes of Ireland, both in the pre-war period, where it dominated the first three years of his leadership, and later during the move towards partition. Yet on becoming leader he had little comprehension of Irish affairs or connection with the groups lining up in its defence, despite coming from an Ulster-Scots background. Any understanding of how his thinking and actions developed towards Ireland must therefore start with an appreciation of the extremely difficult situation that greeted him as leader.

The manner of his ascent, and perhaps the obscurity of his past, denied Bonar Law the authority over the party he now led. For most he had been foisted onto them by an anxious chief whip and party organisation, worried by the prospect of disunity. Opinion was hostile: one junior whip felt after his selection that there was now 'a greater feeling of discontent about than at any previous time'.[2] Two days later there was still 'undoubted discontent amongst those who think they are balked of their prey'.[3] Nor was Bonar Law helped by some obvious deficiencies. Beyond the intricacies of Tariff Reform he had little detailed experience; 'how can he help us without any knowledge of Foreign Affairs, Navy, Church questions or Home Rule, the Lord alone knows'.[4] In addition, he was of Canadian origin with a clear Scottish brogue, who had made his fortune at the Glasgow Iron Ring, was Presbyterian by religion, and, more significantly, without land or connections, characteristics ill-suited for a leader of the Conservative party:

> After the aristocratic elegance and courtly bearing of Balfour, Bonar's commonplace and commercial appearance, his apparently ready-made clothing and almost aggressive lack of distinction made them [the blue-blooded Tories] feel vaguely uncomfortable.[5]

None were more hostile than Irish Unionists, who had wanted Carson and after he withdrew, Walter Long. Now they had a Tariff Reformer, closely associated with the constructive wing of the party, who had flirted with federalism in 1910. *The Irish Times*, on 11 November, could only vaguely reassure readers that 'he is held to be a sound Unionist'.[6] Ronald McNeill thought Balfour's retirement a 'calamity' and was unimpressed with the appointment of Bonar Law 'whose great qualities as

Parliamentarian and Statesman had not yet been revealed'.[7] John Lonsdale went further, admitting he was 'furious' at the outcome. 'In my opinion he is wanting in knowledge of statecraft … he has never been a cabinet minister and is nothing like as able a Parliamentarian as Mr Long and Mr Chamberlain.'[8]

Bonar Law's authority was further limited by the petty jealousies of more experienced colleagues, whose shoulders he had leap-frogged to the front. The speedy return of Balfour overwhelmed the new incumbent for 'the presence of Arthur makes him feel his immeasurable inferiority'.[9] Worse still, Bonar Law shared the leadership with Lord Lansdowne, following the precedent of 1881 when Sir Stafford Northcote led the Commons and Lord Salisbury the Lords.[10] This left command of a future Unionist ministry unclear; it was more than possible the king would have sent for Lansdowne or even Balfour to head an in-coming Unionist government. *The Irish Times* reassured its readers 'that Mr Law will not step into the place occupied by Mr Balfour. He will become simply the leader of the party in the Commons … The question of the general leadership of the party, however, may be expected to remain for some time in abeyance.'[11] While Hugh Cecil felt that 'Bonar Law will not I think really lead, it will be done by a committee'.[12] This weakened Bonar Law's standing, diminishing his status in the Commons and suggesting his tenure was of a temporary quality.

Weakness at the top reflected a deep unease within the party, born of the grave political position they now inhabited. In addition to bitter internal divisions, Tories faced the prospect of four long years of opposition, but without the comfort of fresh ideas or creative policy initiatives to facilitate their return to government. This was all the more dispiriting since they confronted a buoyant Liberal ministry, armed with a full legislative agenda, much of which stood to impair any future Unionist electoral performance, such as land and rating reform, and the abolition of plural voting. More worryingly, after August 1911, the party was unable to exert informal control over political events, as they had since 1906 via the Lords veto. Without this, Tories were powerless to check government measures, and exposed for the first time to the brute reality of an executive able to fully dominate the parliamentary system:[13] 'there is nothing but the cabinet',[14] Selborne told his son, an early observation on what Lord Hailsham would describe seventy years later as a parliamentary dictatorship. But if cabinet was now everything, then, according to Unionists, the destinies of the British Empire and direction of domestic policy lay in the hands of the eighty-two Nationalists, who held the balance of power in parliament and wielded enormous influence over the Liberal government. These speculations suggested they were in the midst of, what Balfour called, a 'ministerialist revolution',[15] and what Bonar Law described as rule by a 'revolutionary committee'.[16] Such opinions spread through the party during 1911–12, weakening Tory conformity to traditional political behaviour and parliamentary niceties, and enhancing the attraction of extreme methods. They even induced some to question the existing foundations of constitutional rule itself.[17] It was clear, then, the party was in danger of spiralling out of a constitutional orbit and becoming unleadable.

Bonar Law's response to these pressures was to fall back on his vigorous public-speaking skills.[18] In the circumstances of the time, with such a well of pent-up frustration in the party, with the 'young Tory braves' keen for a fight and a generally bitter atmosphere in politics, it was less important *what* Bonar Law said than *how* he said it. In this Bonar Law held a great advantage over the pedestrian Long and the conservative Chamberlain – Leo Amery compared his debating style to a 'steel-riveter',[19] and Sir John Simon likened it to 'having handfuls of fine, stinging gravel thrown in one's face'.[20] Bonar Law hit the government and their supporters hard, with rude, robust and sensationalist attacks. At Bootle, he declared the Nationalists 'are just now the mildest mannered men that ever cut a throat or scuttled a ship'.[21] The new style certainly caused trouble, upsetting the more straight-laced Tories, such as Chamberlain, who criticised his accusations of government corruption during his Albert Hall speech in January 1912. Concentrating on style led to some policy confusion, as with his inflated claims during the debate on Lloyd George's National Insurance Scheme, which he later retracted in a letter to *The Times*.[22] These criticisms have been echoed by historians who feel that his 'public recklessness in 1912 cannot be justified'.[23] Yet this is to miss the point, as Lord Balcarres shrewdly noted, 'had Bonar Law confined himself to polite expressions of sympathy and regret, the responsibility resting on his shoulders would be increased tenfold by the ultimate catastrophe'.[24] With reputations still made and unmade on the floor of the Commons, and in an age of rapidly advancing democracy, where platform speaking was so important, these qualities were vital for establishing a standing in the party and a presence in the country:

> the party, in its subconscious way, likes Bonar Law's attitude precisely because it lacks those very qualities which in a Gladstone or a Balfour

> would conform to high Parliamentary tradition ... our friends in the country like Bonar Law because his attitude is uncompromising.[25]

Authority and notoriety were much the same thing for Bonar Law early in his leadership. The die-hards relished a leader who finally was willing 'to call a spade a spade',[26] no small consideration in channelling them back behind the party leadership. Fighting talk also drew Carson and the Ulster Unionists towards him, again tactically important with Home Rule so close. Martial tones were in vogue after 1911 within Unionist politics for which Bonar Law held a premium.

But party's (and leaders) cannot live by bellicosity alone. What Bonar Law required was a single, all-embracing cause to stump the country and rally support. An issue that would not divide the party, yet could offer a sort of Gladstonian moral crusade, to recover popular approval, generate loyalty and paper over discord. Most important of all it was an issue able to return the Conservative party to office; Jenkins writes of them being 'sick with office hunger'.[27] Only government would enable Unionists to reverse Liberal legislation, restore a second chamber, fortify the Empire, ameliorate class friction, remedy internal party wounds and allow Bonar Law to enhance his prestige and authority within his party.

Early on, he championed the issue of government corruption and unconstitutional behaviour. This drew on, what Tories regarded as, a catalogue of recent experiences. These included the government's broken promise on the preamble to the Parliament Bill, that the second chamber would be reconstructed once it lost its veto powers; the patronage system established by National Insurance; the payment of MPs. and the 'unholy bargain' between the government and the Nationalists, who allowed passage of the 1910 budget in exchange for a cabinet commitment to remove the Lords' veto. These were productive lines of attack, that avoided the detail of policy. Yet of more significance, criticism of government corruption and unconstitutional behaviour led into the brewing campaign against Home Rule. For it was over the issue of Home Rule, and the question of Ulster, that Liberal abuse of the constitution was most obvious.

Unionists deployed powerful arguments to support their case. According to their interpretation of parliamentary practice, the Constitution was suspended until government introduced an amending Bill to restore a viable second chamber, recalibrating the natural and historic balance of king, Lords and Commons. To force through Home Rule, or indeed any measure altering the Constitution, under such conditions would be unconstitutional. And all the more so, Unionists argued, since Home Rule was not only part of a 'corrupt bargain' between the government and Nationalists, but had never been before the British electorate in either of the general elections of 1910, and therefore lacked a 'mandate' from the people. Unionists scoured the election messages of Liberal ministers, finding few clear endorsements for such a change.[28] Home Rule was, accordingly, being 'smuggled' through parliament and behind the backs of the people, certainly without their agreement.

Much of this thinking was open to question. The notion of a corrupt bargain was tendentious, since all politics was a process of bargaining. Nor did the notion of a mandate have much basis in constitutional law or convention: the British political system was a representative not a delegatory one. Yet the question of legal precision mattered less than political argument and from this hotch-potch of constitutional rebuke, both valid and bogus, Bonar Law constructed a forceful and useful line of attack. He used it to demand a general election, as the only technique for restoring due constitutional process, before a Home Rule Bill was passed. If no appeal to the people were made, Unionists were both justified and determined to support all means of resisting the imposition of Home Rule: indeed as self-proclaimed defenders of the Constitution they were obliged to do so. Tories were posing as champions of the people, populists behind which lurked the thinly disguised threat of civil resistance. In this Bonar Law drew upon established Conservative suspicious of an unchecked executive, most recently articulated by Lord Salisbury in his referendal theory, that he used to justify the House of Lords as a revising institution.[29] They echoed a Lockean vindication of a 'rightful' rebellion, when a government transgressed the invisible contract it enjoyed with the 'people', and particularly as applied to Ulster. While sponsoring the 'people's' rights connected their arguments with a deeper vein of Tory populism going back to Disraeli, and perhaps even the Reeves 'Throne and Alter' societies of the 1790s.

These were, however, dangerously open-ended constitutional arguments, legitimating any number of un-parliamentary, even un-Constitutional remedies to impede the bill before an election. Tories were effectively declaring it open season on extreme parliamentary tactics because, by their reading, the constitution was suspended. On the other hand, these justifications provided a clear, if novel, constitutional rational that allowed Bonar Law to promise unlimited support to Ulster in its rebellion. Of course his promise was limited by the demand for an election, a constitutional sheet-anchor, in what would otherwise have been unconstitutional support for resistance to a lawfully constituted government. And, presumably, Bonar Law would stand aside and not resist the bill's introduction if, having forced an election on Home Rule he then lost it, with all the consequences that would entail for his authority and leadership?

These ideas on the Constitution and Ireland were evident long before Carson committed himself to Ulster and indeed before Bonar Law became leader. In a letter to *The Times* on 26 July 1911, Bonar Law suggested, in declaring his support for the policy of abstention, that a future Home Rule Bill might be countered by 'delay[ing] ... the Expiring Laws Continuance Bill or the Army Annual Bill ... [to] ... make the continuance of the Government impossible and compel an election'.[30] Two weeks later (8 August) he warned the House of Commons,

> I say this with absolute deliberation if the people of this country decide that they will make the experiment of Home Rule then ... I should say to the loyalists of Ireland 'you have got to submit'. On the other hand, I say equally deliberately if this or any other Government try to force through a measure on which there is good reason to believe that the people of this country are not agreed ... I would never, if I were one of those Irish loyalists consent to have such a system forced upon me as part of a corrupt Parliamentary bargain. I believe if this or any other Government attempts it they will find they have broken up the foundations of society in this country and they will not carry their bill.[31]

It is clear, then, that Bonar Law's approach to Ireland, grew out of the constitutional crisis of 1911.

However, there was a degree of circularity at work in Bonar Law's thinking. For not only did his re-working of constitutional precedence enable him to support Ulster, but support for Ulster would, in turn, help validate his constitutional arguments, by actually impelling the government to an election. Like Carson and the Ulstermen, Bonar Law calculated that if Ulster was determined to stay outside a Home Rule settlement, the government could do very little, particularly confronted by the growing militarisation of the province. To forcibly include northern Protestants would provoke major civil unrest in Ulster and the likelihood of sympathy riots in various mainland cities, such as Liverpool and Glasgow. Force raised the question of agency. The Royal Irish Constabulary were small, openly loyalist and in Belfast, riddled with Orangeism. But employing the army, similarly honeycombed with loyalism was no easy alternative and ill-suited to public order roles.

> They say [Ulster] will not submit to Home Rule. How are they to be made to submit to it? Is that resistance to be overcome by using British soldiers to shoot down men whose only crime is that they refused to be driven out of the Union. To attempt to do that would be to exercise a tyranny as unjustifiable and cruel as had ever been seen in the world.[32]

Such a scenario would be 'impossibly unpopular and an absurd contradiction of the principles of Liberalism', Hugh Cecil observed.[33]

The alternative for government would be some form of exclusion for Ulster from the Bill. But excluding Ulster, although it might well alleviate the threat of civil unrest in the north, was politically hazardous. There was no certainty that the Ulstermen would accept this, and in public at least, they still spoke of resisting Home Rule for all Ireland. Large parts of Ulster were peopled by Catholic Nationalists. Was exclusion, therefore, to be all Ulster or just part; and if part, then where was the cut to be made? Irish Nationalists were even more unlikely to accept partition, least of all a permanent one. Partition undermined their historic claim to a 'seamless' Ireland, with all the wealth and taxable income of Ulster included. Any move by Redmond, leader of the Nationalists, towards exclusion would be contested by others from within the Nationalist movement, and opposed by opinion in the USA from where Redmond obtained much of the party's finance. The attempt to exclude Ulster held as many problems as coercing it into a Home Rule bill.

Prevented from moving forward to grant self-rule to Ireland, yet unable to retreat to a compromise around exclusion, the bill would never reach the statute book. Many Unionists realised the government's dilemma, as Bonar Law informed the Commons, 'the thing is impossible, all your talk about details, the union of hearts and the rest of it is a sham. This (Ulster) is a reality. It is a rock and on that rock this bill or any bill like it will make shipwreck.'[34] Confronted by such a complexity of pressures, the government would be compelled to an election, either as a way of escaping from their untenable political situation or to re-establish public support for their Bill. J. St Loe Strachey, editor of *The Spectator*, saw clearly the tactical opportunities ahead, telling Bonar Law just four days after his selection as leader; Ulster 'will wreck Home Rule (and) drive them either to dropping the Bill or to having a dissolution to get them out of their difficulties'.[35] This was the crux of Bonar Law's approach to Home Rule and the Ulster question, that it could secure an election.

This still left the problem of winning it. Electoral success has been established as the foremost difficulty facing the Edwardian Conservative party.[36] The two solutions which recommended themselves now seemed obsolete. One was the Balfourian method of passive resistance; avoiding controversial promises, facilitating government unpopularity by remaining silent and awaiting the inevitable swing of the political pendulum. The inadequacy of this method lay in the three election defeats under Balfour's leadership and the temper of the party by 1912, which precluded a long-term strategy. Many Unionists simply could not wait for the pendulum to return – although that itself seemed increasingly unlikely – given the aggressive radicalism of the existing Liberal government towards much of what Tories found vital.

A second approach was to inject new ideas into party policy. Peel's Tamworth Manifesto, Disraeli's Imperialism and Social Reform and Randolph Churchill's Tory Democracy demonstrated the effectiveness of this technique. However, new ideas were more likely to cleave the party apart by 1911 than thrust them back into office. Tariff Reform, the party's main constructive policy, caused division and was of declining value by 1912 as prosperity returned. On social policy the Liberals easily outdistanced them, in spite of the attempts by the Unionist Social Reform Committee to project a uniquely Unionist social programme.[37] In any case, their plans were financially hamstrung by a reluctance to increase taxes and the practical flaws in Tariff Reform as a source of revenue. On land policy, the party faced Lloyd George's radical Land Campaign which, it was claimed, would sweep the countryside out of the control of Tory squires. Their own attempts to formulate a policy on land provoked bitter divisions between traditionalists dedicated to the maintenance of the *status quo*, and reformists, such as Lord Milner and Steel-Maitland, who wanted Chamberlainite policies of the 1890s, such as allotments, smallholdings, minimum wages and even rent courts. Unable to agree, Unionists were incapable of offering an alternative to the Liberal government.

With neither option available, Bonar Law guided the party towards a third option to lift them from the electoral trough, an unlimited struggle over the unconstitutionality of Home Rule, and the 'illegality' of forcing it onto Ulster. It was an option that propelled the party sharply to the right and away from previous migrations to the centre, where past (and future) revivals occurred. It was a negative strategy, appealing to what people did not want rather than offering what they did, but no less powerful and attractive because of that. And in these respects it resembled Lord Salisbury's sharp move to the right over Home Rule in May 1886. In short, tough campaigning upon Ulster sprang from an absence of anything as effective, hiding the dearth of positive ideas and constructive planning at the heart of the party by 1911.

On the other hand, a negative Tory line on Ulster could still invoke a myriad of traditional sentiments and popular images; images around which the party ventured to construct or re-activate networks of electoral support. These sentiments and images included the security of the Empire, the democratic rights of minorities, opposition to political deceit, a sense of 'English' fair play, constitutional form and precedence, anti-popery and the defence of religious toleration, employment and economic prosperity, the rights of British citizenship, the protection of property, National defence and resistance to lawlessness. The campaign for Ulster and against Home Rule, represented a classic Conservative appeal to aspirations that cut across boundaries of class, region and religion, and impugned the narrow, sectional, un-English prejudices of Liberals and Irish Nationalists. It was an issue that could rally support in strategically important areas, such as Lancashire, London, Scotland and the North-West. In addition, by defending the rights of Presbyterians in Ulster, against what would be a Catholic-dominated southern legislature, Unionists stood to win the sympathy of Non-Conformists (or at least their abstention) at any future election. 'I am sure you are aware', Tom Sinclair reminded Bonar Law, 'that the great obstacle in our way in defeating H.R. lies in the attitude of English Non-Conformists ... nevertheless ... now that the H of L's question has been dealt with they may now be more willing to listen to appeals from their non-episcopal brethren.'[38]

However, the strategy of extracting an election through the threat of resistance entailed considerable risks. What if the Ulster menace was mere bluff? Everything hinged on Ulster convincing Asquith he could not proceed with Home Rule without civil war. Events so far in the province, and the frequent outbreaks of sectarian unrest, had done little to convince political opinion that Ulster meant business.[39] Bonar Law exerted what influence he had on ensuring the rebellion was more than mere 'opera bouffe'. He increasingly committed himself to their cause, visiting Belfast early in April 1912 and then with his dramatic pledge of support at Blenheim Palace, in July. Tough words and public displays of assistance, lessened the suspicion felt between Ulstermen and Conservatives since the federalist scare in the autumn of 1910. It also raised the morale of the Ulstermen, inspiring them in their activity and furnishing reassurance to those preparing on the ground. Bonar Law loudly and publicly encouraged Ulster to actually 'go to any length'. At best this played a key role in the mobilisation of Ulster; at the very least, he dramatically raised the stakes on Asquith, if he still thought Ulster was bluffing.

Demanding an election raised serious difficulties between the constituent parts of the Unionist coalition. Neither federalists nor the Ulstermen placed much value by an election. Federalists desired a political agreement along devolutionary lines. The Ulstermen sought the destruction of the bill or the government, and failing that, a settlement whereby Ulster was left under the parliament at Westminster. The Ulstermen were not to be constrained by a general election, reliant as it was on the fickle opinion of the British public. This points to their intention of influencing political attitudes at Westminster, amongst both Liberals and Conservatives, where they believed a solution to their problems would be won. In harnessing everything to an election, Bonar Law and the Tory leadership were following a slightly different course to Carson and the Ulster Unionists, a distinction he outlined to the Commons on 16 April 1912;

> if this bill were openly submitted to the people of this country there would be a difference between the Unionists in England and the Unionists in Ireland. Now there is none. We can imagine nothing which the Unionists in Ireland can do which will not be justified against a trick of this kind. And you will not succeed.[40]

And because the Ulstermen gave a lower priority to an election, the danger for Bonar Law was that they might pursue an independent line by angling for separate treatment from Asquith. This scenario was conceivable, given the centrality of the Ulster question, by 1912, to the success or failure of Home Rule, and the visibility of partition as a possible basis for compromise. The idea of a compromise between Ulster and the government had already been mooted during cabinet discussions on the bill in February and March 1912 by Lloyd George and Churchill. For Bonar Law, an agreement between the government and the Ulstermen would be impossible to reject, not least from the effect on public opinion. Yet acceptance eliminated the central Conservative demand for an election. To avert this, Bonar Law publicly connected the Tory offensive to the cause of Ulster. He established cordial relations with the Ulster leaders, instilling trust and pledging co-operation, to deter the Ulstermen from ploughing their own furrow. Fulsome, and seemingly open-ended, support from Bonar Law raised the Ulster leaders' estimation of how far the Tory leadership would go and what they would support. This, Bonar Law hoped, would diminish the likelihood of Carson and Craig plumping for the lesser option of a settlement with Asquith, if the greater option, of destroying the bill in its entirety and removing the government, seemed possible. The Ulstermen could always return to the 'narrower' option, if no election materialised or if its result was not to their liking:

> The Ulster members had to keep in view the ultimate policy to which they were already committed ... The likelihood of failure to bring about a dissolution before the Bill became law had to be faced.[41]

In addition, Bonar Law 'queered' the pitch upon where a compromise between Ulster and the government might be laid. The gulf between what the Ulstermen would accept and the Nationalists be willing to offer was generally thought unbridgeable. Bonar Law helped to insure this. His biting and hostile language against Home Rule, hardened Nationalist resolve and moved them in an equally uncompromising direction, so restricting Asquith's ability to manoeuvre them in a moderate direction. Earl Grey touched the essence of this when he warned Bonar Law that 'the refusal of the Unionist party to even consider Home Rule made it necessary for Redmond ... contrary to his own inclinations to fall back upon the extreme party'.[42] Bonar Law's bitter and die-hard stance, heightened sectarian and political tensions between the Ulstermen and the Nationalists, helping to destroy Asquith's line of retreat of separate treatment for Ulster.

Yet, it was in Carson and Craig's interest to firmly embrace the Tory leadership. The Tory leadership also had the ability to reach agreement with the government, perhaps upon the basis of a pro-order coalition to impose a solution onto Ireland, as was suggested during the 1910 Constitutional Conference and again in the autumn, and which, to a degree, operated in 1920–22. This course found sympathy with leaders such as Balfour and Lansdowne, as well as the likes of Chamberlain and F.E. Smith. And as the political atmosphere worsened after 1912, with the political crisis over Ireland joined by industrial and suffragette protest, and naval threats from Germany, so the idea of co-operation became more enticing to many in the party. Bonar Law never moved towards this, though it was something the Ulstermen had to keep in view. An uncompromising stance convinced Asquith and those sympathisers within his own party that such a pro-order alliance was not possible. Adversarial politics over Home Rule polarised the two parties, thus precluding any centrist or collusionist inclinations and keeping Asquith fastened to his acute predicament of civil war or an election. 'Which horn of the dilemma', Strachey wrote in *The Spectator*, 'they will impale themselves upon, it is not for us to say positively but that they must be impaled on one is clear.'[43]

Conservatives and Ulstermen, therefore, clasped each other in a shotgun marriage of mutual convenience. This still left the problem of powerful forces within Unionism alarmed by such a close association, namely Southern Unionists, federalist supporters and moderates. Bonar Law had to move with caution in Ulster's direction, ensuring the other elements in Unionism were not upset or alienated. Accordingly in his first major public speech, at Bootle, he avoided any direct reference to Ulster: 'There will be no shrinking from strong action … from any action which we think necessary to defeat one of the most ignoble conspiracies which has ever been formed against the liberties of free-born men.'[44] Similarly at the Albert Hall in January 1912, he kept his attack broad: 'we who represent the Unionist party in England and Scotland have supported and we mean to support to the end the loyal minority'.[45] His speeches in Belfast on 9 April 1912 and on the first reading debate on the 16 April, were more explicit in their pro-Ulster sentiment. But it was not until his speech at Blenheim Palace, in July 1912, where he gave an unequivocal pledge of support to Carson's efforts, that Ulster came to dominate his public attacks on Home Rule.

In the six months before the introduction of Home Rule, in April 1912, Bonar Law moved slowly towards his line of attack against Home Rule. It developed from the intersection of various pressures: party divisions, electoral failure, the mobilisation of Ulster and rise of a die-hard campaign around Carson and Craig, personal political weakness and deficiencies in policy. Avoiding the charms of federalism and the sterility of older attacks on Home Rule, which held Ireland as 'unfit' to rule itself, Bonar Law resisted Home Rule on clear constitutional grounds that it could not be advanced until the people had spoken on the matter. This provided enormous width to support Ulster in its activities; indeed its threats of rebellion would help move Asquith to just such an appeal to the people. To say the least, this was an extreme line of opposition, certainly one which neither Chamberlain nor Long, if selected leader, would have adopted. Lurching back to the negative Toryism of Lord Salisbury did, however, bring immediate political benefits for the struggling Bonar Law, at the expense of setting party politics upon a trajectory that would shake the foundations of the parliamentary system and transport the British state to the brink of civil war.

CHAPTER THREE

Home Rule and Unionist politics, 1912

INTRODUCTION

THE UNIONIST party's lurch to the right over Ireland became much clearer once the government introduced its Home Rule bill on 11 April 1912. Tories now began an intensive operation to de-rail the bill inside the house and with some success, as when they defeated the government on a finance resolution in November causing parliament to be suspended for a week. The shift rightwards resulted in several unsuccessful attempts at a compromise, with the Agar-Robartes amendment requesting the exclusion of the four Ulster counties of Armagh, Antrim, Londonderry and Down from the bill, and later an amendment from Carson calling for the exclusion of all nine Ulster counties. More famously, the struggle within the Commons was accompanied by a campaign outside the house which over the summer of 1912 achieved new heights of rhetorical excess, most notably with Bonar Law's pledge at Blenheim Palace on 27 July 1912 and the signing of the Solemn League and Covenant in Belfast on 28 September.

Not all within the Unionist alliance welcomed this lurch to the right. Federalists grew restless at the intemperance of their leaders while Southern Unionists became increasingly apprehensive at the possibility of independent action by Ulster. Despite these tensions, the first parliamentary circuit of the Home Rule bill was the high-point of Bonar Law's pre-war leadership. By-elections were won, the government were visibly shaken and the party was enthused. Most rewarding, the campaign against Home Rule looked as if it could well unseat the government.

'WE HAMMER HOME RULE:'[1] INTRODUCTION OF THE BILL

With the introduction of Home Rule in April, whatever grandiose strategic decisions Bonar Law and the Tory leadership took during the winter of 1911–12 about resisting Home Rule gave way to the slow parliamentary grind of opposition through the Commons. The bill was similar to Gladstone's Home Rule bills of 1886 and 1883: it called for an Irish parliament, composed of a Lower House of 164 representatives and an Upper House of 40.[2] The assembly would have power over local affairs such as education, fisheries, the Post Office, Customs and Excise and Judicial appointments. Reserved to the Imperial Parliament were control of the Army and Navy, Foreign policy, the temporary command of the Irish constabulary, taxation,(though there were some powers to raise taxes), Land Purchase, pensions and National Insurance. Through the Transferred Sum, the Imperial Exchequer would grant to Ireland monies to finance its local services, with an Exchequer board to oversee management and financial relations. Westminster was to retain an absolute veto over all Irish legislation, a right parliament had over all colonial governments but used rarely. A residue of forty-two Irish representatives were to remain at Westminster, avoiding the confusion of the 'in/out' clause in the 1893 Act. As with its two predecessors, no special treatment was offered to the northern Protestant areas, Asquith announcing that 'we cannot admit the right of a minority of the people ... to veto the verdict of the vast body of their countrymen'.[3] Interestingly, he pitched the 1912 bill as 'the first step and only the first step in a larger and more comprehensive policy',[4] in other words the beginning of a federated United Kingdom, a clear indication of the importance and support federal ideas enjoyed.

Promoting the bill as a stepping stone to full federation exposed it to Unionist attack as a sop to anxious federalists. 'It is put forward', Carson declared, 'simply for the purpose of pretending that you are only giving to Ireland something which you would also give to England and Scotland ... you are only pretending.'[5] If the government's plan really was Home Rule all round, 'was there a mandate for this at the last election? Was there a mandate for Home Rule for England?'[6] In any case, granting Ireland power over the Post Office and Customs and Excise was 'introducing diversity into unity',[7] and 'depart[ed] from all English speaking federal practice. Why when the federal scheme is completed and we have before us a systematic edifice of a separate England, Wales, Scotland and Ireland [should] one of these should have its own patronage and its own post office.'[8] And was it not a curious form of federation that dealt solely with Ireland and ignored the rest of the UK? 'What would have been thought of the founders of the American Constitution', Balfour asked the Commons, 'if they decided first on the powers of Massachusetts and left the powers of New York undecided for some remote future'.[9] Few federalists regarded the bill as anything more than self-rule for Ireland. 'I differ from you about Home Rule in the abstract', Lord Dunraven wrote to Carson, 'but I agree to a great extent with your views on the present bill.'[10] Establishing that there was little federal substance to the bill restricted support for it from these quarters.

A second angle of Unionist criticism was the financial arrangements of the bill.[11] *The Spectator* judged that, apart from Ulster, 'finance is the most important of all the questions raised by the Home Rule bill'.[12] Unionists set out to show these as unworkable and unfair. The reserved services, such as National Insurance and Pensions threatened to cost £5 million, a figure that could not be met by Irish tax revenues, the threshold of which was £3 million. This left a bounty of £2 million, which added to such invisible expenses as the cost of Naval and Military expenditure and contributions towards the National Debt and Foreign representation, cost an extra £4 million, according to *The Spectator*. This brought the total bill for granting Home Rule to Ireland to £6 million. Taxpayers were unlikely to find this a comforting thought, while government claims that Home Rule was in line with colonial precedent were shown as bogus. More embarrassingly, it contravened the fundamental principle of no taxation without representation. 'I do raise the strongest objection', Chamberlain protested, 'to voting British money for an Irish Parliament in Dublin to spend, not as we direct, but as they choose and as they direct.'[13] Other areas of its financial arrangements were also weak. Hayes-Fisher, MP for Fulham, demonstrated the danger they posed to future Irish prosperity and especially Irish credit.[14] Leo Amery, explored the complicated tax relations between Britain and Ireland, arguing they amounted to the Irish Exchequer having the power to raise taxes and customs, but not to lower the Imperial ones already in operation, a situation pregnant with complications in exchanges between the Irish and Imperial Chancellors of the Exchequer. 'In the domain of finance', Amery declared, 'this bill is not going to lead either to economy, co-operation or finality.'[15] Nor were the government's fortunes made easier when, on 19 April, it rejected its own advisory committee on Irish finance, the Primrose committee, when it recommended control of its own taxation. After several months of Unionist attack upon the bill's finances, there was much force behind *The Spectator*'s analysis that 'if the bill is bad from a constitutional point of view it can only be described as mad from a financial one'.[16]

Other lines of attack proved fruitful for Unionists. One was the so-called constitutional 'guarantees' of the bill, to ensure fair treatment for protestants over matters of religion and education, safeguards which Unionists revealed to be 'mere flummery'. Lord Selborne pondered 'the value of guarantees in a case like this which can only be enforced against a recalcitrant Irish Government and Parliament by force?'[17] Could a British government ever seriously coerce an established Irish parliament? The guarantees were simply decorative, a conclusion that enabled Unionists to publicise the fears and vulnerability of Ulster, and justified their determination to stay under the parliament at Westminster, a demand the government would find difficult to overturn. As Harry Lawson, Conservative MP for Mile End, inquired of the government, 'how are you in these days, these democratic days in this democratic age and in this democratic country to force a million men into a system which they refuse to join'?[18]

But it was the method by which the government were introducing Home Rule that drew from Unionists the sharpest attack, a criticism unique to the struggle of 1912. What was at fault was less *what* than *how* the bill was being passed, in disregard of all constitutional precedence. The usually mild Austen Chamberlain asked the Commons, 'what moral right has the Government to claim obedience to legislation of this character passed in this way? What were the preliminary steps which they paved their way? A conspiracy hatched in secret, nurtured in fraud and trickery by which you snatched support from the electors.'[19] At St Andrews Hall in Glasgow, Bonar Law hammered out this theme more explicitly. 'There is a determination in certain eventualities to resist the Government, a determination the seriousness of which no one recognises more fully than I do ... [The Government] are responsible *not because of their policy but because of their methods, not on account of what they propose to do but in the way in which they propose to do it*[20] [my italics].' Here again was the line of division between Ulster Unionists and Conservatives: the former would resist, whatever the government's methods in applying Home Rule or however conscientiously they were guided by parliamentary convention.

PARLIAMENTARY WARFARE

During the first months of the bill's life Unionists had much the best of debate. *The Times* noted, as parliament was breaking for Whitsuntide (23 May to 4 June 1912) 'the remarkable change in the position of the Government over the last six months'.[21] Signs of ministerial apprehension were clearly evident. Both Churchill and Sir Edward Grey, during second reading, had acknowledged Ulster as a serious obstacle and subscribed to some form of separate treatment, remarks that agitated the Nationalists. Some Liberal backbenchers also displayed cold feet. Sir George Kemp, Captain Pirie and Agar-Robartes, all abstained on both divisions of the bill, while Sir Clifford Cory went through the opposition lobby.[22] An up-beat Bonar Law pondered the government's troubled position; 'I am at this moment', he exclaimed, 'at a loss to understand what the professed object of the Government is and I think many Hon. gentlemen opposite would like to know.'[23]

Yet the bill entered committee stage on 11 June unchanged. One acute problem for the government was the tightness of the parliamentary timetable, with three major bills (Home Rule, Welsh Disestablishment and Franchise Reform) all demanding passage before the end of the session. They were constrained, however, by the declining number of days left and by Asquith's declaration that debate on Home Rule would be 'free and unfettered'. *The Times* drew two conclusions; either one of the bills must be dropped (but this would be 'fatal to the solidarity of the coalition');[24] or 'we may thus before long expect to renew our acquaintance with "guillotine" and "Kangaroo"'.[25] Prior to the summer recess, the government persevered without recourse to the guillotine, although this entailed, uniquely, prolonging committee into the autumn.

Unionists mobilised to capsize this cramped timetable. They tabled various amendments. For example, Ronald McNeill, Lord Tullibardine, MP for West Perth, and James Hope, MP for Sheffield Central, all moved for the postponement of the bill until a referendum, its likely rejection advertising a lack of trust in the electorate and validating Unionist claims that Home Rule was being smuggled in behind the backs of the people. Interestingly, the most significant amendment came from the Liberal side. On 11 June 1912 Agar-Robartes, MP for St Austell, moved for the exclusion of the counties of Down, Armagh, Antrim and Londonderry[26] from the bill, against a background of by-election disappointments and growing unease within Liberal quarters about the situation in Ulster. The amendment revealed the level of discontent on the Liberal backbenches, when a normal government majority of 110 collapsed to 69: indeed its rejection had only been assured by a full Nationalist turnout. *The Times* sensed 'considerable disquietude' amongst ministerialists,[27] while at St Dunston's Lodge on 28 June, Bonar Law reflected that 'so far things are going well with us. I am convinced they are going to be much better for it seems to me that every day shows more clearly that the Government are getting tied up into a knot which cannot be severed by any method except suicide.'[28]

Yet the amendment posed serious problems for the Unionist leadership. To abstain or reject it, having championed the cause of the northern Protestants, would expose them to charges of expediency and provide the government with the moral justification to continue with their bill as it stood. Unionists would advertise their unco-operative and unreasonable character, a poor impression to foster if their central purpose was to secure and win an election. On the other hand, to embrace the amendment, however good for public relations would, if accepted, remove the need for an election. And perhaps more divisively, acceptance signified that Home Rule for the rest of Ireland was admissible, a recognition liable to create much anger amongst traditional Tories and Southern Unionists. Whether the amendment was, as *The Times* initially saw it, 'nothing more than a tactical move without substance or serious import',[29] it still presented Bonar Law with a difficult choice.

After consultation with Carson and other leaders, Bonar Law decided to support it. Replying to the chief secretary, Augustine Birrell, who dismissed the amendment, he declared 'I am going to vote in favour of this amendment. I am going to vote in its favour not for a moment that it would take away my opposition to Home Rule ... But while we oppose this bill root and branch ... we will support any amendment which, bad as the bill seems to us to be, would make it less bad than it was before the amendment was introduced':[30] a negative endorsement of the lesser evil. Balfour and Hugh Cecil followed his line, as did Carson on 13 June 1912. Tactical considerations in favour of acceptance had been paramount, and particularly the belief that the Nationalists would reject it. Indeed Bonar Law went some way to ensure a Commons majority against the amendment, by declaring his support, rather than offering a free vote, thus securing a straight forward division on party lines.

For the Ulstermen, the need to play the parliamentary game, advertising to the government their willingness to compromise and appealing to British public opinion, had triumphed over their commitment to all-Ireland Unionism. After an acrimonious conference with Irish Unionist colleagues at Londonderry House on the 11 July, where McNeill refers to 'sharp differences of opinion' between Southern and Ulster Unionists, Carson approved the amendment.[31] In his speech of the 13th, which was full of qualifications, he endorsed the amendment following the Speaker's request to be more relevant.[32] 'I can only say', Carson replied, 'with great respect that I am surprised if I am not entitled to show why these counties in Ulster cannot trust the majority and give that as a reason why they should be excluded from this bill.'[33] McNeill justified acceptance as a necessary precaution 'to prevent if possible the passage of the Bill to the Statute book, and if that should prove impractical to prevent its enforcement "in those districts of which they had control"'.[34] But it also marked something of a point of departure; 'the first time (Ulster Unionists) publicly accepted the idea of a separate treatment for themselves as a possible alternative policy'.[35] Certainly Craig saw it in this light, interpreting the government rejection as 'a declaration of war against Ulster', and thus permitting them to 'take a step forward in their campaign' and preparations.[36]

Up until this point, Southern Unionists had, somewhat hesitantly, accepted concentration upon Ulster as the best tactical line in the campaign to destroy Home Rule, trusting Carson that he was simply 'trying to do what is best for them'.[37] James Mackay-Wilson, a prominent Southern Unionist and elder brother of Sir Henry Wilson, told a Belfast audience that 'without Ulster's agreement, Home Rule is impossible. We look to you to make it so'.[38] But concentration upon Ulster looked suspiciously like a dearth of opposition elsewhere, something they struggled to repudiate. Several Unionist demonstrations were held across the South. One at Cork in April, was rather optimistically held to have 'dispelled the fiction that opposition to Home Rule is confined to Ulster',[39] and J.B. Powell, secretary of the IUA, referred to southern Unionism as a force which 'had to be reckoned with'.[40] Lord Midleton, already emerging as a champion of southern loyalists, claimed after demonstrations in Cork, Waterford, Sligo and Limerick that although 'Ulster holds the field ... Unionists outside Ulster have rallied as they have never done before'.[41] The Agar-Robartes amendment dealt a blow to this nervous brotherly co-operation.

Southern and some die-hard Unionists were outraged by the Ulstermen's support for partition, fearing Carson's approval represented 'the larger aspects (of Unionism) gradually dropping away'[42] to leave greater independent action by Ulster. Midleton felt that 'leading politicians in England regarded the South as a losing game'.[43] 'I could not betray my friends in the south',[44] Walter Long told Bonar Law on 4 June 1912, and three days later, he warned 'by clever tactics we shall disgust our friends in the rest of Ireland and seriously weaken our position in Great Britain'.[45]

To Lady Londonderry he attacked Carson, perhaps observing a new role for himself as a defender of wider Unionist interests:

> I am very glad you have written as you have done to Carson. I can't imagine what has come over him … He and others may turn and twist their actions, the bulk of the people will say 'we told you so, Ulster was bluffing' … if accepted it would be sheer madness and would split our party to its foundations.[46]

Long struggled to rally opinion against the amendment. Speaking at the Albert Hall on 14 June, he assured the audience (though aimed at Bonar Law) that 'no bribe would buy them and no temptation would seduce them'.[47]

However, Long was a lone dissentient. Most of the leadership, including Lansdowne, recognised it was tactically essential to support the amendment and Carson was careful to assuage ruffled Unionist fears during debate: 'we do not accept this', he reassured them, 'as a compromise of the question. There is no compromise possible because he [Asquith] offers what would be merely a simple act of justice to a portion of Ulster, why should we on that ground abandon our position in regard to a policy which we believe harmful to Ireland.'[48] Bonar Law also tried to calm fears by establishing contact with influential Southern Unionists. In response to Mackay-Wilson's concerns, Bonar Law offered some comfort:

> I can assure you that the point of view which you put before me is always present to my mind. When however one is engaged in a great conflict it is necessary to use the means which are most effective; and after all it is not Ireland which we hope to influence but England and Scotland … There is no difference, I am sure, of view on this question between yourself and me; *it is simply a question of the best way in which to win the fight.*[49] (my italics)

Such overtures clearly worked for no revolt materialised against the amendment. A little crest-fallen, Long now quickly fell into line and by the 19 June he was even telling the Commons that by supporting the amendment 'they would be in a stronger position to stand up for their brethren in the south and west if they were outside an Irish Parliament'.[50] Yet events for Carson, and for Bonar Law, had certainly revealed the difficulties of their position. According to Carson's critics, it appeared circumstances were compelling the leader of Irish Unionism to nail his colours more firmly to Belfast's mast. He countered these charges of betrayal by stressing the tactical, 'wrecking' nature of his support, intended simply to split the opposition and destroy the bill. Nor should we necessarily question his justification and position as an Irish Unionist fighting to defeat Home Rule, not just to save Ulster. Yet the fact remains, Carson was under growing pressure trying to straddle both southern and northern Unionism.

Despite the intense debate and argument within Unionism, the amendment proved beneficial for them. It publicised Nationalist refusal to accept some form of separate treatment or partition for Ireland. As *The Times* put it, 'Mr Redmond would never accept Home Rule without the inclusion of Ulster. He claimed Ulster and therefore he must either get it or the Government must go.'[51] Such Nationalist obduracy stoked frustration amongst Liberals and was reflected in the government's heavy reliance upon Nationalist votes for defeating the amendment.[52] Bonar Law seized upon such dependence. 'I am not going to say anything about the subserviency of the Government. There is no need to tell the country about that. Everybody has seen it ... they are carrying Home Rule at the dictation of the Nationalist party.'[53] The Agar-Robartes amendment brought into sharp focus the Irish 'straightjacket' that was tightening around the government: on the one side, intimidated by Ulster if they continued with their present bill, on the other, Nationalists watchful and determined against any back-sliding. It was this 'vice which was going to squeeze Asquith to an election'.[54]

Liberal disillusionment increased through the remainder of the summer session and manifest itself in a falling attendance. *The Morning Post* wrote of 'a fatal disease which pervades the Liberal ranks'.[55] On 25 June 1912, just six days after the rejection of the Agar-Robartes amendment, the government majority fell to twenty-two on a budget resolution, and a month later (25 July), it was down to just three on supplementary estimates. 'If our men had played the game better', Robert Sanders a junior whip lamented, 'we should have beaten them easily.'[56] The short summer recess did little to raise Liberal spirits. Unionists dominated the headlines during the holiday period, with Bonar Law's dramatic pronouncement at Blenheim and the signing of the Ulster Covenant. The momentum established by the Unionists stood in stark contrast to the government. There was no triumphal crusade across Britain to rouse support for Home Rule and the only prominent ministerial speech, from

Churchill at Dundee on 12 September 1912, advocated a federal alternative to Irish Home Rule.

When the House reassembled on 4 October the government faced a very tight parliamentary situation, with the extra pressure of a Trade Union bill added to the already stretched legislative programme as 'a sop to the Labour party'.[57] Four major bills now required passage through parliament. It was clear to all that 'the Government enter upon a difficult and overcrowded session with no very great political capital and no very great driving force behind them'.[58] To accelerate the legislative process, two changes were introduced. First, the present sitting was extended into the next year, making March 1913 the end of the 1912 session, an 'extraordinary expedient' that revealed 'what straits the Government are reduced and with what cynical contempt of constitutional practise ... some people are prepared to act'.[59] This sparked bitter exchanges between the parties, in an already acrimonious political environment, after the summer's fireworks. But such ill temper was nothing compared to the effect had by the second change, the introduction of a closure resolution on 10 October 1912, to speed up progress on the Home Rule bill. Closure inspired a violent response from Unionists. 'This is the first fruits of your Parliament Act', Bonar Law declared, 'and the fact that this resolution is proposed at all is the clearest evidence that Act can never work unless the majority are willing to make this house cease altogether to be a legislative assembly and to become instead a machine for registering the decrees of the Government.'[60] The closure resolution reinforced Unionist arguments concerning unconstitutional behaviour by the government, who were now forcing their measure through, contrary to parliamentary precedence, prime ministerial guarantees and the opinion of the people. *The Times* viewed it as 'totally destructive of the powers of the House of Commons' and hoped Unionists would confine their fury to 'Parliamentary protest'.[61] Feeling certainly ran high in the party; 'quiet staid men like Bigland', Sanders wrote after the debate on closure, 'got absolutely wild. Monsell very nearly came to blows with Eustace Fiennes as they went out.'[62] However, such was the ineffectual position of the Opposition party that little could be done except violent words and to continue their campaign of disrupting and 'spoiling' the government timetable.

Since the introduction of the bill in April, Tories had tried to disrupt government business by utilising all manner of parliamentary tactics. The key to this game was a refusal to pair and a constant scrutiny of attendance, in the hope of catching the government short on a division. The likelihood of this was increased by a well-oiled team of whips, under the leadership of Lord Balcarres, who generally fatigued government supporters through well-planned 'rushes' to London, secret pass words, members hiding in the Commons toilet or lingering expectantly at St Stephens tavern, for the all important snap division. Such pressures were likely to result in a 'snap' defeat, or if they were especially fortunate exhaust the government sufficiently enough to 'throw in the sponge'. Walter Bridgeman, another junior whip, observed that the Liberals 'are thoroughly uncomfortable. They never know when we are going to turn up.'[63] This resulted in running the government close on two divisions in the summer, which might have gone the other way 'if our men had not been late'.[64] By the autumn session, with a new and inexperienced Liberal chief whip, Percy Illingworth, and with Liberal members already flagging under the strain of Unionist tactics, conditions seemed ripe for a strike. It came on 11 November 1912, with a surprise amendment by Sir Fredrick Banbury on a finance resolution to the Home Rule Bill, which caught the government short in the lobbies by twenty-two votes.

The snap defeat marked the triumphant climax to six months of hard work by Balcarres. It brought to a head within the party the desire for some type of direct action in the House, in the form of a walk-out, unruly behaviour, 'pantomime histrionics' or even a replay of the famous 'Cecil' scene of August 1911. The closure resolution in October had pushed some Unionists over the edge. Balcarres sensed that 'many of them especially Irish Unionists are anxious to do so on the ground that nothing short of suspension following turbulent scenes will impress England with the depth of their conviction'.[65] And *The Times*, two days later, reported rumours of 'violent measures or violent action'.[66] Bonar Law hinted at the likelihood of party disorder on 25 October. 'It is intolerable to many of our supporters who, I know, are not satisfied either with the position or with our action. They want something dramatic. They hold and there is something to be said for their views, that a revolutionary committee … can only be overthrown by a counter-revolution.'[67] Fearing the public response to these methods, Bonar Law managed to control his party with a tough and bitter reply to Asquith's closure motion that was enough to temporarily assuage the aggressive atmosphere (Balcarres wrote of it containing many 'angry passages').[68] However, the government's snap defeat in the Commons, and their subsequent attempt to rescind the vote, a high-handiness Unionists believed was 'contrary to all precedent and practice', finally broke the reserve and control of Tories.[69]

During the debate to rescind the defeat, the House heard Asquith in relative silence, but ministers following him were shouted down. Sir William Bull, MP for Hammersmith, was told to withdraw after calling the prime minister a traitor, and 'the tumult became so continuous that the House was adjourned'.[70] The sitting resumed an hour later, but tempers had not cooled. Sir Rufus Isaacs was howled down, causing the sitting to be suspended for the rest of the day. As the chamber emptied, McNeill threw a copy of the standing orders at Churchill, hitting the First Lord on the head, though not damaging the weighty tome. Sanders, a junior whip considered the atmosphere such 'that it would have taken very little to make a general fight' along the lines of 1893.[71] Although others, including Bull, considered it had been badly stage-managed and only just avoided dissolving into farce.[72] The next day, in a calmer House, Asquith agreed to follow parliamentary precedent and to 'negative his own financial resolution and then introduce another'.[73] Parliament was then adjourned for the rest of the week to allow tempers to subside but tightening the timetable even more. Comment on the Tories' action was generally supportive, most concluding the fray was reasonable, given the government's 'outrageous methods';[74] but repetition was another matter. 'I hope', Bonar law confided to Lord Stamfordham, the king's private secretary, 'the proceedings in the House of Commons will now go on in the ordinary way.'[75] Not all rejoiced at the methods. Dicey, Vinerian Professor of Law at Oxford, constitutional expert and fanatical Unionist, complained that 'the cause of Unionism may be ruined' by such action.[76] *The Times* also 'regretted that the opposition allowed themselves to be goaded into the unseemly demonstrations ... and it was probably an error in tactics as well',[77] although five days later they insisted, 'the opposition have good reason to be proud of the success with which they have upheld the practice and the customs of the House'.[78]

For the die-hards, the 1912 campaign inside the House was everything they hoped from their new leader. With such partisan assaults on the government, all reminiscent of the no-surrender movement of July and August 1911, they could relish a leadership that spoke forcefully and plainly, and was able to capture the public imagination. 'The country will turn gratefully', *The Morning Post* believed, 'from lawyer politicians ... to the plain man with the courage to speak his mind.'[79] Importantly, activism by the leadership tied the recalcitrant members of the right behind the party. But resorting to unconventional and un-Parliamentary methods, to rally discontented Unionists, was fraught with dangers for Bonar Law.

The speedy launch into second reading, only two weeks after completion of first reading and Asquith's closure resolution in October, witnessed Bonar Law and Balcarres straining to keep command of the party. When the prime minister tried to reverse the snap-defeat of his government in November, control was only maintained by orchestrating grave disorder in the House. Regulating and yet satisfying the right was a difficult balance to strike and always held the very real potential of dissolving into acrimonious, uncontrolled chaos.

And yet despite all the fireworks and the war of attrition inside the House of Commons during the summer and autumn of 1912, Home Rule progressed majestically along its path. By 12 December the committee stage was completed, with a further seven days given over to report and then third reading on the 15–16 January 1913, before the bill moved upstairs to the Lords. The bill remained largely as it had been when introduced back in April and public opinion was still little stirred by events. Parliamentary theatricals over the first circuit of the bill betray not Unionist strength and resource but frustration and weakness.

'FREEZING THE LIBERAL BLOOD':[80] UNIONISTS TAKE TO THE PLATFORM

'The battles at Westminster are seldom of decisive importance … An opposition must therefore not only oppose in the House of Commons but must devote its best efforts to rallying public opinion in the country'.[81] Since late 1911 the UUC and IUA, had been engaged distributing literature, canvassing electors and arranging speakers, across the country, and in conjunction with the Ulster Defence League, a group financed by prominent British sympathisers and chaired by Walter Long. By-elections were an obvious focus for their energies. For example the St Rollox by-election in February 1912 witnessed ten canvassers and two agents descend on the constituency,[82] though without success. And with the approach of the holiday season, canvassers switched their attention to popular resorts.[83] By September 1912, after a full year's work, over 91 constituencies had been 'worked', 2,178 meetings addressed, and 517,119 doubting voters canvassed by the UAI.[84] As the Unionist leadership engaged in platform pyrotechnics, a slow, hum-drum war was being waged by an army of Union enthusiasts, much of which had only the faintest of impacts upon British public opinion.

From the public platform, Carson was the most popular Unionist leader, though well supported by others, especially his sidekick Smith. Carson caught the public's attention, with his appetite for the heroic gesture, 'his stage-Irishman' mannerisms,[85] his air of dogged determination, complemented by his hard, chiselled features ('Carson, with his face, was bound to be a Christian martyr; he would not have been born like that otherwise'[86]). And as his public stature, and notoriety, rose so his influence on the Tory right grew. J.S. Sandars, assessing various political fortunes at this time, felt that Carson had 'advanced' while 'Bonar Law [is] looking on and Austen resting'.[87] Between October 1911 and January 1912, the Tory leadership took the fight to the country with a series of speeches in the north. Carson toured Scotland. Walter Long spoke in Manchester and at the party conference in Leeds on 17 November 1911 he moved the resolution against Home Rule. Despite their mutual detestation, Smith shared a platform with Long at Manchester, before moving on to Glasgow. These sporadic platform addresses culminated on 22–3 January 1912 with a campaign through Lancashire, timed as a prelude to Bonar Law's keynote speech at the Albert Hall on the 26th and the opening of parliament in February. Interestingly, at this early stage and before a Home Rule Bill had even been presented, the Unionist leaders offered slightly different interpretations of the task ahead of them. Walter Long and Lord Midleton focused on the party's opposition to Home Rule for the whole of Ireland rather than just Ulster. Austen Chamberlain recommended a devolutionary scheme as a compromise on Ireland while Carson and Smith stuck firmly to Ulster grievances.

The campaign outside was galvanised just days before the bill was introduced, when Bonar Law and Carson addressed an enormous anti-Home Rule rally in Belfast on 9 April. For McNeill it represented 'the Unionist party of G.B. met and grasped the hand of Ulster loyalism', a grasp that until very recently had been decidedly loose.[88] Nervous, and overwhelmed by the size of the meeting, Bonar Law delivered a disappointing speech, although the most significant aspect was not his words but the 'symbolism in his presence'.[89] Carson, on the other hand, more attuned to his audience, provided a rousing oration, full of vigour, declarations of loyalty and resolution against a 'corrupt' foe, that resonated perfectly the sentiments and style of Ulster Protestants.[90] On 10 May Bonar Law spoke again, this time to the Primrose League, whom he assured that '[Ulster] shall not trust us in vain'. He also went further in his sponsorship, prefiguring the type of pledge he would make two months hence at Blenheim; 'we shall take any steps – whatever steps seem to us likely to be effective – to put an end to the conspiracy which is directed against them'.[91] On the same evening Carson spoke to the 1900 club introducing an element of sedition into the unfolding debate; 'what would be the effect on the Army? Many officers would resign; no Army could stand such a strain,'[92] language that for, Will Thorne, a Labour leader, warranted his removal from the Privy Council.[93] The idea of Army mutiny was echoed by the Duke of Bedford, who claimed, rather bizarrely, that although army officers had to obey orders if commanded to march north, they might refuse them 'at the moment of deployment'.[94]

Despite these seditious warnings, the country stirred little. Robert Sanders observed in May 1912 that 'there is no sign of any considerable feeling against the Bill in the country'.[95] By mid-June, Leo Amery was no less pessimistic; 'we must get steam up quickly if we are ever to get the country interested and the Government out before 1914'.[96] And *The Times* noted that 'the general public are apparently looking on in mere bewilderment – if not in mere boredom'.[97] National Insurance was a bigger political issue while Welsh Disestablishment was, according to Sanders, more bitterly resented than Home Rule.[98] Awakening public opinion to the supposed horrors of Home Rule was proving a difficult nut to crack. To make matters worse renewed sectarian violence broke out in Belfast. Tensions had been running high since Churchill's visit in February 1912, when he had been forced, by the UUC and general disquiet in the city, to speak not at the Ulster Hall as intended but at the Celtic Road football ground.[99] Come the bill's introduction, in April, 'feeling there (was) hotter than it (had) ever been before',[100] sparking some sectarian attacks. But it was in late June 1912 that violence fully erupted in the Belfast shipyards ('the inflammable zone').[101] It was sparked by the strange fracas at Castledawson on 29 June, where a group from the Ancient Order of Hibernians broke up a Protestant Sunday school outing. There followed the usual sequence of assaults upon Catholic workers in the Belfast shipyards, their eviction from the workplace and disorder in Nationalist parts of the city. Events suggested a lively summer as the marching season approached. Sectarian outrages were a profound anxiety to Carson and Bonar Law. They undermined the image of northern Protestants as the aggrieved party and, more seriously, presented the government with an excuse to clamp down on the Ulstermen's preparations in the province. Hence Carson, on 11 July, urged 'self control and discipline'[102] for the 'twalfth'. Smith, speaking on the twelfth, urged Ulster to 'maintain that impression of self-restraint and reserve force'.[103] Unionist leaders eagerly sought to blend sedition with self-control.

Confronted with the problems of dwindling public interest and increased tensions amongst northern Protestants at the seemingly unstoppable path of Home Rule, Bonar Law responded with his famous Blenheim Palace speech on 27 July 1912. The timing was determined by a speech from Asquith on 19 July, re-affirming the government's commitment to Home Rule and offering little comfort to Ulster: enraging the Ulstermen into civil commotion provided useful moral authority for the government. It was imperative, then, that Bonar Law not only replied to Asquith but gave reassurance to Ulster that their struggle was undertaken with determination by the Conservative party. Bonar Law might also have been reasserting his own influence and prestige in the party. This was against, on the one hand, a campaign whose tone and pace were set by Carson, and on the other, to subdue recent federalist and moderate Unionist rumblings, alarmed by the ease with which Carson had hi-jacked the Unionist response to Home Rule. Buoyed up by news of a Unionist victory at the Crewe by-election the day before, Bonar Law delivered at Blenheim Palace a speech unique in British political history. He began by questioning the legality of what the government were trying to do:

> We do not acknowledge their right to carry such a revolution by such means. We do not recognise that any such action is the constitutional Government of a free people. We regard them as a revolutionary committee which has seized by fraud upon despotic power ... We shall use whatever means seem to us likely to be most effective'.[104]

Having said this he unreservedly committed the party he led to disobedience of the law, even civil war, if the government did not hold an election before imposing Home Rule:

> In my opinion if an attempt were made without the clearly expressed will of the people of this country ... to deprive these men of their birthright they would be justified in resisting by all means in their power, including force ... and I say now, with a full sense of the responsibility which attaches to my position, that if the attempt be made under present conditions I can imagine no length of resistance to which Ulster will go in which I shall not be ready to support them

and in which they will not be supported by the overwhelming majority of the British people'.[105]

It was the language of 1689 or 1830–32. 'I never hoped for such a strong statement from Bonar Law', Lady Craigavon wrote elatedly in her diary, 'it really does put heart into one.'[106] A shell-shocked Asquith denounced it as 'reckless rodomontade',[107] and Churchill, worried at the long-term consequences, fiercely denounced it, accusing Bonar Law of a 'frantic manner' which '[is] foreign to the instincts of the party which he leads'.[108]

In analysing the speech we must be cautious of Asquithian moral indignation, the political purpose of which was to portray Bonar Law in as bad a light as possible. Certainly Blenheim injected an extremism into political dialogue. Asquith and Bonar Law clashed in the Commons over the speech with Bonar Law refusing to retract any part of it and indeed repeating the pledge inside the House, to the accompaniment of loud cheers from his own side. Yet most of what he said had been taken from previous speeches, particularly his speech on 26 January 1912 at the Albert Hall and in the Commons on 16 April. His Blenheim pledge also had a strange, plagiaristic element to it, echoing a speech given by F.E. Smith on the 22 January; 'there is no length to which Ulster will not be entitled to go, however desperate or unconstitutional in carrying on the quarrel ... in any resistance to which Ulster might be driven ... she would command your support and she would command my support'.[109] Bonar Law had spoken from a written sheet, unusual for him and indicating the care with which he chose his words.[110] And his pledge was firmly tied to the constitutional sheet-anchor of an election, a line used on several previous occasions. His tough words were not unique but part of a trend, behind which lay the same objectives he had pursued since 1911 – firstly of driving home to the public the awful position Ulster was placed in as a result of Home Rule and secondly of intimidating the government into a dissolution by demonstrating the impossibility of implementing the bill. In the process of reiterating these dramatic observations he helped re-enthuse his party at the end of a tiring session; 'the call of a bugle' was how *The Morning Post* regarded it.[111] Furthermore, as Lady Craigavon's diary implies, Blenheim sought to calm the right wing of the party, after his support for the Agar-Robartes amendment and to control Ulster, tying her closer to the Conservative leadership and bringing a halt to sectarian violence.

Bonar Law's Blenheim speech set the scene for an even bigger demonstration of Unionist resolution with the signing of a Solemn

League and Covenant on 28 September 1912 by loyalists through-out Ulster.[112] As early as 17 August, details of the demonstration were published in the press, listing dates, venues and speakers.[113] It was designed as huge theatrical spectacular, full of mock ceremony and public acts of loyalty to the cause, with the covenant a sort of blood oath. A good omen to the preparations was news of the overturning of two key Liberal seats, N.W. Manchester on the 8 August and Midlothian on 10 September. 'When a Liberal Government is beaten in Midlothian', Bonar Law gloated, 'the end of that Government must be at hand.'[114]

Carson arrived in Belfast on 16 September. For the next two weeks he led a team of Unionist leaders on a speaking campaign across Ulster, culminating on the 28th with the signing of the covenant at the City Hall in Belfast. The covenant tied its signatories to 'using all means which may be found necessary to defeat the present conspiracy to set up a Home Rule Parliament in Ireland'.[115] It committed the signatory to defend all Ireland and not just Ulster from a Home Rule Parliament, a statement designed to settle Irish Unionist fears but without inhibiting the Ulstermen in their separate preparations. These dramatic events continued on the mainland. Carson arrived at Liverpool docks to be greeted by a crowd of 150,000 singing hymns. The same day he spoke at Shiel Park, described by *The Times* as 'Belfast all over again' and, in the evening, to the Liverpool Conservative Club.[116] Later that night he travelled north to another conclave of Orange sentiment, Glasgow, where he addressed another mass meeting. The press relished the street theatre, something for which Carson, with his flair for the melodramatic, was uniquely qualified. The intention was to capture the imagination of the British public, and *The Times* certainly believed 'that these Northern gatherings have brought that conviction home to many thousands of Englishmen',[117] while the covenant was 'a definite and irretrievable step in the opposition to the Home Rule bill'.[118] Two days later, Bonar Law felt it had 'killed Home rule, as I always felt sure it would',[119] and Carson concluded 'our action has made a profound impression through-out the U.K.'.[120]

We might question just how much effect it did have. For all the theatricals and fireworks, nothing had actually changed. Carson's September 'jihad' and the covenant were good entertainment but of little practical value in defeating the bill. Although the political temperature had been raised, the bill had not been re-routed from its parliamentary course. Public opinion had been interested even intrigued, but scarcely roused, and still appeared largely unconcerned. Considering the fortunes of the

Ulster campaign a month after the covenant, Lord St Aldwyn felt that 'there must be a very different state of feeling on the subject if it is ultimately to be prevented from becoming law'.[121] Sanders also believed the summer and autumn campaigns against Home Rule had not rallied the English constituencies.[122] In addition, perhaps its most significant consequence was in publicising the dangers threatening Ulster rather than in extending a degree of control over the province. This was all the more necessary following renewed rioting in the shipyards during July and at the Celtic football ground on 14 September, where over 100 people were injured.

At a broader level, Unionist tactics had fatigued the government and accomplished a notable triumph on 11 November, but Home Rule remained intact and the government had not been forced to an election. Once all the smoke had risen, by the New Year, a stagnant parliamentary condition persisted. We might push this argument further. Liberal apathy during the summer and autumn of 1912 was less the result of dissatisfaction with the government than the product of a crowded legislative timetable and the loss of so skilled an operator as Elibank as chief whip. Furthermore, Unionist recourse to parliamentary trench-warfare suggested frustration at their own essential powerlessness. As these conclusions began to dawn on Conservatives and Ulstermen, so the early unity, forged from late 1911, slowly began to dissipate.

TORY MODERATES AND FEDERALISTS

Elements in the party sympathetic to a compromise were dismayed at their leaders' extreme language and unlimited pledges of support for Ulster. *The Times*, often a barometer of opinion amongst party backbenchers, reprimanded Bonar Law for his immoderation, describing the Blenheim speech as 'grave and explicit, perhaps in view of its gravity more explicit than was altogether desirable or necessary'.[123] Balcarres observed a group 'of straight-laced and ill-informed purists' who were upset by the leaderships' actions.[124] Many were particularly upset by the sectarian undertones to the Tory leadership's opposition. Lady Ninan Crichton Stuart criticised Bonar Law for his attacks on Catholics[125] and Aubrey Herbert, newly elected at the December 1910 election, was 'saddened' by the 'strong and abusive line with regard to Irishmen and Catholics'.[126] To meet these concerns, Bonar Law invited the Duke of Norfolk, a leading

Anglo-Catholic, onto the platform at Blenheim, a 'significant and even symbolic' ploy to avoid the loss of any Catholic support.[127] It was also from these moderate quarters that pressure came for the exclusion of Ulster. They had supported the Agar-Robartes amendment in June and reciprocated the sympathy which Churchill and Grey showed towards a compromise. Such opinion was more established in the House of Lords, from where the Duke of Sutherland and the Earl of Mar urged Bonar Law to seek a solution.[128] Unfortunately, despite these modest developments moderate Tory opinion never crystallised into a strong movement. Much of the Unionist press savoured the spasm of 'bloodletting' after two years of hesitancy and Balfourian 'flour and water'. As a group, the moderates lacked political weight, or a recognisable focus within the leadership. Balfour was the obvious choice having endorsed the exclusion of Ulster during the committee stage.[129] However he declined to give a lead, aware that moderation was not practical politics in 1912, when the party was appreciating its first experience of unity and success for nearly three years. Nor were first circuits the ideal time for compromise. These considerations might explain the absence of a moderate backlash against extremism of 1912.

Many federalists were also suspicious of the tone and direction of the campaign against Home Rule. F.S. Oliver told Bonar Law, a week after Blenheim, that 'public opinion ... is very perturbed by and opposed to certain things which have been said in regard to Ulster not only by Carson, Smith and others but also by yourself';[130] 'I don't think the country will stand unconstitutional weapons'.[131] And to the party chairman, Steel-Maitland, Oliver pressed for less outrageous behaviour; 'urge your Tom fool followers to keep off two things – religious intolerance and treason. Carson has done more harm to Irishmen in the last months than Redmond has'.[132] Avoiding the passion of the platform, federal activity concentrated upon disproving Asquith's claims that his bill was part of a wider devolutionary change. Oliver published several articles demonstrating the bill was a contradiction of federal beliefs, as did Garvin, in *The Observer*.[133] Sir Gilbert Parker, a Unionist and federal supporter, mounted a series of attacks in *The Morning Post* under the title of 'Home Rule the Colonial analogy'.[134] In the House, Chamberlain, Harold Mackinder and Leo Amery all refuted that the bill had any true federal basis. These attacks insured few federal sympathisers were gulled into regarding Home Rule as a stepping stone to a wider federal reconstruction. Asquith unwittingly encouraged this with his slip in the Commons on 9 May 1912 that 'no cast iron pattern would be appropriate' to a new federal structure, implying his scheme was of a specific rather than general application.[135] As a consequence, the next day *The Times* commented that the idea of the bill as a first stage to full federalisation 'has ludicrously broken down'.[136]

In addition to negating the bill, some more positive federal activity was evident during the 1912 session. Both Churchill and Sir Edward Grey put out 'feelers' during the second reading to which Austen Chamberlain reciprocated with support for a local government solution and offered suggestions on how the present bill might be re-drafted upon a more viable federal basis. Through the entreaties of Moreton Frewen, a keen federalist and friend of Bonar Law, federalists and round-tablers enjoyed access to the Tory leader.[137] Down this channel Frewen, through June, pressed the views of Lords Dunraven and Earl Grey, by proposing a more constructive path and less hostility towards the Nationalists. He even mooted the idea of some form of co-operation with the independent Nationalists, William O'Brien and Tim Healy.[138] This notion of co-operating with the independents, around a compromise on Irish self-government and resolution to the Land question, had first been suggested in October 1910.[139] Now, in an atmosphere of bitterness and menace, it offered Tory devolutionists and federalists an Irish component in a wider coalition of constructive moderate politicians. Of course such schemes were largely the idle speculations of men outside the normal run of party politics. Constructive approaches towards Ireland seemed a long way off in such a polarised political environment.

On the other hand, Bonar Law's speech at Blenheim, did help rekindle federal interest within higher political circles. It was Churchill who tried to set this initiative in motion. Churchill along with Lloyd George, Grey and Birrell, had recognised Ulster as the major obstacle to Home Rule as far back as 1911. He was also a close friend to F.E. Smith and many round-tablers, and an eager enthusiast for the 1910 coalition plan, which he clearly hoped to resuscitate at some point in the future. Blenheim provided him with such an opportunity. Churchill's first move was to drive a wedge between what he (wrongly) assumed to be the moderate, law-abiding majority of Tories and their new extreme leadership. In a series of articles and speeches he questioned the attitude and tone Bonar Law was adopting. 'Surely these are strange tactics for the leader of a great party. Surely they are peculiarly inappropriate tactics for the leader of the Conservative and constitutional party ... Why not win honourably? Why not win patiently? ... Why squander the estate in disputing the inheritance? Why capsize the boat in jostling for the tiller?'[140] And to Garvin he lambasted the Tory leadership, 'I am shocked at the threats of Ulster violence which are made by Conservative leaders, have they no policy for Ireland except to make it ungovernable?'[141] Churchill also used Blenheim to organise federal and devolutionary sympathies towards a new initiative. He contacted Edward Grigg and Lionel Curtis, leaders of the round-table movement, spending a weekend with them at Cliveden and then, in August, inviting them on board the Admiralty yacht, *The Enchantress*. Following the dismal by-election results from N.W. Manchester and Midlothian on 10 September, Churchill decided to force the pace with a speech at Dundee on 12 September. Here he launched his 'heptarchy kite' of regional parliaments, a policy proposal that for one historian created 'furore in both parties and thrust federalism to the forefront of political debate'.[142]

Churchill's 'kite' at Dundee, coming after a summer of mounting apprehension in federal circles, served to rally constructive opinion. Moreton Frewen repeated his appeals to Bonar Law for co-operation with the O'Brienites; 'the Dunraven influence and the attitude of our newspaper has got this small party fairly in revolt against the Home Rule Bill'.[143] Dunraven himself urged Bonar Law to move away from 'the violence of Carsonism' and towards 'a conference of some kind on the whole constitutional question'.[144] 'Moderate opinion is in Ireland desperately shy and in the face of the violence of the Molly Maguires on the one side and Carsonism on the other the most that can be expected of it is silence.'[145] Lord Hythe, a confidant of Dunraven, complained to Bonar Law that 'the party of which you are the leader are sacrificing the party, the interests of England and the Empire to the Ulstermen ... Settle the H.R. problem on Canadian or federal lines.'[146] He followed this up with a letter to *The Times*, reiterating that the Irish 'problem' would only be solved along Canadian lines.[147] To add fuel to this growing federalist pressure, twenty-four Dublin businessmen called for a conference of the parties to agree constructive settlement, 'deeply deplor(ing) the distortion and embitterment of the whole question by a revival of sectarian prejudices and animosities'.[148] More intriguingly, a letter appeared in *The Times*, referring to the Conference of 1910, when both parties had come close to a devolutionary solution for Ireland and suggesting, correctly, that Lansdowne and Chamberlain were privately opposed to the hard line Bonar Law was taking towards Ulster.[149] The leaked information was of value in publicising those federal sympathisers within the leadership and so strengthening the momentum that was building up over the late summer of 1912.

By October, support for a constructive solution to the Irish question was now more vocal within Unionist circles than it had been six months earlier. However it still proved insufficient to move the leadership. The mood of the party remained wedded to the frantic tone set by Bonar Law and Carson. Few Tories were yet inclined to publicly oppose this line, however much private misgiving they may have felt. In any case, the 'tactical' federalists, such as Oliver, Milner, Amery, Selborne, Wyndham and Chamberlain, still believed that a strong campaign now would not harm the federalist cause but would in the longer term create the political impasse from where the opportunity to construct a truly federal bill could develop. More damagingly for the federalist initiative was that many of these same federalists were increasingly preoccupied, by late 1912, with a revival of interest in tariff reform. This would explain Chamberlain's reluctance to offer a response to Churchill's overtures or to play a more active role. With the tariff issue suddenly tipped in his favour, following Bonar Law's dramatic reversal of Balfour's referendum pledge in November, Chamberlain was not going to rock the boat on Ireland only to sink tariff reform.

'THIS IS NOT MERELY A CRISIS, IT IS A DISASTER'[150]

The first circuit of the bill had been a successful period for Bonar Law. He had strengthened his position by a tough, incisive performance in debate and gained notoriety on the platform. He had tempered extreme threats from his brooding right wing with strong populist appeals for a general election and had forged party unity by a common, tough struggle against the unconstitutional position taken up by government in introducing Home Rule. In this, he had made Ulster a central plank of the party's attack on Home Rule, encouraging the Ulstermen in their preparations and granting a high profile to their cause. He had also observed the strength of Nationalist influence over the government, recognising them as a stubborn impediment to any compromise, particularly against the exclusion of all or part of Ulster from the bill; Redmond refusing to see Ireland as anything but a one nation. And for the government, demoralised, rattled and at times split, it had been the most unsuccessful and exhausting year since 1908.

However, by the end of the year despite all the pressure, the government's position on Home Rule had not changed. The bill was still on course in the same form, with the ministry firmly in power. How were Unionists going to force an election if intimidation and dire warnings of civil strife failed to produce such a result? This presaged trouble ahead for Bonar Law; splits in the Unionist alliance could easily widen and encourage protest against his tough line. And moderate and federalist sections had only tolerated his strategy whilst it held out the possibility of success. A second problem was the situation in Ulster. By late 1912, the *threat* of Ulster, so critical to the whole Unionist position, was clearly not working. Sectarian violence of the summer and autumn hinted Ulster could well 'collapse in some opera bouffe fiasco, police court proceedings, cabbage garden rebellion or so forth'.[151] Moreover, the threat might dissolve (and the government were perhaps hoping on this) through 'the difficulty of keeping Ulster at the boil for this period [two years]'.[152] How was Ulster to be made into a serious 'threat'? If this prescribed increased militarisation, would it really 'scare' the government into changes? And how would British public opinion react to such a development? Would Ulster be able to avoid lawlessness in the process? Ultimately, how could English and Scottish public opinion be roused with the apparent failure of Ulster theatricals so far? All these would concern the Conservative leadership over the coming session.

But most dramatically, for Bonar Law in particular, the problem of tariff reform reared its fractious head.[153] In November 1912, under sustained pressure from tariff reformers, Bonar Law and Lansdowne decided to publicly discard the referendum pledge, as agreed at the February shadow cabinet. The decision threw the party into chaos. A majority in the party resisted removal of the referendum. With its epicentre in Lancashire, they pushed instead for dropping the food taxes entirely, a stand against the leadership's stated policy. Bonar Law had boxed himself into an impossible corner and with little choice he offered his resignation to the party. Over December 1912 the party was convulsed in division, with Bonar Law forced to uphold his line, against a party majority keen to drop food taxes instead.

The thought of losing Bonar Law galvanised the Ulstermen to his defence. Carson and McNeill rallied the party to their leader, organising a memorial of support and drawing the distinction between the stated policy of the leadership and the actual position of the leader (a policy once used to remove and then execute Charles I). The semantics provided just the sort of escape clause needed from a highly embarrassing situation. Bonar Law was allowed to remain leader whilst delicately pirouetting against the tariff reformers and dropping the food taxes, a courtesy that had not been extended to Balfour in 1911. Perhaps the most interesting conclusion to draw from the affair concerns the actions of the Ulstermen. None had supported him in his leadership bid just a year earlier, indeed all had been violently opposed, yet by early 1913 no other leader would do. Not only does this suggest a vulnerability and even fragility in Ulster's position but just how vital Bonar Law now was to their cause.

CHAPTER FOUR

Stalemate and the sovereign, 1913

INTRODUCTION

THE FIRST parliamentary circuit meandered to a weary close on 14 February 1913, before the shorter session was launched on 10 March. Unionists began on a low ebb. Their leaders, Bonar Law and Lansdowne, were weakened by recent party convulsions over Tariff Reform. The government's Home Rule bill had altered little, despite the intense struggles of the first circuit. It was also increasingly evident that the issue did not arouse the same popular passion as it had in 1886 or 1893. The loss of Londonderry city to the Nationalists, at a by-election on 30 January 1913, seemed an eerie omen of the way ahead. More ominously, alternative issues revived or emerged to distract attention from Home Rule. Tariff Reform once again divided the party during the early months of 1913. Also Lloyd George launched his long awaited Land Campaign which exercised many on the constructive wing of the party, particularly after the sweeping success of Liberal land-reformers in the by-elections at N.W. Norfolk in May 1913 and Hanley in July.[1] It was the Marconi scandal, embroiling Lloyd George and Rufus Issacs in deep political scandal, that for most of the 1913 session was 'the chief, in fact the only excitement'.[2] Much of this lost enthusiasm was a consequence of the Parliament Act that dictated a bill had to begin its remaining two circuits in the form it left the Commons after the first. This effectively rendered the second and third circuits meaningless, for the Commons were now unable to alter the bill, except with government approval in a separate amending bill. The parliamentary process had for Unionists been reduced to farce; 'it certainly looks as ingeniously silly as putting a bill which may not be amended, through stages intended for its amendment'.[3] Austen Chamberlain reflected on the Common's powerlessness, 'we are like Strasbourg geese which are fed to make pate de foie gras'.[4]

Under these circumstances, alternative methods of defeating Home Rule were considered. On one side, tentative moves towards a compromise gained strength and support within the party. At the other extreme, militancy increasingly took hold of the Ulster campaign with the formation of the Ulster Volunteer Force, supported on the British mainland by prominent Tory politicians. The Tory leaders were also forced to consider other methods, particularly the use that could be made of the king and his powers of veto, a manoeuvre widely debated amongst Unionists and in the press. This culminated in July 1913 with a memorandum sent to the king by Lansdowne and Bonar Law, arguing that his power to change ministers, with the sole object of requesting a dissolution, was simply 'reserved' rather than 'abolished'.[5] For many this was a terribly hazardous precedent to establish, indicative of the growing desperation felt within Unionist circles.

ULSTER PREPARATIONS AND THE TORY RIGHT, 1913

With the failure of the 1912 session, the Ulstermen sought new methods to raise their profile. One was an amendment demanding the permanent exclusion of all nine Ulster counties from the bill. It was presented by Carson on 1 January 1913 and was safely pitched beyond what Asquith could accept. Thus it had the air of a tactical ploy, designed to advertise the unfairness of Liberal policy and to legitimate, in the eyes of British public opinion Ulster's 'full forward policy'.[6] A forward policy meant in the circumstances of 1913, preparing detailed plans for a provisional government, with its own military force, the UVF, to assume charge of Ulster if the attempt was made to impose Home Rule upon them. By the end of January 1913, the UUC had accepted its own Special Commission's report on the structure for a provisional government,[7] allowing planning to continue apace. By May, Carson was able to declare at Willowfield Unionist Club, 'we have never stopped day or night making such possible preparations as will enable us firmly, determinedly and with success to carry out the Covenant into which we have entered'.[8]

The most portentous development was formation of the UVF, under the generalship of Sir George Richardson.[9] The force was limited to 100,000 men, organised on a local basis along British army lines of regiments, divisions and battalions with medical, signalling, and dispatch rider corps.[10] The UVF undoubtedly acquired a strong camaraderie and loyalty to its leadership, although this did not stop inter-regional or inter-locality rivalries, and, as the force grew, strains developing between central command and the local divisions. Finance was an on-going problem. The Sir Edward Carson Fund, begun in 1911, had to be extended, and a five-man committee was appointed to explore possible fresh sources of income.[11] One vital source of cash came from sympathetic Unionists on the British mainland, channelled through the Ulster Defence League (UDL), following a 'cap-in-hand' deputation from the IUA in February 1913. Much of the money went towards procuring arms, prompting Craig's declaration in March that the time had 'now arrived when £10,000 would be a thousand times better spent on rifles than education'.[12] Actually getting arms into Ulster was proving difficult. On 3 June 1913 twelve cases, amounting to nearly 1,000 rifles, were seized at Belfast docks.[13] Three weeks later four large cases of arms addressed to 'people in the north' were seized at Drogheda.[14] And at the beginning of July Lord Leitrim's steamer was intercepted, having left Glasgow with 2,000 rifles rumoured to be on board, although nothing was found.[15] Without guns, the UVF was an army on paper, which perhaps was part of the Ulster leadership's original thinking behind it. As with the Belfast meeting of April 1912 and the signing of the Covenant, plans for a military force were intended to scare the government and awaken British public opinion, not to actually engage the forces of the British crown. Carson certainly hoped the UVF would remain a propaganda weapon, though he was acutely aware of the dangers of it becoming an actual 'fighting' body under the stimulus of his and others' rhetoric if the government failed to move.[16] Thus spring 1913 saw the Ulster street theatre take a paramilitary turn, decamping from Belfast city to the scattered village halls across the province.

Preparations in Ulster gained encouragement from many right-wing Tories. In January 1913, Lord Willoughby de Broke recommended the formation of a group to aid Ulster,[17] which on 27 March was realised with the creation of the British League for the Support of Ulster and the Union (BLSUU).[18] The League claimed the support of 120 MPs and 100 peers and was led by prominent members of the Reveille and Halsbury Clubs. The Duke of Bedford became chairman, with Willoughby de Broke secretary and amongst its leadership the 'old gang' of 1911, which included the Duke of Northumberland, Comyn-Platt, a close friend of Carson, F.E. Smith and Basil Peto.[19] The League established local branches across Britain to drill and equip young men for active service in Ulster, believing, as Basil Peto the vice-president explained, that 'there were in this country many men who did not desire to see Ulster fight her battle alone if the

Government carry the Home Rule conspiracy to the bitter end'.[20] They also provided much needed financial assistance to the Ulstermen, exploiting their contacts within society.

The League gave more than just financial help or vague promises of men. Many of its leaders became central figures in Ulster's preparations. Ronald McNeill, for example, was an influential mover on the Tory backbenches, responsible for generating a more determined spirit of resistance within Conservative circles. Colonel Hickman, Tory MP for Wolverhampton South and with strong connections at the War Office, had been instrumental in securing the services of Sir George Richardson[21] and acted as an unofficial recruiting officer for the UVF: he would later be a member of the Ulster provisional government. Another, Sir William Bull, MP for Hammersmith, helped facilitate the passage of arms through Britain to Ulster, utilising various safe houses of his and organising transport.[22] Bull's connection is of interest given his closeness to Walter Long and his involvement with the UDL, as it reveals the degree of overlap between the various groups and individuals fighting Ulster's cause. Such connections as these helped reinforce Ulstermen in their preparations. They also helped to diminish any movement by the Ulstermen towards partitionist solutions. They were, after all, a league for the support of Ulster and the Union, the two standing strong together, the former engaged in the preservation of the latter.

The formation of the BLSUU was rooted in the altered political atmosphere of 1913. The apparent apathy amongst many backbench Tories, the growing calls for a devolutionary or federal settlement, and the public interest in the Marconi and the Land issues bred a conviction that the party was not doing enough to defeat Home Rule. With Carson's amendment in January 1913 and the moderate tone evident during the Lords debate on the bill in March, some on the right detected the seeds to another betrayal along the lines of 1911: leaders would speak tough but when the time to act came they would compromise. The rumour even spread in January 1913 of secret agreements. An alarmed de Broke sought denial from Bonar Law that 'negotiations are succeeding between you and the government'.[23] As it grew over the spring and summer of 1913, the League was a clear warning to their leaders against compromise. Yet there is little reason to believe there were grounds to these fears or that the Tory leadership were hostile to it. Willoughby de Broke's letter to *The Times* on 27 May 1913, announcing the League 'intend[ed] to stand by [Ulster] until at least we have had an opportunity of voting against the repeal of the

Union', clearly brought the group within Bonar Law's justification for unconstitutional behaviour.[24] Also late in September 1913, de Broke reassured a worried Robert Cecil that 'those who are acting with me think that the stronger the forces arrayed against Home Rule the more likely the Government are to *avoid the extreme touch and to appeal to the constituencies*'[25] (my italics). The League followed the same approach as Bonar Law and the leadership of using violent threats to intimidate the government to an election. And far from being a dangerous company of extremists, the League actually worked to control matters. It channelled right-wing frustration behind a structure, so was able to contain the more outrageous spirits that were still running high after the extremism of the autumn session in parliament. The League performed for the Tory right what the Covenant did for the wilder elements within the northern Protestant community.

The becalmed atmosphere of 1913 led the Tory right into considering other methods of de-railing the Home Rule bill. One such method (to be considered later in the chapter) was the use that could be made of the king. After all if, as Tories believed, the government's failure to restore a second chamber left the Constitution suspended and with no check on the executive, so those once dormant or decorative parts of the British Constitution – notably the royal prerogative – might now have a new role to play. Equally dangerous was the growing discussion in right-wing circles concerning the role the army might take in matters. This, as mentioned earlier, was not new. But in the stalemate environment of 1913, and after the violent words of the 1912 session, such a topic had greater force and relevance. Carson in July spoke of Home Rule as likely to 'smash the army into pieces because it will divide the army between men who under no circumstances will be willing to fight against us and men who may for other reasons be willing to carry out such work'.[26] Liberals, of course, pounced upon this as incitement to mutiny and raised the cry of interference with the army, though they were also forced to counter Unionist warnings of the coercion of Ulster by dismissing the likelihood of a situation ever arising whereby any part of Ireland would be coerced into the bill.[27] Tory speculation on army matters and how they might be turned to their benefit focused in on the idea of suspending the Army Annual Act when it entered the Lords. The Act sanctioned army discipline during peace-time, so its suspension would, it was widely believed, prompt an immediate dissolution of parliament.[28] This was justified on the basis that, with the Constitution suspended, anything went, and by the growing

Unionist concern that the army would, necessarily, be the instrument to impose Home Rule onto Ulster. The idea of suspending the Army Act had first emerged in July 1911 from Goulding and Garvin, as a means to frustrate the Parliament bill and, somewhat presciently, from an unknown Bonar Law in the summer of 1911, as a method to delay Home Rule.[29] By early 1913, Hugh Cecil revived interest in the stratagem, recommending it to Lansdowne but receiving little encouragement. By June 1913 Cecil went further, circulating a memorandum amongst Unionist leaders, showing how suspension of the Act[30] could be safely effected. Cecil was aware of the dangers involved but felt if public opinion was handled carefully and less radical moves attempted first, such as the king warning Asquith he would withhold his assent, the Act could be safely suspended. However, nothing came of Cecil's suggestion at this stage, largely because moves to involve the king were already underway and more sensitive leaders, such as Lansdowne and Lord Salisbury, fretted at the public and party reaction such a move would have.

MODERATES, DEVOLUTIONISTS AND FEDERALISTS

At the start of 1913, with the apparent failure of extremism and the political stalemate brought on by the Parliament Act, circumstances appeared favourable for the slow search for a federal compromise. This sentiment was fortified from two directions – first, from amongst leading Unionists in the House of Lords, where anxiety at their leaders intemperate language produced a growing demand for moderation. This was clearly evident in the Lords closing debate on the Home Rule bill, at the end of January 1913. Calls for a settlement came from Lords Dunraven, MacDonnell and Brassey, while Earl Grey made a forceful plea for a federal system of rule.[31] Mild speeches also came from Tory leaders such as Curzon, St Aldwyn and Devonshire, all of whom seemed intent on reducing the present temper between the parties. 'Do you think' Curzon asked,

> that we equally with you would not like to clear the decks of all the troubled questions of Irish administration, finance, Land and education which so often have taken up the time of the House of Commons? Of course we would. The interests of our country as well as our party demand it.[32]

Lord Lansdowne, already a little discomfited by the extremism of the summer and autumn of 1912, also effected a calmer approach. Lord Aberconway noted the new moderate tone: 'The question of Home Rule today has, I am glad to say, been approached entirely from the point of view of detail.'[33] This angered Ulster Unionists and Tory die-hards, not least given Curzon's prominence in the debates – the man who had betrayed the 'Ditchers' in 1911. Willoughby de Broke struggled to re-inject a bitter note into the debate: 'you have found yourselves up against a thing (Ulster) that no promises of Peerages or presents of money can possibly dissipate or do away with'.[34]

Second, moves towards compromise resulted from developments in Ireland. The formation of the UVF, early in 1913, worried many Unionists as to the implications they were creating for themselves. Lord Salisbury informed Bonar Law that he 'strongly disapproved of Home Rule for Ireland but I cannot support political lawlessness and I shall either disenfranchise myself or vote Liberal at the next election, rather than encourage armed resistance in Ulster'.[35] More subtly, in June 1913, Alfred Lyttleton spoke in praise of a more constructive approach to the problems of Ireland, mentioning particularly the work of Horace Plunkett.[36] His moderate tone was echoed by the All for Ireland League, an organisation formed in 1910 and dedicated to healing divisions in Irish society. It was led by the maverick Nationalist William O'Brien and Lord Dunraven, but enjoyed the patronage of certain influential individuals, J.L. Garvin, T.M. Healy, M. Frewen and F.S. Oliver. At the All for Ireland League conference in March a resolution was passed in favour of an Irish Convention to settle the Irish issue by consent.[37] O'Brien also wrote to *The Times*, praising a recent speech by Long as a 'call for peace and conference'. He even went as far as to publish a letter he had received from Bonar Law as revealing a 'marked encouragement from that quarter without whose assent a conference there cannot be'.[38] O'Brien believed a resolution to the crisis could only be won by bringing the political parties, both in Britain and in Ireland, together and achieving a settlement through conciliation. Unfortunately his initiatives had little immediate impact. The parties stood too far apart, since the bitter autumn session and with personal recriminations over the Marconi issue.

Despite the poor reception to O'Brien's public entreaties, in private, however, opinions were altering and discreet overtures being made between certain party leaders. Churchill, undeterred by his failure to rouse federalist sympathisers in the autumn of 1912, mounted a fresh attack on

Bonar Law in February 1913 against his recent speech in which he speculated on the role the sovereign might play a part in frustrating Home Rule.[39] Churchill's concerns found an echo with some Unionists, most significantly from a brooding Chamberlain, still smarting at Bonar Law's climb-down over tariff reform earlier in the year. Since April Chamberlain had attended several round-table moots, with which Churchill also enjoyed close links. Both were also known devolutionists and had been alarmed at the tone and direction Bonar Law was taking the party in. As long ago as August 1912, Chamberlain had expressed his concerns on Bonar Law's Blenheim Palace speech to Lansdowne; 'like you I should have expressed myself differently, but I hope that Ulster will offer a stubborn, passive resistance'[40] (clearly Lansdowne had already expressed similar views to him). It was now through H.A. Gwynne, editor of *The Morning Post* and close associate of Chamberlain, that Churchill began to make contact with Chamberlain, hinting at some type of co-operation, which Chamberlain passed on to Lansdowne.

> G. [Gwynne] thinks that they [George and Churchill] both would like a coalition; but of this I gave no encouragement, saying that I did not think anything of the kind was possible whilst they stood committed to the Home Rule bill. If they were ready to come down to three or four Provincial councils … it would be a different thing.[41]

Of interest is Chamberlain's belief that a settlement could be constructed around the devolution of power within the UK, in a stance that essentially reflected the proposals recommended by Churchill in his Dundee speech of September 1912.

Chamberlain again dithered, still proving too apprehensive for the type of departure Churchill envisaged, and perhaps, at this stage, because of his preoccupation with tariff reform. Such reservations did not inhibit F.E. Smith. After his 'oratorical fireworks'[42] of 1912, Smith had melted into the background from where he could begin to explore the centre-ground for a settlement. He remained in close regular contact with Lloyd George and Churchill and, significantly if a solution was to be assembled, in close communication with Carson. Churchill and Lloyd George recognised Smith (and perhaps even Carson) to be a force working, ultimately, for a compromise, which might explain Churchill's disproportionate concentration on Bonar Law as the wild, intemperate leader, despite the equally sanguinary hue to Carson's rhetoric. What might have served to build bridges between these individuals was the Marconi episode. The decision by Smith and Carson to defend Isaacs and Lloyd George in their libel action against *Le Matin* newspaper angered Unionists and outraged the Ulstermen.[43] 'There is a good deal of feeling', Sanders noted, 'about Carson and F.E. appearing for Godfrey Isaacs in the Chesterton case';[44] Sir George Younger also felt that 'this feeling is very strong among our men'.[45] During his campaign in Scotland, in mid-June, Carson was publicly criticised by the chairman of the Edinburgh Conservative Association, Sir John Stirling-Maxwell,[46] and Smith felt it necessary to justify his action in a long letter to *The Times* on 17 June.[47] These were harsh judgements. Both men undoubtedly cherished the independence of the bar. Carson was also professionally close to Isaacs and no doubt, as H.M. Hyde suggests, 'friendship ... and the strong traditions of the Inns of Court may have played their part'.[48] Carson's most recent biographer believes he acted nobly; 'he had sacrificed political gain to the traditions of the bar. He had placed profession above party; he had placed professional bonds above the demands of his adopted Ulster.'[49] These seem fair assessments but it may also have been, for both Carson and Smith, an effective way of absenting themselves from the bitter Marconi censure debates, so sending the 'right' people the right signals. Isaacs told Carson, 'you behaved to me with all that nobility which is characteristic of you',[50] while to Garvin, Lloyd George spoke of 'his higher conception ... of his [Smith's] character' as a result of Marconi.[51]

Such a gesture towards Lloyd George, with his known sympathy for a settlement on the Irish question, was always likely from Smith, given his own political sympathies and the pragmatic manner he had 'picked up' the Ulster issue in 1911. But Carson was a different proposition and we might speculate that his decision reflected an increased awareness of the full gravity and delicacy of his position by 1913. With the Ulstermen in full preparation for their armed rebellion, following the formation of the UVF, and while he fully endorsed the righteousness of their cause, Carson never lost sight of the constitutional dangers of the situation and the political necessities that might well be forced onto him. If the government did not collapse or did not drop Home Rule, he would have to begin the search for a compromise. To this end, Marconi perhaps advertised his good intentions, without saying anything concrete or compromising his position as leader of the Irish Unionists. It was a difficulty he would again encounter; looking to advance the compromise process while remaining publicly aloof from such manoeuvring. Of course this does not imply Carson was now a thoroughgoing partitionist or devolutionist, for his deeper aspirations remained those of an all-Ireland Unionist, with Ulster still a tactical wrecking mechanism to save the Union. But alternatives had to be explored!

By the early summer of 1913, then, hesitant gestures on both sides were hinting at an emergent consensual spirit beneath all the fiery rhetoric and public displays of determined opposition by the key political leaders. An exchange, of sorts, was tentatively in motion, to the extent that future attempts to find a compromise fell on ground already traversed. Indeed the initiative might have been stronger but for the deaths, in 1913, of two significant Tory devolutionists, George Wyndham and Alfred Lyttelton, a blow to any push to moderation. Also Milner and Oliver still thought the moment tactically too weak to advance federal alternatives, as much because most constructive Unionists were busy formulating policies in response to Lloyd George's Land campaign.

IRISH UNIONISM SPLINTERS

The first months of 1913 generated anxiety among Irish Unionists that Ulster was looming too large in the offensive against Home Rule. The Covenant in September 1912 and Carson's amendment in January gave the impression of Ulster as the sole obstacle to the bill, with no credible resistance being offered outside the northern Protestant enclaves. Lord Midleton, a Southern Unionist peer and owner of several thousand acres in the west of Ireland, complained in *The Times* that 'the Prime Minister, admitting the animus against the bill in Ulster, has assumed that the Unionist population in the other three provinces views the bill with composure'.[52] To remedy this, and with the help of the Duke of Devonshire, he arranged loyalist meetings throughout the South, although his efforts '[had] hitherto been very feeble'.[53] G. Stewart, chairman of the IUA, warned Carson that 'we Southern Unionists are badly in need of encouragement'.[54] And to James Campbell he remarked that 'things have never been in so critical a condition as they are now. If Mr Bonar Law does not hold us together it is hard to say what might happen.'[55] So concerned was Stewart that on 14 March 1913 he led a deputation of leading Irish Unionists to Bonar Law to register their anxieties:

> A great feeling of uneasiness exists amongst the Unionists of the south and west of Ireland at the present crisis. We believe that this

> feeling is due to a very large extent to the attitude of the leaders towards Ulster and the feeling which is stated to exist in England, that there is no opposition to Home Rule except the opposition of Ulster.[56]

All-Ireland Unionists imagined that over-concentration on Ulster led inexorably towards a compromise upon the basis of the exclusion of Ulster from the Home Rule bill, while the rest of Ireland would be left to languish under a Dublin parliament. Dicey warned Long that the government were 'meditating some unexpected trick with a view to divide the Unionist opposition. Is he thinking of some concessions to Ulster? We must certainly be prepared for this'.[57] And Midleton, concerned at the over-emphasis upon Ulster cautioned Hugh Cecil that 'if it were possible to exempt Ulster from the Home Rule bill we should be guilty of a most outrageous crime against the loyalists throughout the south'.[58] These fears came to a head at the meeting of the council of Unionist clubs, where Lord Templetown was worried enough to publicly disclaim all rumours 'of compromise, of devolution or of a separate Ulster, they would have none ... that while it was for their leader Sir Edward Carson to state the policy of Ulster, he ventured to think that what he [Templetown] had stated was unquestionably the views of the Unionist clubs of Ireland'.[59] These anxieties suggest a clear and growing cleavage between the Ulstermen and the rest of the Irish Unionist movement: note Templetown's reference to Carson as 'their' leader, formulating policy just for Ulster. Sensitive to these developments, the Ulster Unionist Council passed a resolution at its meeting of 19 February 1913 'that the position of Unionists in the south and west of Ireland has not been lost sight of and when the time comes, have the support and sympathy of Ulster brethren'.[60] Carson, as the leader of *Irish* Unionists was acutely conscious of these worries; 'I think they are disturbed over the question of compromise', he informed Bonar Law.[61]

But Southern Irish Unionists were in a difficult position. To allow Ulster to continue to dominate Unionist opposition to the bill would raise the profile and practicality of partition as a possible compromise. On the other hand, Southern Irish Unionists were unable to offer the Tory leadership anything as effective as the problem of Ulster with which to defeat Home Rule. They were limited, then, to encouraging the Conservative party towards greater activism in opposing *all* the bill, itself not an easy task given the negative effect of the Parliament Act in engendering listlessness and apathy into many Tories. Dicey counselled Long in April 1913 that 'nothing but great energy both in leaders and followers will avert this calamity'.[62] And later that same month, 'what I deprecate is the saying … that somehow the passing of the Home Rule bill would be prevented; such feats we all know are not achieved somehow but by energy and concerted effort'.[63] Bonar Law tried to inject enthusiasm into his troops throughout the 1913 session, principally through a tough rhetoric. And as late as June he was still ploughing this furrow:

> in my deliberate opinion … the best chance of avoiding civil war … is to convince the ministers that we are in earnest and that if they attempt to carry this through under present conditions they will find themselves face to face with resistance of more than half the nation. I think they are now beginning to believe it, then I think it is impossible for them to persevere.[64]

This request for greater energy flared up in May 1913 over what tactics to use during the second reading debates (9 and 10 June 1913). Bonar Law and Carson planned a walk-out of the chamber and abstention in the division lobby, to effect an 'unusual' protest. Both Long and Midleton objected to this passive resistance on the grounds that 'it would not be understood in the country if no vote were given by those chiefly affected on the second reading'.[65] Long felt that the policy gave the appearance of resignation and 'the electors will surely think that our opposition to the bill is played out'.[66] Bonar Law and Carson back-tracked in deference to Southern Unionists' doubts and allowed the second reading to pass as normal.

Alongside their repeated calls for greater energy from Tories, Irish Unionists urged them to direct their fire upon the demand for a dissolution of parliament. This request, despite Bonar Law's meticulously precise rhetoric, had been a little smothered by the dramatic events of 1912. Bonar Law's clear reiteration of this, through 1913, now offered Irish Unionists an (admittedly) meagre amount of reassurance to counter-balance his over-concentration upon Ulster. Dicey harangued colleagues to make the demand for a dissolution their first priority,[67] and in private he pestered Bonar Law to 'openly and avowedly to agitate for a dissolution and raise the perfectly legitimate cry of an appeal to the people'.[68] Lord Curzon declared to the Primrose League on 2 May 1913 that 'our demand is that the matter should be put to the test'.[69] And Midleton reminded Bonar Law that 'those who are behind the scenes in Ulster believe that such terrible events are impending that nothing very much matters here [London]. This may prove to be so, but is it not just as much our duty as a party to exhaust all constitutional means of opposition before a rupture ...?'[70] Perhaps a little over-optimistically, Long began preparation of a manifesto of policy initiatives (land, housing, Insurance), obviously with an eye on an election campaign in the near future.[71] Prioritising the demand for an election may also have mollified Conservative apprehensions at the unparliamentary line Bonar Law appeared to be pursuing. An election would safely defuse the brewing sense of catastrophe, and whether the Tories won or lost, at least save the parliamentary system from irreparable and irreversible harm.

Of course, greater concentration on an election exposed differences between the Ulstermen and the other parts of the Unionist coalition. Bonar Law had already drawn attention to this during his speech in the Commons on 16 April 1912, though its full effect had been lost beneath the excitement of the first parliamentary circuit. Now, with the bill well into its second circuit of parliament, this distinction came increasingly into view and was a subject used by the Liberals to divide the Unionist forces. Sanders noted during a debate in October 1912 that 'Lloyd George tried to draw Bonar Law as to whether he would approve of resistance if at a general election the country decided for Home Rule. Bonar Law refused to be drawn. But as a matter of fact he has said both publicly and privately that in that case he would not support resistance. There he differs from Carson.'[72] And in reply to a question from Asquith, Bonar Law explained the value of an election.

> I cannot say what the attitude of Ulster will be but I can at once say what my attitude will be if I am leader of the Unionist party ... if that is done we shall not in any way, shape or form encourage the resistance of Ulster. I say that without hesitation ... if you put it before the people of this country as a clear issue, then it is a problem for Ulster and not for me.[73]

For Ulster, an election, whether won or lost, would not deflect her from defending her interests. This was hinted at by Carson during the second reading debate in June 1913: although 'he preferred to fight this battle out with the whole of the Unionist party behind him, rather than, as they might have to fight it out eventually, alone in Ireland'.[74] Lord Londonderry expressed it more bluntly: 'If Home Rule is granted it is absolutely certain there will be civil war in Ulster', to which Lord Morley responded, 'even after a general election?' 'In any circumstances', came Londonderry's retort.[75] As the issues clarified themselves, by 1913, the Ulstermen and the Tory party were shown to stand slightly but significantly apart. This posed the danger to Bonar Law of independent action by Ulster, and perhaps their exclusion from the bill if they could hammer out a separate agreement with the government. The Tory leader struggled to off-set these differences with a tough, combative style and by focusing in on Ulster's grievances (aware all the time that this stood to alienate Southern and more traditional Unionists). Winding up the debate on 16 January 1913 he affirmed, 'the reality of this situation does not consist in discussions in this house. It does not consist in your majorities ... It consists in the resistance of Ulster. That is the reality of the situation.'[76] And to the huge rally at Craigavon on 12 July, Bonar Law repeated his Blenheim Palace pledge: 'whatever steps [Ulstermen] might feel compelled to take, whether they were constitutional or whether they were unconstitutional, they had the whole of the Unionist party under his leadership behind them'.[77] Such public displays of loyalty did much to keep the Ulstermen within the Unionist alliance and lessened the likelihood of them pursuing their own agenda.

Finally of great significance to Irish Unionist fortunes was the position of Lord Lansdowne who, after being relatively quiet for much of 1912, now emerged as champion of traditional Unionist concerns. Lansdowne had already, during the Lords debate on the bill in January 1913, expressed his willingness to accept the verdict of the people if Home Rule were put before them. This commitment he reinforced on 15 July 1913 by introducing an amendment in the Lords demanding an election before any further progress of the bill. This moved him closer to other traditional defenders of the Union, Lords Midleton, Salisbury and Walter Long, against what they all saw as the dominating and dangerous concentration upon Ulster. These developments suggest support for Ulster was weakening within some Tory and Unionist quarters; an indication perhaps that even if there were no election, assistance for their rebellion was not automatic, despite Bonar Law pledging the party to go to their aid. And unlike Bonar Law, Lansdowne had never offered unconditional or conditional support for Ulster, nor did he cloak his analysis with blood-curdling threats of civil catastrophe. Thus by 1913, Lansdowne began to surface as a counter-weight to Carson within the Unionist leadership, with

Bonar Law the fulcrum between them, a tension which would become more acute during the autumn.

THE KING AND IRELAND, 1913

Pressure to revive the king's prerogative powers as a method of defeating the Home Rule bill came from several quarters in 1913. It appealed to the Tory right, already suspicious that the king had not done enough to save the House of Lords in 1911. Moreover, as Salisbury argued, although 'no one wishes to drag the king's name into party-politics but vital national and Imperial interests are involved which justify our laying our case before his majesty'.[78] And if national interests were in jeopardy, then an active role for the king seemed a small danger by comparison. For moderates, royal intervention was a better, indeed more constitutional, option than sanctioning Ulster to rebel or take up arms against the government. Others calculated that involvement of the king might well prompt another conference of the party leaders, as in 1910. This particularly appealed to Southern Unionists who, short of a Unionist government, regarded a conference on Ireland between the leading British parties as perhaps the only way to find an all-Ireland settlement that avoided exclusion. Nor were such observations lost on federalists.

Involving the king had, for Tories, a justifiable constitutional rationale behind it. For them the constitution was, by the preamble to the Parliament Act, in 'suspension' and as Lansdowne argued, 'under a suspended constitution the old customs cannot have the same force'.[79] Or rather, within an unbalanced parliament, old customs like the crown's power would have more force as the only mechanism to now counteract executive power. Furthermore, Lansdowne pointed out that the wording of the Parliament Act prescribed usage only on bills 'which had during two years been supported by a majority of the House of Commons and had also received the stable support of the constituencies'.[80] The question of 'stable support of the constituencies' implied, according to Unionists, some type of appeal to the people. And 'the question whether the last condition has been fulfilled can hardly be left entirely for decision by the government of the day, and it will certainly be argued that some responsibility must also rest upon the crown'.[81] Unionist arguments for a more dynamic role for the king were not lacking in constitutional force, indeed they drew the backing of Sir William Anson and Dicey, and were firmly rooted in the wording of the Parliament Act and the manner in which the government had ignored its preamble.

Such ideas had circulated in Unionist circles since the Parliament Act. Carson informed Lady Londonderry as early as August 1912 that although the king could no longer exercise his veto he was fully entitled 'to call on his P.M. to relieve him of an impossible situation'[82] before giving his assent. Similarly, Edward Saunderson urged Lady Londonderry to use her influence with the king; 'if you put your mind to it to make the little man put his foot down. He has a great opportunity. He will either be a man or a mouse. Let us hope he will be the power.'[83] And at the same time Lord St Aldwyn, in *The Times*, 'doubted if ministers dare advise the king to give the Royal assent to the measures and thought that if they did they might be told to consult the country'.[84] Bonar Law placed himself at the head of this initiative. Following the snap division victory on 14 November 1912, he wrote to Lord Stamfordham, the king's private secretary, hoping to move the king to re-assess his position.

> Sooner or later … we shall have to decide between breaking the Parliamentary machine and allowing these terrible results to happen. When faced with a choice of such evils as these we shall not hesitate in considering that the injury of the House of Commons is not so great an evil as the other.[85]

As if these alarmist views were not enough, he added:

> the Speaker felt he had to intervene and there is always the risk that the time will come when the nation will expect His Majesty to take, in regard to the whole nation, the same attitude which has been taken by the speaker.[86]

It seems clear that Bonar Law was capitalising on the recent draconian actions of the government to impress upon the king a Tory understanding of present constitutional developments, a vital education if he was to be employed at some future date. Also if Bonar Law was going to justify Ulster resistance, and possibly armed rebellion, then all alternative courses of action for securing an election had to be explored, and more importantly, shown publicly to have been explored. Encouraging the king to act was Bonar Law traversing constitutional or semi-constitutional paths before unconstitutional ones took precedence. Thus on 24 January 1913 he followed up his private speculations to the king with a speech at Edinburgh, where he hypothesised on the presentation of the bill for royal assent, asking his audience,

> what would then be the position of the sovereign of this country? Whatever he did half of his people would think he had failed in his duty … that any loyal servant should put his sovereign in such a position would have been, till a year ago, incredible … but … can we be sure that the present Government will not commit that crime?[87]

Bonar Law's public suggestion of royal intervention helped generate debate upon the subject within the Unionist alliance, while bringing more pressure to bear on the government as to the consequences of continuing with their bill. January 1913 saw Bonar Law dramatically raise the political stakes in his struggle to force an election.

The government's reaction to Bonar Law's speech was hostile. Churchill referred to Bonar Law's 'criminal advice',[88] and Herbert Samuel judged his comments a 'grave constitutional offence' and 'unwarrantable'.[89] For some Unionists it was an equally dangerous recommendation. Lord Esher, a close confidant of the king, thought it 'a new departure' and not one he particularly liked.[90] For Strachey, editor of *The Spectator*, it was 'a mad movement', got up by 'Garvin and the other hotheads' who were simply 'gambl[ing] with the Monarchy'.[91] Strachey used *The Spectator* to rally opinion against the move and even distributed a critical memorandum to Unionist leaders,[92] but with little impact: opinion amongst Unionists was shifting firmly in favour of some type of action by the king. As an alarmed Stamfordham noted, 'I fear the feeling that [the King] should take some action will not be confined to the Diehards and Garvin'.[93] Nor was it. In May 1913 Carson echoed Bonar Law's statements: 'every monarch rests upon certain ground so long as he makes his maxim "the will of the people shall prevail". But no monarch rests upon certain ground who says the will of a coalition Government must prevail.'[94] Yet more surprising, Lansdowne, Balfour, Long, Salisbury, Hugh and Robert Cecil all gave private if cautious support to the idea.

There were differences between the Unionist leaders but these centred not upon the viability of the move but upon how it might be successfully effected. Some postulated that the king might shake away the accumulated dust of two centuries and exercise his veto on the bill, the threat of which would, so many Unionists believed, force Asquith to dissolve. 'His

Majesty', wrote Long (an early advocate of this line), 'might decide to tell the Government that he would not assent to the bill without a dissolution.'[95] In May 1913, Steel-Maitland informed Bonar Law of a petition which Carson, Chamberlain, McNeill and Locker-Lampson were organising to present to the king in the autumn, imploring 'that your Majesty may withhold your Royal assent to that measure until the Parliamentary electors of the UK shall have had an opportunity … of making known their wishes'.[96] And as late as 12 September the new Tory chief whip, Edmund Talbort, reported that the idea of a petition was still popular in leadership circles, not least with Bonar Law himself.[97] Salisbury as well recommended use of the veto in a letter to Sir George Younger: 'Does not the king's coronation oath … not give Unionists the right to ask his majesty under the circumstances to withhold his signature when the H.R. for Ireland … Act [is] presented to him?'[98] For others, wielding the royal veto was both perilous and tactically flawed – 'suiting Asquith's game uncommonly well' – by offering him an election on the basis of 'King versus the People', so throwing 'the crown after the coronet' while for the party it 'would utterly destroy us at the polls'.[99] Dicey worked hard to steer Unionist opinion on the royal prerogative into less dangerous waters. Rejecting use of the veto, he argued the king was better advised to invite Asquith to dissolve. If he refused, it would then be a 'perfectly constitutional manner' to dismiss what were technically 'his' ministers and call fresh ones, with 'wholly and solely' the aim of an immediate dissolution of parliament.[100] Also Dicey advised that instead of public pressure on the king, Unionist leaders should work the initiative more subtly, 'let[ting] it be known that they are prepared at any moment if called to office to carry through a dissolution even though this measure may meet with Parliamentary opposition'.[101] What had to be avoided was Bonar Law's more brutal, high-profile approach to manoeuvring the crown. Bonar Law accepted these considerations, reassuring Dicey in March that

> I do not think that it is a question really of using the veto, but in my view the one constitutional right which the sovereign undoubtedly still possesses is that if ministers have given him advice of which he does not approve, he should then see whether he cannot get other ministers who would give him different advice'.[102]

Balfour and Lansdowne also supported this line. Replying to entreaties from Strachey to mobilise moderates against any such initiative,

Lansdowne admitted the veto would 'be a great mistake', but found little problem with the King changing ministers to procure a dissolution.[103]

During 1913, then, momentum built up within the Tory leadership that a certain, specified response from the crown could indeed be employed. It was not, however, until July that Bonar Law and Lansdowne sought to channel this momentum into positive action. On 31 July, and in reply to Lord Stamfordham's request for their views,[104] they sent the king a joint memorandum outlining his constitutional role with regard to the Home Rule bill and in light of the Parliament Act. The memorandum synthesised Tory arguments as they had evolved in debate and discussion since Bonar Law's speech in January 1913. It argued that while the veto 'has no doubt fallen into desuetude' and

> as a constitutional monarch he can only act upon the advice of a minister, it has never been questioned by any constitutional writer that if the king is not sure that in the advice which they have given him his ministers have the support of his people, he has the right to change his advisers, to give his new ministers the power to dissolve Parliament and so to ascertain whether or not they have the support of the country.[105]

The memorandum sought to familiarise the king with Unionist reasoning on his powers and prepare him for future use of his prerogative. In particular, it aimed to foreground the demand for an election before the bill was given royal assent. It represented a more subtle approach than Bonar Law's and Carson's platform intimidation, revealing the cautious hand of Lansdowne.

What gave the memorandum force was its arrival at a moment of mounting pressure on the king, from the platform, in the press, from informal talks with leading privy councillors, peers, and Tories, and with the air thick with 'rumours of probable agitation in the country; of monster petitions; addresses from the House of Lords; from Privy Councillors; urging me to use my influence to avert the catastrophe'.[106] This constant speculation left the king increasingly anxious at his own plight. Birrell, meeting him on 24 July, was forced to discuss the Irish problem for nearly an hour during which the king referred to government policy as 'drifting'.[107] And on 11 August, obviously stirred by the memorandum from Lansdowne and Bonar Law, the king wrote to Asquith urging that a resolution to the present imbroglio be found, and indicating his approval for an election.[108]

Whether it was politically wise to implicate the king was of course highly debatable. On the one hand employing the king, to either change his ministers or exercise his veto, centred upon securing an election and was not a method of simply destroying the bill or the government, as Liberal comment portrayed it. The tactic, therefore, conformed to Bonar Law's approach towards Home Rule and rested firmly upon the constitutional rationale which the Tory party had operated according to since 1911. However, it was fraught with dangers for the party. How would public opinion react to the revival of the royal prerogative? Would they accept or understand the constitutional subtleties espoused by Unionists or regard it, as Liberals would surely represent it, as a thinly disguised Tory plot to overturn an elected government? An election on 'People versus the King', rather than Home Rule, would be a far from attractive proposition for Unionists to run on. For Bonar Law, there was the added danger that involving the king would as likely result in another conference of the party leaders, as in 1910, as it would in an election. And yet despite these pressing concerns, the Unionist leadership, including Lansdowne, Balfour, Long and Salisbury, who under different circumstances would have recoiled from the suggestion, clearly thought it was a practical line.

CHAPTER FIVE

Unionist politics and attempts at compromise, 1913

INTRODUCTION

BY LATE August 1913, pressure for a political solution to the Home Rule struggle reached a climax. After months of Tory counsel, the king pressed for a conference of party leaders, as evidenced by his memorandum of 11 August.[1] From another direction devolutionists, such as Earl Grey and F.S. Oliver, and moderates from across the political spectrum, were mobilised into action by the Ulster Unionists' alarming declaration on 23 September 1913 of a Provisional Government to come into force across Ulster the moment Home Rule became law.[2] Not least, in regards to developments in Ulster, those leaders who had already made tentative moves towards a settlement – Smith, Churchill and Chamberlain – redoubled their efforts. Ironically for the compromise initiative, it was the Ulstermen who were increasingly convinced that the exclusion of their province from the operation of the bill was an avenue they had to traverse. These pressures for a settlement were aided by the political circumstances of the autumn of 1913, with parliament not sitting, MPs away from Westminster and a six-month interregnum before the next parliamentary session opened in February. These were perfect conditions for the forces of compromise to broker a deal.

It was Lord Loreburn, the ex-Liberal lord chancellor, who energised these various currents with a letter in *The Times* on 11 September calling for a 'settlement by consent'.[3] The letter attracted much interest within high political circles and set in train a series of extremely delicate manoeuvres that led, finally, to a secret meeting between Asquith and Bonar Law. The meeting took place on 15 October 1913, at Cherkley Court, home of Bonar Law's friend, Max Aitken. As Bonar Law entered discussions, he came under sustained pressure from Carson, Smith, Balfour and the Ulstermen for a settlement upon the exclusion of Ulster. Others, notably

Lansdowne, Long and Salisbury resisted this course, some recommending instead an All-Irish solution upon the devolution of power. And yet others, including many Irish Unionists and the Tory die-hards, desired no solution at all. Bonar Law was in a very difficult position between these various demands and forced to manoeuvre hard. But he never lost sight of his ultimate objective of securing an election. This required not assisting a settlement, as historians have generally pictured him doing at this stage, but frustrating and avoiding one.[4]

MOVES TOWARDS A COMPROMISE, SEPTEMBER 1913

Lord Loreburn's call for an 'exchange of opinions' between the party leaders was the first public break in the partisan fireworks, and all the more significant because Loreburn had been a convinced Home Ruler during cabinet discussions on the bill in 1911.[5] It might well be that Loreburn was acting under orders from Asquith, to open a line of communication with the opposition, without publicly initiating a discussion or endangering Nationalist support and government credibility.[6] It was certainly the case that a conference of leaders had already been suggested privately by the king and it was more than probable that Loreburn's announcement was sanctioned, if not influenced, by the king himself. Indeed in the period after the letter was published, it was the king who forced the pace of events. He invited Lansdowne to Balmoral early in September 1913, believing him to be a moderating force within the Unionist leadership. The king pushed exclusion as a basis for a conference and even as a long-term agreement on the Irish question, only to encounter a cool response from Lansdowne. Undeterred, the king sounded out Bonar Law during his scheduled visit to Balmoral on 15 September. On his way north, Bonar Law visited Lansdowne at Meikleour, his Scottish estate, where he learnt the current direction of the king's thinking. Once at Balmoral, the king urged Bonar Law to take up Loreburn's request; 'H.M. seemed much impressed by Lord Loreburn's letter and was, I thought, hopeful that a conference might take place'.[7] Perhaps to sweeten this pill the king proposed to write to Asquith recommending an immediate election and 'would reserve the right to make public after the event as a justification of his own action'.[8] Bonar Law had to box clever, aware that to reject the king's suggestion of a conference would be politically risky, not least if Tories expected the king to pressure Asquith to an election or exercise his prerogative powers in the future. Instead, Bonar Law gently side-stepped the idea of a meeting by outlining to the king the problems involved with a conference and particularly with the scheme of exclusion. In place of exclusion he recommended an election as the best and only solution in the circumstances: 'I reminded him also that the Unionist leaders had equally pledged themselves if there were an election and the people decided in favour of Home Rule, not to encourage or support the resistance of Ulster.'[9]

The king's attempts to lay the basis for a political settlement were helped by the arrival of Churchill and Balfour at Balmoral.[10] Churchill came with instructions from Asquith to explore the grounds for a compromise.[11] Despite all his preconceptions, Churchill found Bonar Law concerned by the present situation and willing to examine various options. Again, Bonar Law could not simply repulse these soundings, fearful of upsetting the king and aware that a disinterested attitude might encourage a compromise to hatch behind his back, not least with the Ulstermen. Bonar Law left Churchill with a positive impression, although he did not under-rate the dangers they faced.[12] Balfour arrived at Balmoral immediately after Bonar Law, but with Churchill still in attendance. Though no longer leader, Balfour still retained much authority in the Tory party and enjoyed close working connections with the king and with the government, as witnessed over its army reforms.[13] By the summer of 1913 he was increasingly alarmed at political developments and particularly the threat of rebellion in Ulster. This apprehension had already encouraged him to offer himself as a possible caretaker prime minister, if the king needed a non-partisan ministry to call for a dissolution. Not surprisingly, then, the king found Balfour 'serious and very sympathetic' about current circumstances and in favour of exclusion as the best route out of their present dangers. Balfour's sympathy for exclusion encouraged Churchill, informing Asquith, who in turn urged him to open a dialogue with other moderate Tory leaders.[14] Balfour's stance might even, for Churchill and Lloyd George, have raised hopes for a fresh attempt at coalition. For Bonar Law these developments were a serious threat. With Balfour (as well as the king) behind a settlement upon exclusion, the silent, moderate Tory backbenchers could well rally against the leadership's extreme tactics. He was forced, therefore, to appear receptive, to fellow-travel with compromisers in order to avoid marginalisation or loss of influence.

However, of most significance in these moves towards a settlement were the Ulster Unionist leadership, who began to press their case for a compromise upon the basis of Ulster's exclusion from the bill. This was not a new departure. Their largely tactical amendment in January had demanded all nine Ulster counties be cut out of the bill. Now by the autumn, the nature of this demand shifted from being a tactical ploy to a possible basis of agreement. This shift was fuelled by several developments. The end of the second parliamentary circuit for Home Rule in July 1913 had witnessed no meaningful alteration to the bill. Also, as a consequence of a sequence of arms seizures over the summer, notably in a warehouse in Hammersmith,[15] Ulster's military committee were forced to suspend their purchase and importation of guns. Arms for the UVF thus remained limited, while the guns they already possessed offered only a narrow military capability, differing in calibre, design and ammunition. If asked to fight, it would have been, 'indescribable confusion and disaster in action'.[16] Such military weakness was compounded by renewed sectarian rioting in the province, most seriously in Derry during August. In addition a compromise had always been implicit in what the Ulstermen were doing, if, in the last resort, the bill survived their public attacks and the government did not collapse. By the time the Ulstermen made their public declaration of a provisional government on 23 September 1913, their leadership were therefore acutely aware of the vulnerability of their position and looking towards a settlement.

It was these considerations, alongside Carson's own political and constitutional reservations and 'feeling more and more the responsibility of his position',[17] that convinced him this was the moment to strike out for a compromise. Carson now viewed exclusion less as a tactic to destroy Home Rule than as a means to quell tensions within Ulster and satisfy the growing demands of its representatives for salvation from a Dublin Parliament.[18] On 20 September, three days before he publicly approved the setting up of the provisional government, he wrote to Bonar Law in reply to an account of Bonar Law's talks with Churchill and the king;

> I am of the opinion that on the whole things are shaping towards a desire to settle on the terms of leaving Ulster out … my own view is that the whole of Ulster should be excluded but the minimum would be the six plantation counties and for that a good case could be made. The South and West would present a difficulty and *it might be that I could not agree to their abandonment, although I feel it would be the best settlement if Home Rule is inevitable* … I am fully conscious of the duty there is to try and come to some terms[19] (my italics).

Impressed by Bonar Law's exchanges at Balmoral, Carson now clearly backed a settlement with the government, even one well short of the nine-county limit outlined in January. Two years of extreme rhetoric had brought the first solid glimmers of a political settlement.

Carson's inner thinking on these matters was fleshed out in a five-page memorandum which accompanied his letter to Bonar Law. This outlined the tactical options available at the present,[20] with the clear intention of convincing Bonar Law that exclusion was the basis of a viable settlement. This he justified on several grounds. First, because a refusal to negotiate (if, that is, an offer to do so was made from either the king or Asquith, and clearly Carson believed one to be imminent) would mean 'great injury to the cause would follow',[21] alienating public opinion and upsetting the king. Second, Carson argued that Southern Unionist objections could no longer stand in the way of Ulster defending their own interests, especially since they could offer no substantial resistance on their own behalf. Finally, he suggested devolution as a long-term solution to the Irish problem, as the least detrimental to party unity, but with exclusion an immediate and necessary prerequisite to calm Ulster's fears. The offer of devolution is interesting, perhaps revealing the influence of Smith, who helped write the memorandum. It suggests that Carson's commitment to exclusion for Ulster was never an end in itself, merely a temporary, if vital, move to salvage a rapidly deteriorating situation. In January 1912 at Omagh he declared Ulster would 'take matters into their own hands and keep it in their own hands *until they were admitted back to what was their birthright*'[22] (my italics). In other words, his stance was one of exclusion pending re-entry into the Union. Devolution appealed to Carson because it looked beyond exclusion to a more permanent arrangement, the beauty of which combined his Southern Unionist prejudices with Ulster's partitionist realities.

Yet Carson's predicament was a delicate one. It was all well and good trying to convince Bonar Law of the need to negotiate and of the necessity of exclusion, but if no conference or meeting between party leaders took place, his entreaties would be for nothing. Moreover, to move too quickly would destroy Irish Unionist support, impair the credibility of Ulster's resistance and undermine his own bargaining position. Like Asquith, Carson had to be 'seen' to come to the conference table in a position of strength not desperation. Whatever his private concerns, his public stance had to remain tough. To these ends Carson needed a well-connected operator to make overtures, plant ideas, put out feelers, foster an optimistic atmosphere and generally construct the groundwork for a political settlement, a role for which F.E. Smith proved uniquely suited.

Smith was already aware of the tentative developments. He had Carson's ear and knowledge of his private views – they had spent the first three weeks in September campaigning together in Ulster and Smith had shared Bonar Law's correspondence even though addressed to Carson. As recently as 26 September 1913 Smith had written to Lloyd George recommending that the time was ripe for a settlement[23] while on 5 October he had urged Churchill to show support for exclusion in his speech at Dundee on the 8th. Smith also pressed Churchill to open channels with Carson (and thus with Asquith): 'Carson is most reasonable. I think he would be glad to meet you.'[24] More crucially, Smith made contact with the king at the army manoeuvres towards the end of September. Here he conveyed to the king the impression that most Tory leaders were eager to settle around exclusion, especially 'Carson [who] is all in favour of such an arrangement and thinks a solution on these lines could be arrived at which would be acceptable to his friends',[25] and promised to relay Carson's 'precise views ... as to contracting out Ulster'. Smith had no doubt that 'Carson would be quite ready to agree to leaving Ulster out and was sure a satisfactory solution could thus be arrived at',[26] but went further and pressed for the idea of a conference arranged by the king. '[Smith] said that the Unionists would not accept an invitation to conference from the government; the king was the only person who could initiate such a meeting'. The effect of these disclosures was dramatic. The king was greatly encouraged and the next day Stamfordham wrote to Bonar Law suggesting a conference.[27]

It seemed clear, then, that by the start of October, the pace towards a conference was quickening. Harcourt-Kitcher, editor of *The Glasgow Herald*, informed Bonar Law of a recent meeting with Lloyd George,[28] who argued the case for a settlement on exclusion and 'seemed to think that his colleagues would be willing on this matter'.[29] An anxious Lansdowne felt this to be yet 'another indication that events are moving in the direction of a proposal for the exclusion of Ulster pure and simple'.[30] His fears were born out by a communication from Lord Stamfordham urging the Tory leadership to accept the exclusion of Ulster. '*There is good reason to believe*', he told Bonar Law, 'that it would be satisfactory to H.M.G. if the Opposition should intimate ... that they would undertake to put down an amendment to the H.R. bill excluding Ulster but giving her a right to come in after a term of years and invite a conference on that understanding.'[31] On 7 October Stamfordham tried again, this time urging Bonar Law into negotiations with Asquith. 'The king as you know will do everything he can to help and the P.M. who arrived yesterday is evidently ready and anxious to arrive at a satisfactory settlement.'[32] These were clear, direct requests from the king to the Tory leadership to explore the basis of an agreement with the government, requests they could not easily ignore.

Within the Unionist camp, the momentum for a settlement continued. On 4 October Carson returned to London[33] from Belfast, only too aware of the strength of feeling amongst Ulster Unionists for exclusion. The next day he met Bonar Law, who noted the advance in his position of 20th. 'He [Carson] naturally is feeling more and more the responsibility of his position as it comes nearer the time when there is a likelihood of bloodshed.'[34] Carson was forthright in impressing upon Bonar Law that 'the leading men in Ulster ... desire a settlement on the lines of leaving Ulster out'.[35] This he had agreed to support having spoken to a group of Dublin businessmen:

> He [Carson] then said to them why is it that there has been nothing this time of the organised opposition to Home Rule which was shown by the Unionists in the South on the two previous occasions? There has been no resolution by the Dublin chamber of commerce; and he said further, can you undertake now, that when you go back to Dublin such organisation will be organised and come into the open. They had to reply to him that they could not give such an undertaking, for the Unionists dreaded the effect of it on their businesses ... He then said to them, 'tell me exactly what you want me to do, and as far as possible I shall do it. Do you want us in Ulster to say that we will resist Home Rule by force of arms even though the government offer to exclude Ulster' ... They, of course, replied that they could not expect the Ulster people to do ... these things.[36]

The implication of his conversation was clear; it was time to cast the Southern Unionists adrift[37] and if Bonar Law did not support this they would be willing to pursue their own course independently of him.

It was clear, then, by early October that a considerable movement had emerged eager for a conference of party leaders and for a settlement to the crisis upon the basis of exclusion. Powerful elements within the Tory leadership had shifted from hardline resistance towards compromise. The idea won favour with Bonar Law's close confidant Beaverbrook, party wire-pullers such as Lord Balcarres and Steel-Maitland and younger, more constructively-minded backbench Tories. And sections of the press, notably *The Times*, *The Daily Mail* and *The Express* clearly scented an atmosphere of growing compromise and approved of it. In the circumstances, the most prudent line for Bonar Law to follow was to appear receptive to such ideas, to keep all his options open and watch for events to unravel themselves. He did not have to wait long, for on 8 October he received an offer from Asquith to meet secretly.[38] This olive branch was reinforced by Churchill, who in speaking at Dundee on 8 October praised exclusion as a viable solution.[39] Curzon greeted his speech with enthusiasm and pressed hard for a similar commitment from Bonar Law; 'a definite offer has been made by W.C., incomplete, obscure nor wholly satisfactory, perhaps perilous. But it cannot be refused nor can it be passed over.'[40] And two days later Carson threw his approval behind Churchill's and Curzon's. 'It is hard to see, if separate treatment was given to Ulster, how I could be justified in asking men to go on preparing for resistance where their only object could be to obtain that which was offered to them.'[41] Against this onslaught, Bonar Law was forced to bend towards the exclusionist wind.

FORCES OF RESISTANCE

Bonar Law's position was complicated by a growing reaction from the right, horrified at the sympathy expressed by certain Tories for exclusion. Die-hards believed it would damage their public stance and the morale of the party. Willoughby de Broke harangued Tory leaders against any thought of a compromise over Home Rule. In a speech at Liverpool, early in September,[42] he demanded renewed determination to defeat Home Rule in its entirety, rather than chasing what he saw as Liberal 'hares' of a compromise. Within the leadership it was Lord Lansdowne who began to emerge as the leader of those Tories hostile to exclusion, despite long being perceived as a moderate. Lansdowne, as a Southern Irish Unionist, shared their conviction that exclusion for the north simply meant Home Rule for the south and thus represented an acute danger to their property, their religion and what remained of their local political standing. He was also aware that if an agreement were reached upon exclusion, he would have the unenviable task of ensuring safe passage for the amended bill through the Upper House. Nothing could have been more dangerous to his position or more destructive to his authority than smoothing the way for Home Rule for Southern Ireland. The disunity in the Lords in 1911 would pale by comparison and was already a source of concern to him, with Lord Willoughby de Broke rallying the die-hards and Lords Midleton and Barrymore giving a voice to growing Southern Unionist discontent. In place of a settlement upon exclusion Lansdowne put his faith in the demand for a general election. Not until much later in the crisis, when the government were under even more pressure, should a compromise be contemplated and only then along the lines of mild all-Ireland devolution or extended local government, both of which avoided the partition of Ireland and desertion of Southern Unionists.

Lansdowne's apprehension that a quick-fix solution around exclusion was developing increased during September and October. His visit to Balmoral alarmed him, while the king, in turn, found Lansdowne 'not very satisfactory'.[43] Bonar Law's report on his royal audience and discussions with Churchill, as well as Lansdowne's own talks with Balfour and Curzon in which 'Balfour had apparently given a considerable amount of encouragement to this idea (exclusion)',[44] heightened his trepidation. The Home Rule crisis was, it appeared, shifting its footing from a determined call for an election, towards a conference upon the exclusion. Lansdowne struggled to steer Bonar Law away from this; 'I am inclined to think that the practical difficulty of an arrangement ... (exclusion) ... would be even greater than you suppose. I doubt whether it would be possible to obtain for it the requisite measure of approval from Unionists of the South and West of Ireland.'[45] Three days later, on 23 September, he sent Bonar Law a four-page letter, warning against exclusion. 'The idea of a conference on these lines fills me with alarm and I gladly call to mind that you made it clear that we could not entertain the project unless it were consented to by loyalists of the South and West. Nor could we do so without some kind of authorization from our own party, many of whom would ... regard us as guilty of betrayal.'[46] He then cautioned Bonar Law against haste and hinted at a more satisfactory basis if a conference was unavoidable; 'I told [Balfour] that I thought it would never do to assume at this stage that a general election was out of the question and I regarded the idea of a *restricted* conference with the utmost alarm.'[47] In other words, a conference on with no fixed agenda, unrestricted in his own guarded words, was acceptable but certainly not a narrowly defined meeting centred upon exclusion. On the 26 September Lansdowne again argued the timing for a conference was wrong[48] and tried to separate Bonar Law from Carson:

> I have always felt that we have to be extremely careful in our relations with Carson and his friends. They are 'running their own show' and there is some advantage in our being able to say … that we are in no sense responsible for their proceedings … The fight which they are putting up in Ulster is, from a *party point of view*, much the most important factor in our calculations.[49]

Lansdowne's views tallied with Bonar Law's earlier belief that the Ulster Unionists and the Tory party were fighting for slightly different ends. But unlike Bonar Law, whose primary aim was to use Ulster to win an election, Lansdowne's first concern was to preserve a connection with all-Ireland, something he believed devolution to be compatible with though exclusion was not. He was thus keen to move Bonar Law away from a conference upon the basis of exclusion. On these grounds he severely criticised F.E. Smith, for drawing the king into a 'fool's paradise' over the chances of a compromise,[50] and attacked Carson, who he clearly blamed for the drift in affairs: 'the actual language used by Carson to F.E. or by F.E. to the king, it is interesting to collate them with the language of Carson's letter to you'.[51] To subvert the movement towards exclusion Lansdowne used the misgivings of Lord Salisbury to influence Bonar Law. 'I had a few lines from Salisbury two days ago which show that he and probably others are getting a little restless',[52] a warning that selling a compromise to the Lords would present the leadership with a situation similar to 1911. He also petitioned Walter Long for support. On the 3 October he warned Long 'what I am most afraid of is an attempt to manoeuvre us into a position in which we might be made to appear obstructive and unreasonable – we might find ourselves in such a position if we were to be offered the exclusion of Ulster, subject to our acceptance of the bill as it stands'.[53] Long agreed and two days later relayed his anxieties to Bonar Law. 'Personally I do not believe in a conference except after an election or on condition that the bill is withdrawn.'[54]

Yet these warnings proved unable to galvanise the Tory leadership against exclusion. Despite his letter of 5 October, Long remained silent during this period. This was partly the result of his slow recovery from illness and partly because of his precarious position, with many of his closest colleagues, such as Sir Harry Samuel and Sir William Bull keen supporters of Carson and heavily involved in Ulster Unionist activities. More sympathetic to Lansdowne were Lords Ashtown, Bedford and Barrymore who were outraged by suggestions of a compromise. Lord

Barrymore, sensing moves afoot, wrote to *The Times* on 10 October, attacking the drift of events towards exclusion and sounded a note 'of warning which we cannot disregard'.[55] Lord Midleton, a leading Southern Unionist, rejected any compromise, warning Bonar Law that 'some of my friends in Ireland, outside Ulster, are a *good deal concerned* at the turn matters are taking and the concentration of men's minds on the exclusion of the four Ulster counties ... It should certainly be made very clear that ... our appeal to the constituencies is against H.R. for any part of Ireland.'[56] (alarmingly Midleton even broached the idea amending the Army Annual Act[57] to forestall a compromise). These sentiments were echoed by James Campbell, Carson's colleague at Dublin University, who believed 'our policy is to declare that on this question we will ... sink or swim together'.[58] Lord Arran similarly felt that 'this idea of a compromise on the H.R. bill on the basis of the exclusion of Ulster ... cannot be accepted by Covenanters except by breaking their oath which they have taken before God'.[59] So alarmed was Willoughby de Broke by rumours of the exclusion of Ulster that he immediately began to rally support from die-hard colleagues in the upper chamber. Resistance in the upper house was to be expected. Southern Unionism was heavily represented in the chamber, while many peers expected an exclusion clause to be introduced in their house, according to the new guidelines of the Parliament Act. Indeed many Tory peers began to discern parallels to Liberal tactics used during the Parliament Bill crisis of 1910–11, where to ensure passage of their legislation they presented the Lords with 'Hobson's choice'. Either they passed the bill (or in this case an amendment for exclusion) or the Lords would suffer acute public odium from their refusal to sanction a compromise that removed the threat of civil war. If the Lords followed the latter course they offered the government a useful electoral platform of peace in Ireland versus the sponsorship of civil strife in Ireland at the hands of die-hard Tory peers.

Learning of Asquith's offer for secret talks on 10 October, Lansdowne re-doubled his efforts to persuade Bonar Law against a settlement. Although an informal 'tête-à-tête discussion' between Asquith and Bonar Law was probably unavoidable, he stressed 'a conference is quite another matter' and would present Bonar Law with 'an extremely difficult hand of cards to play'.[60] Recent government moves were simply a trap to 'throw upon us the odium of having obstructed a settlement'.[61] And he again drove a wedge between Bonar Law and Carson, by hinting at party rebellion:

> He [Carson] evidently means to fight on his 'inner-lines' and it looks as if he does not anticipate much articulate objection from his brother Unionists outside Ulster ... These Unionist 'outsiders' would find their voices if they were to discover suddenly that they had been left in the lurch and their cry would find a vociferous response amongst our own Diehards.[62]

Two days later he was even more forceful: '*it will be impossible for us to agree to any course which would involve a betrayal of our friends, whether in the South and West of Ireland or in "larger" Ulster*. Quite apart from the party disadvantage of such a betrayal, it would I am sure be, on its merits, odious to most of us'[63] (my italics). Lansdowne, like Carson, was trying to shift Bonar Law towards his way of thinking.

THE TRIALS OF LEADERSHIP

A conference, with the real possibility of agreeing a settlement, worked against Bonar Law's central strategy. It offered a viable alternative to the grim choice he had constantly threatened the government with since early 1912: either they call an election or Ulster, with the help of the Tory party, would resist Home Rule even if it provoked civil war in Ireland. However, Bonar Law could not simply refuse to enter a conference, for to do so would risk undermining public support for the Tory position. It would enable the government to contrast their own moderate, reasonable credentials against Bonar Law's belligerence, and alienate the king, who had done so much to lay the groundwork for the present accord. Equally dangerous, a refusal to negotiate (or even just to meet Asquith) could well rupture the Tory alliance with Carson and the Ulster Unionists, who were privately pushing hard for a settlement. By September 1913, the situation was pregnant with danger for Bonar Law.

One point working in his favour was that many observers, including Bonar Law, believed the idea of excluding all or even just part of Ulster (which the king, Carson, and Churchill had all touted) could never provide the basis for a compromise on the Home Rule issue. The complexities of the issue combined with the entrenched views many felt towards it, gave some the impression that it offered a suitable basis to 'wreck' proceedings and to actually *prevent* an agreement. This had been the substance of Strachey's advice to Bonar Law on 15 November 1911[64] and had been implicit in his acceptance of the Agar-Robartes amendment in June 1912 and the Carson amendment in January 1913. Underpinning these assumptions lay what Bonar Law imagined to be the resolute hostility of Irish Nationalists to any type of partition of Ireland; as Redmond declared 'Ireland for us is one entity'.[65] Yet without Nationalist support for such an alteration, any government attempt to compromise along these lines was dead in the water. Moreover, the issue of exclusion avoided the discussions taking place upon the basis of a devolutionary or even a federal arrangement, a scheme popular amongst the leaders of both political parties. And since it held out the opportunity of an all-Ireland solution, something that might well appeal to moderate Nationalists. It was clear to Bonar Law that negotiations upon the basis of devolution for Ireland stood a good chance of success. If, then, a conference was probably inevitable, Bonar Law perceived that one convened upon the basis of exclusion would give rise to the widest variety of obstacles, with the least likelihood of success. Working from this basic premise Bonar Law felt able to enter a conference and even in certain company express sympathy for exclusion, secure in the knowledge (so he believed) that it would fail.

Such an understanding of the situation provided Bonar Law with an important tactical advantage over the government. By expressing a positive approach to developments, he was able to negate their attempt to identify the Tory leadership as unyielding and extreme. This allowed Bonar Law to reassure the pro-settlement forces within Unionism, a posture that neutralised the threat from Balfour, as a leader of the moderate sections of the party, and helped maintain his co-operation with Carson and the Ulster Unionists. This latter consideration was imperative for Bonar Law; he could not allow Ulster to drift away at this critical moment. 'You know that I have not only so strong a personal friendship for you', he told Carson, 'but so much belief in your judgement that I do not think in any case I would go on with the proposal to which you were strongly opposed ... as you know I have long thought that if it were possible to leave Ulster as she is ... that is on the whole *the only way out*.'[66]

Of course, supporting exclusion did raise serious problems. Could he be sure, for example, that Nationalists would reject it as a basis for compromise, especially if Asquith watered it down sufficiently with restrictions on time and area? Earlier Nationalist obduracy was no concrete guarantee to continued resistance, at this more intense phase of crisis. Furthermore, a conference on exclusion would provoke grave party opposition, as was already clear from the die-hard warnings of Long, de Broke and Salisbury.

To placate these elements Bonar Law tried to soften the demands for a settlement. He reminded Carson of the difficulties exclusion raised right across the Unionist Alliance.[67] And he worked hard to dampen the king's fervour for a compromise. Already on 26 September Lord Stamfordham had informed Bonar Law that 'the king is ready to help in any way possible to arrive at a satisfactory solution',[68] and on 1 October, 'the king is every-day more anxious to bring about a conference especially in view of the trend in Ulster'.[69] He even invited Bonar Law to initiate an exchange between party leaders, assuring him of the government's readiness to negotiate. Bonar Law sought to lower the king's expectations. He disputed it was the opposition's role to initiate a conference[70] and challenged Smith's assertion that Carson was keen for one, informing the king that although he did not regard as impossible the proposal for a conference even with the idea of having some form Home Rule provided Ulster was excluded; but he was very far from being sanguine as to the possibility of such an arrangement'.[71]

It was also imperative that Bonar Law assuage the anxieties and concerns of Lansdowne. To this end he offered a guarantee that Unionists in the South and West remained a vital consideration to his opposition. 'I pointed out to him [Churchill] even more clearly than to the king the impossibility of our considering leaving Ulster out unless there should be a large measure of consent to it among the loyalists in the South and West.'[72] And a week later he confirmed that 'agreement from the South and West would be essential'.[73] Bonar Law also attacked Smith, a particular hate-figure of Lansdowne's after his 'loose talking' to the king. In reply to Lansdowne's suspicion that 'F.E. Smith had not been discreet',[74] Bonar Law retorted that 'F.E.'s talk with the king seemed to me just about as unwise as anything could be'.[75] He went further: 'Stamfordham's letter makes me feel that I made a mistake in sending the copy of the talk at Balmoral to Carson'.[76] Bonar Law was clearly keen to assure Lansdowne that the two of them stood shoulder to shoulder (an assurance he had similarly given Carson). Thus on the 24th he could write to Lansdowne, 'I have received from him [Carson] a reply … and I am rather surprised to find that, on the whole, he takes pretty much the same view of the position *that we do*. There is nothing now *for us* to do except to wait.'[77] Playing up his personal loyalty to Lansdowne was vital to preserving his support, at a moment when the actual direction of policy was beginning to divide them. 'There is nothing I am more anxious about than that I should make no move of any kind without your approval.'[78]

Unfortunately for Bonar Law, momentum for a settlement gathered pace, from early October, amongst many Tory leaders, Ulster Unionists and sections of the press. 'Since I have come to London I have seen Curzon, Bob Cecil and Walter Long (who is very much better) and all of them (including Walter) I think would welcome a settlement much as in other conditions they would have objected to it.'[79] The attitude of Long was particularly significant, as an influential figure carrying weight in party circles and who tended to reflect backbench party opinion. Against this onslaught Bonar Law was forced to move further towards exclusion, going beyond his rather neutral stance taken up in September. Writing to Lansdowne on 4 October 1913 he now believed that 'probably I have looked upon the solution of leaving Ulster out much more favourably than you have'[80] and sounded a more pessimistic tone about an election; 'we must not forget, however, that even if we can force an election (and I think we can) difficulties are not removed. It is not certain that we should win it.'[81] These more direct suggestions he still qualified by confirming 'that such a solution is a last resort and nothing would seem to be more foolish than to give the enemy the idea that we were not only ready but anxious for a settlement'.[82] Bonar Law accompanied this letter with an eight-page memorandum,[83] (much of which echoed Carson's arguments), which was designed to win Lansdowne over. He began by noting the lack of resolve shown by Southern Unionists. 'If this really represents the position it seems to me obvious that we are not justified in risking civil war for the sake of people who will take no risks even of a financial kind for themselves, and I do think it shows clearly that they have become more or less reconciled to the idea of Home Rule.'[84] Bonar Law then considered the various options available. Continuation of the government's present policy of Home Rule to all Ireland would be 'utterly impossible', for to coerce Ulster into the bill would be the 'worst possible condition'. Alternatively, if the Tories forced an election and lost it, 'the position would be desperate'. Yet even if they won with what would realistically be a small majority, 'our position would be impossible'. 'These considerations ... make me feel that if it is possible to secure a settlement by consent we ought to secure it even if it should be a settlement which we dislike.'[85] He continued:

> there are only two possible bases of settlement; first, a general system of devolution; and second, a form of Home Rule for Ireland from which Ulster, or part of Ulster, should be excluded. The first of these

> alternatives is not in my opinion possible, and it is only the second *which can be seriously considered*'.[86]

As an analysis of the situation, its purpose was to persuade Lansdowne towards his way of thinking in a tense and changing political environment. It was not, necessarily, a reflection of what Bonar Law actually felt, for something of his deeper thinking can be gauged from a passage towards the end of the memorandum, initially crossed out and then re-inserted later on (he was obviously concerned that it should have the right effect):

> There are of course many difficulties. What would the government mean by Ulster? Sir Edward Carson believes that his supporters in Ulster would accept nothing short of the whole province ... It may be that if there were to be a division, the Nationalists themselves would prefer that it should apply to the whole province, but if we found that the government would only consider the exclusion of the four or possibly six counties ... we ought not to enter a conference, *for nothing could be worse for us than that we should be put in the position of having to refuse an offer which the people of this country would regard as fair and reasonable.*[87] (my italics)

Two things are revealed here. First, an awareness that defining Ulster would cause serious difficulties between the Nationalists and government. The 'geographical puzzle' he mentioned, could be a conundrum undermining any exclusion formula. Second, there is an almost fatalistic sense that they had little choice but to accept an offer if made, for to obstruct it would destroy their public standing. Concerns for public support were paramount to Bonar Law, for his central aim remained that of keeping the party popular, in expectation of a general election. Subtly, then, while we can see a shift in approach, style and emphasis in Bonar Law's position by early October, continuity with his long-held ambitions can also be detected; namely a continuing desire to prompt an election, to keep in with public opinion and to avoid a solution to the crisis.

Bonar Law's concern to appease Lansdowne was also based upon his prediction that the noble Lords' obstruction served to weaken his Law's negotiating position, at precisely the moment when an image of moderation was needed to face down Asquith. If Bonar Law was unable to appear 'genuinely' reasonable then the government was provided with the room and the security 'to offer us terms which they know we cannot accept and then throw upon us the odium of having obstructed a settlement'.[88] This was all the more dangerous since Asquith might have taken his chance of an election at this point, fighting it not on the issue of Home Rule but on whether their solution to the crisis should be accepted or not, a far less attractive political stance for the Tories to oppose. It was imperative, therefore, that Bonar Law moderated Lansdowne's resistance before his meeting with Asquith. To these ends he gave a detailed account of 'the line I should take when speaking to him [Asquith]' in order to calm Lansdowne's anxieties.[89] He also reassured him that 'even, however, if all these conditions were fulfilled and though we did enter into conference, we would not be under any obligation before to agree to a settlement; and we might find it impossible to agree to it if we found that the Unionists in the south and west were vehement in their hostility to it'.[90] Once again Bonar Law gave hostages to fortune by tying his policy to Southern Unionist reactions. But such a firm commitment might also suggest he had little hope of anything concrete emerging from his talk with Asquith.

INTO CONFERENCE

When, therefore, Bonar Law finally met Asquith on the 15th he faced many conflicting pressures. Within the Unionist alliance he was acutely aware that influential sections favoured a compromise, and that a weary (if not bored) public opinion would not react well towards the party that obstructed a settlement. However, many in the party were also poised to raise revolt if a compromise transpired – even the knowledge that he was meeting Asquith was enough to exacerbate party tensions. A second problem lay with Bonar Law's estimation of Liberal tactics. On the one hand he believed the government would find it almost impossible to settle with the Nationalists upon the basis of the exclusion of part of Ulster; recent speeches from Redmond and Devlin had revealed for many just how much they disliked exclusion. 'I understand', Balfour told Bonar Law, 'that Redmond has quite explicitly rejected any suggestion of excluding Ulster from the operations of the bill. If he means all he says – and presumably he does – Asquith will find himself in a very delicate situation.'[91] This was encouraging. But Bonar Law could never be wholly sure Asquith would not somehow square the Nationalists to a compromise formula which, if 'the people of this country regard as fair and reasonable', he would be unable to refuse.[92] Churchill had reckoned back in September they could get Redmond to agree to a meaningful concession, perhaps along the lines of a devolutionary or even federal restructuring of the UK; this after all had been hinted at by Asquith when introducing the bill in April 1912. And with the current strength of forces in favour of a reasonable settlement, its success seemed a real possibility, whatever the difficulties involved in appeasing the Nationalists.

A third problem for Bonar Law was that he was not a natural negotiator, indeed he had hoped to take either Lansdowne or Chamberlain with him. Bonar Law was a plain-speaking, blunt platform orator, inexperienced in close-quarter negotiations and now facing the prospect of engaging the highly experienced and wily Asquith in face-to-face talks. Yet Bonar Law did possess great foresight and a clear understanding of the issues at stake, as well as what he regarded as a coherent bargaining position. That strategy centred on a realisation that exclusion would prove impossibly troublesome for the government to effect, given its weakness in three areas. First over the definition of the area to be excluded: was it all nine Ulster counties or just the four where Protestants had a sizeable majority or perhaps a compromise between these two of six counties? Second upon what was actually meant by exclusion, particularly whether it was to be a temporary or permanent exclusion from the operations of the Home Rule bill. And third how far would alterations to the original Home Rule bill render it such a different bill that a whole new bill would need to be introduced? In other words, there were for Bonar Law three areas where Liberals and Nationalists could disagree with each other and upon which the negotiations might well collapse. In light of this Bonar Law hoped his meeting with Asquith would highlight the acute political difficulties involved in reaching a satisfactory settlement, so forcing the government back into its dilemma of a choice between civil war or a general election.

Asquith and Bonar Law's first conversation at Cherkley Court was exploratory in substance. Bonar Law began by requesting a general election as 'the real way out', sweetening the pill by 'pledging ourselves to support Ulster to the utmost if there were no election, that pledge was contingent, and if an election took place and the government won, our support would be withdrawn'.[93] At the same time he repeated his threats of disorder, 'we should have to try by all means to force an election and to be successful we should have to take means which would be distasteful to all us'.[94] Bonar Law continued to reduce the Home Rule struggle to a choice between civil war or an election. Beyond these predictable opening salvoes Bonar Law was canny in immediately focusing their discussions of possible compromise formulas onto the idea of exclusion. 'On *my* part the conversation then took the form of *my* pointing out how difficult such an arrangement (exclusion) would be for us, and I called his attention to these difficulties.'[95] Although conveying the negative aspects of such a solution, the important point was that they were now talking about exclusion and not a 'larger' or more 'unrestricted' type of political settlement, which he feared. He had, in other words, narrowed the debate, leaving Asquith under the impression that exclusion was the avenue down which Bonar Law might travel towards a successful compromise. He (Asquith):

> repeated his declaration of our position ... 'subject to the agreement of your (B.L's) colleagues whose concurrence is essential to you, if there were not a general outcry against you in the South and West of Ireland, if Ulster (which we can at present call X) were left out of the bill, then you would not feel bound to prevent the granting of Home Rule to the rest of Ireland'. I accepted that statement as correct and that is where the interview ended.[96]

After the meeting Lansdowne was incensed at Bonar Law, believing he had been far to free and easy with his opinions to Asquith. 'The most important paragraph in the memorandum is that with which it concludes. Read literally, it rather suggests to my mind the idea that we are ready to ask our colleagues, if Ulster is left out of the bill, to agree to a proposal for "the granting of Home Rule to the rest of Ireland" ... I do not think I could bring myself to concur in such a proposal.'[97] Yet given Bonar Law's concerns and objectives before the meeting, we might actually consider his performance a success. He repeated his desire for an election[98] and backed this up with the threat of extreme consequences if none was forthcoming. More importantly he avoided discussion of an all-Irish solution and targeted exclusion as the only basis upon which a settlement by consent might come. Thus he had focused on a project he believed stood the least chance of success. In addition, Bonar Law had shown a willingness to negotiate. Asquith now had no room to label the Tory leadership as obstructive in the public mind. This had been a concern for Bonar Law. Indeed he even speculated that Asquith, unable to placate the Nationalists, would make a 'dummy' compromise offer, not with the intention of settling the issue but solely to advertise Liberal reasonableness while provoking a Tory rejection, and so provide the government with suitable grounds for a snap election. As Bonar Law explained to

Lansdowne, 'even if we did decline to enter a conference … when they (the government) had made up their minds with the consent of the Nationalists to exclude Ulster, they could then definitely make that proposal public and appeal to the country with this new proposal and I should have very little hope of winning an election under such conditions'.[99] A show of agreeableness from Bonar Law removed this manoeuvre from Asquith's armoury; and in removing it, Bonar Law forced back onto Asquith the onus of finding a viable compromise that had as yet evaded detection, namely of marrying Nationalist interests with Ulster Unionist fears.

However, Bonar Law's moderation was qualified. He threw powerful obstacles in the way of any smooth bargain on exclusion, such as the agreement of his colleagues, the concerns of Unionists in the South and West of Ireland and the problem that, with Home Rule solved, Welsh Disestablishment would pass quickly through under the Parliament Act. More significantly, he did not move the discussion onto defining what was meant by exclusion or how much of Ulster was to be excluded:

> In the course of conversation he spoke of the 'North East counties'. I was afraid of that line of discussion and said that I had not seriously considered what was meant by Ulster. He showed that he had carefully considered that, for he had figures for the different counties and I passed from that subject without going into it at all, for it is quite evident to me that he had in his mind only the four counties.[100]

Nor can we level against Bonar Law the charge, implicit in Lansdowne's reaction, that he was manoeuvred into admitting the principle of exclusion while receiving nothing in return from Asquith. Support for the Agar-Robartes and Carson amendments had already conceded this principle. And from Asquith, Bonar Law wanted little: his strategy was based on the assumption that the Liberals and Nationalists would split over exclusion, and this required patience and nerve on his part, not information.

Bonar Law's first meeting with Asquith should therefore be considered a success. Of course this is not to argue that all was now well or that Bonar Law himself was confident of the future. For in a very pessimistic covering letter to Lansdowne, shortly after his meeting, Bonar Law revealed momentary doubts;

> I do not like the position and I'm sure that the next move will be for Asquith to sound out the Nationalists. There is therefore a very great

> danger that we shall be invited into a conference in which they have made up their minds to exclude Ulster. They would, I am sure, be reasonable in their definition of Ulster ... that the four counties remain in the Union and as regards the two counties a plebiscite should be taken ... I don't think Carson could possibly accept this solution; and yet it would be so reasonable that I think we should be in a hopeless position if we had to refuse it.[101]

Perhaps Bonar Law still feared Asquith would secure Nationalist agreement to a compromise; 'if he [Asquith] or the government decided on any course which commanded the support of their own party the Nationalists would have no choice but to accept it'.[102] Yet such fears do not reflect Bonar Law's settled thoughts, but simply lingering and transient qualms. For three days after his meeting Bonar Law revealed to J.P. Croal, a close friend and editor of *The Scotsman*, 'my view is that it is all to the good that we should seem to be open to compromise and that irreconcilableness should come from the Radicals as a result of their connection with the Nationalists'.[103] More positively still, 'my own impression however is that Redmond cannot agree to the solution of excluding Ulster; and if so everything in the nature of moderation on our part will be an advantage'.[104] Bonar Law now appeared confident and surefooted, once again believing that the attempt to find a political solution would come to nothing and that his task was to avoid the party being labelled obstructive. Reinforcing Bonar Law's belief that the government would find it impossible to exclude Ulster, the Tory Chief-Whip, Edmund Talbot, stated that the speaker 'has said that the exclusion of Ulster would entail a new bill'. And from Croal he received an optimistic reply on the 21st that 'if the government were to act on the lines of the (Churchill's) Dundee speech there would be open feud between them and the Nationalists'.[105] Such views buttressed his own belief that exclusion, whichever way it was applied, would not prove the basis for a negotiated settlement.

CHAPTER SIX

Secret parleys and party strains, autumn 1913

INTRODUCTION

THE INTERVENING three weeks between Bonar Law's first meeting with Asquith and their second meeting on 7 November 1913 were rich in speculation and suspense. This was fuelled by Asquith's deeply ambiguous speech at Ladybank on 26 October. Balfour, perhaps hankering after the type of non-partisan role that would characterise his later career saw in it the seeds of an alliance with the government. Lansdowne and Chamberlain, on the other hand, detected a tentative proposal for proceeding along devolutionary lines for a settlement, clearly against the substance of his meeting with Bonar Law on 15 October. And from yet another angle, Lord Milner interpreted his speech as nothing less than disinformation, with Asquith 'merely playing with the question'.[1] After much discussion amongst the Unionist leadership, Bonar Law replied to Asquith's declarations with a speech at Newcastle. Bonar Law delivered a neat, measured but decisive response to the prime minister, giving the appearance of being open-minded towards a compromise yet, at the same time, repulsing any definite move towards one.

Perhaps the most significant development of this period was the emergence of a powerful movement against the exclusion of all or part of Ulster as a basis for a compromise. The movement had several different foci. One was Lansdowne who, alarmed by Bonar Law's apparent recklessness during his meeting with Asquith, sought to steer any future discussions away from exclusion and towards an All-Irish devolutionary settlement. A second was Austen Chamberlain who emerged alongside Lansdowne in a common anti-exclusion stance, although Chamberlain was keen to move events well beyond simple devolution towards a more far-reaching, federal reconstruction of the British Constitution. From another direction Walter Long, sensing a hardening of opinion on the

Tory right, looked to stiffen Bonar Law against a compromise altogether and in so doing echoed the views of Milner, Willoughby de Broke and Hugh Cecil. For Bonar Law this movement of opinion within the leadership against exclusion as a basis for settlement was extremely dangerous, despite being made up of groups (federalists, devolutionists and die-hards) that ordinarily had little in common with each other. For one, the support of Carson and the Ulster Unionists could well evaporate if the Tory leadership ignored their preference for a settlement based upon exclusion. Furthermore, Bonar Law's concern had always been to appear reasonable and open to a compromise with the public, so as not to be outmanoeuvred by Asquith. Grave dangers clearly lay ahead for Bonar Law. Yet, ironically, Asquith's failure to move over this period towards a viable compromise plan, also served to convince Bonar Law that his tactical line was correct. 'He is quite at sea and does not in the least know what he can do', Bonar Law could tell Selborne at the end of December.[2]

Bonar Law and Asquith met for a third time on 10 December 1913. After this last and largely futile meeting (and between Asquith and Carson on 16 December and 2 January 1914) the initiative towards finding a settlement ended. Bonar Law asked Asquith for permission to publicly announce this fact, which he did in a speech at Bristol on 15 January 1914. The interlude between their last meeting on 10 December and his Bristol speech witnessed much frenzied activity within Unionist circles. During this time the idea developed that Asquith was not simply drifting along but shrewdly wasting time in the hope of splitting the Unionist forces, following a course similar to that of 1910. Growing mistrust of the prime minister hardened party opinion against any further attempts to find a compromise or even to have contact with him. Nineteen fourteen therefore opened with the parties far apart and a settlement to the Home Rule crisis little advanced on the political position in September.

'CHANGING THE ISSUE': CHAMBERLAIN, LANSDOWNE AND DEVOLUTION

By mid-October Unionist supporters of federalism began to mobilise against a compromise based upon exclusion. From being rather marginal during the highly partisan parliamentary sessions of 1912 and 1913, federalists now emerged as a powerful force at the very centre of political debate. They were encouraged by Churchill's Dundee speech of 8

October 1913, with its heavy hints of compromise. 'Very courageous', thought F.S. Oliver, 'and I should say not only that he means to stick to it but that he has the P.M. behind him.'[3] As significant was Carson's earlier letter to Earl Grey on the 26 September ('which shows that he [Carson] is prepared, provided the present bill is withdrawn, to accept federalism').[4] This ignited much enthusiasm in the federalist camp, for the clear implication was that Carson was not, after all, averse to a constructive solution for Ireland and was not, as Lansdowne alleged, fighting solely for Ulster.[5] His attitude sprang from a recognition, present by the summer of 1913, that federalism might offer him a means to satisfy the interests of Ulster as well as the fears of Southern Unionists, and thus a solution to the divergence between his private all-Ireland sympathies and his public role as leader of the Ulster revolt.

Buoyed up by this revelation, federalists worked hard to raise the profile and potential of federalism as a way out of the existing impasse. Oliver sent Geoffry Robinson, editor of *The Times*, Carson's letter to Grey as evidence of a more positive attitude among leading Unionists, and urged him to give support for the federal initiative which had been hinted at by Churchill just two days before.[6] Robinson also received letters from Grey and Dunraven, similarly requesting that his paper champion federalism.[7] Earl Grey was active elsewhere: in late September he implored Haldane to turn towards federalism[8] and on 15 October he invited Henry Page-Croft, influential on the Tory right and president of the United Empire Club, to 'build up an interesting programme (of speeches) for the winter in the hope of focusing the attention of Unionists upon the federal principle'.[9] Despite these efforts, Oliver was forced to admit by mid-October that 'things have not gone particularly well so far … nor at the present time very hopeful and unless some push is given from the outside … are likely to drift into a deplorable impasse'.[10]

Oliver's despondency sprang from several key problems. One was a continued disagreement over what was meant by federalism. Rather embarrassingly this became public when Dunraven and Grey had letters published in *The Times* on 25 October, advocating fundamentally different schemes. As Oliver moaned to Milner, 'what strikes me rather with wonderment about them all is that they don't seem to have thought much … of the actual way out. They don't seem to have realised or visualised what federalism or anything else means. Consequently things are in a very fluid and uncomfortable condition.'[11] Another dilemma for federalists was the timing of their initiative, and particularly the fear that Unionist leaders would commit themselves too early. 'At this juncture it would be fatal ... if the Unionist party proclaim in advance their willingness to accept federalism then of course federalism will become their maximum demand and they will have to be content with something less.'[12] Federalism had to be embraced, but held back until the ideal moment. Moreover, a federal solution ran counter to the tough line being pursued by the Tory leadership of forcing an election. Not only did this throw the weight of party opinion against them but Oliver realised that an election before a settlement was actually ruinous to the success of their cause; 'one can hardly hope that the temper of politicians and the conditions generally will be favourable for success *after* a bitter electoral struggle, as they are at the present time'.[13]

But more problematic for the federalists was that they lacked someone of sufficient influence at the top of the Unionist party to set the initiative rolling. 'The difficulty ... [is]', Oliver told Grey, 'of getting the thing begun'.[14] He even urged Grey to take the lead as 'someone whom they all trust to go between them, to bring them together and to give them ideas'.[15] But Grey, though widely respected, was not a front-rank politician. What was needed was a strong advocate within the Tory leadership. Carson, who though privately sympathetic and who in the long term might have regarded Federalism as a solution, could not publicly move from his stand upon Ulster. F.E. Smith was a 'believer' and his speeches and actions had shown some courage in furthering the cause of a settlement, but he was trusted even less by his own side than by the Liberals. Balfour was certainly sympathetic towards finding a solution, envisaging a pro-order, anti-Irish alliance of the party leaderships to impose a settlement on Ireland. He recognised that future co-operation in parliament between the parties would be necessary to push through 'the Home Rule measure, mutilated as it will be' against 'the *representatives of Ireland*'. He even speculated that 'if Home Rule and the Welsh Church were out of the way the differences between the two parties (putting T.R. aside) would seem to be mainly as to the methods by [which] Social reform ... and Constitutional revision ... were carried out'.[16] Balfour's fondness for coalition government was growing steadily against a backdrop of mounting crisis. But, crucially, he believed in exclusion not federalism as the only viable solution to the present stalemate. Lansdowne was mistrusted on the right and, though keen to change the basis of discussions away from exclusion, was no federalist. The obvious choice was Chamberlain but he was abroad until 20 October 1913, and in his first contact with Oliver for over a month thought the present moment inauspicious for a conference upon a federal basis.[17]

The situation changed following Asquith's speech at Ladybank on 26 October, with its albeit rather vague suggestion that a conference on federalism might be the way to proceed. The day after, Moreton Frewen urged Bonar Law to respond positively to Asquith's federal hints and run with such a scheme. He believed such a course would draw support from Tim Healy[18] and the handful of other moderate O'Brienite Nationalists, so embarrassing Redmond and increasing support in parliament for a constructive alternative to exclusion. More practically, Oliver again wrote to Robinson, pressing him to 'play-up' the moderate parts of Asquith's speech in *The Times* and to focus attention on the feasibility of a federal political settlement.[19] The same day he contacted his friend Murray Macdonald,[20] a Liberal MP and known supporter of the Empire, to establish links with moderate men in the Liberal fold and hoped 'that the lunatics on both sides of politics may be blessed by providence with a lucid interval somewhere between now and next summer'.[21] He even assured Macdonald that Carson's real intention 'is a serious attempt to settle the whole thing'.[22] Oliver also maintained contact with Churchill, from whom he received encouraging sentiments on the prospects for a constructive arrangement. 'I think', wrote Churchill, 'that there is a strong undercurrent setting in a good direction; and that many of the obsolete Victorian quarrels are passing altogether from men's minds.'[23] Lastly, Oliver persuaded Chamberlain to play a bigger role in the federal enterprise. 'The great advantage of Austen is that when once he grips an idea and accepts it he doesn't wobble. I regard him as the greatest standby at the present juncture'[24] (note Oliver's use of standby, implying that Bonar Law's leadership might need to be overturned before an alternative federal line would succeed). Drawing Chamberlain back into politics was no mean feat. Since early 1913, Chamberlain had been disillusioned and had drifted without a cause to champion, following Bonar Law's dramatic U-turn over tariff reform. By the summer of 1913 the idea of federalism as a solution to the Irish Question increasingly attracted him as a new constructive policy (though not enough to prompt any positive action on his behalf). For one, it was a solution associated with his father, who had offered it as an alternative to Gladstone's first Home Rule bill. Federalism also offered Chamberlain the lead to the swelling group of Unionists, alarmed at Bonar Law's extreme tactics and keen for a settlement. And moving against Bonar Law over Irish policy probably satisfied his lingering pique at the reversal of Unionist policy on tariffs.

Keen to move matters forward, Oliver invited Chamberlain to dinner[25] on 22 October 1913, enclosing a copy of the Grey–Carson letter to mull over in the meantime. Chamberlain found it 'highly important', mentioning the substance of the correspondence to Lansdowne on the 23rd.[26] Encouraged by signs of interest, Oliver went further, flattering Chamberlain that a meeting between him and 'the aged Squiff' could be arranged and 'might do good',[27] even suggesting he arrange an informal dinner at Aubrey Herbert's, a close friend of Asquith.[28] Chamberlain proved responsive: 'don't do anything unless you hear from me again. At present I am trying [to get] what support I could get among my own friends.'[29] Although not keen to meet Asquith (he knew of Bonar Law's meeting with him whereas Oliver clearly did not), Chamberlain had been moved by the Ladybank speech and was now ready to provide the type of leadership Oliver was looking for. By the end of October, then, Oliver had done much, tending cross-party contacts, stimulating a groundswell of pro-federal opinion and easing Chamberlain out of his self-imposed wilderness and into a more active role to replace exclusion with federalism as the basis for compromise.

Unbeknown to Oliver, Chamberlain's support had already been solicited by Lansdowne, who had been deeply troubled by Bonar Law's meeting with Asquith and his apparent endorsement of exclusion as a basis for settlement. 'I do not think I could bring myself to concur in such a proposal',[30] urging in its place that future discussions proceed along devolutionary lines.[31] Furthermore, by late October, Lansdowne was increasingly worried that a settlement over Irish Home Rule was becoming connected to Liberal ideas for attracting the agricultural labourers.[32] Speculation on what these involved had emerged over the previous year and included minimum wages for rural workers, local wage boards and even fixed rents and secure tenure for farmers, changes that, for Lansdowne and most other landowners, represented a revolution in the ownership of property. But it was not until Lloyd George's speech at Swindon on 21 October that the Liberal Land Campaign was formally launched – what Lansdowne referred to as 'the most unscrupulous proclamation that I have ever encountered'.[33] The timing of the pronouncement was, he thought, of most significance for it indicated the government was preparing a popular platform for an election in the not too distant future. This, however, required the rapid settling of Home Rule as a hot (and potentially unpopular) political issue, if it was not to lose the government votes, which in the circumstances of October 1913 suggested a snap compromise deal with the Ulstermen upon exclusion. The return of Chamberlain now gave Lansdowne the opportunity to construct an alliance against such a development. Though Chamberlain was a federalist, he recognised that such views were sufficiently compatible with his own plans for all-Ireland devolution, to act as a bridge to their political co-operation and provide him with a counter-weight to Bonar Law and Carson. After all Chamberlain was someone with influence and standing amongst Unionists in the Lower House who enjoyed close relations with Carson, Smith and Churchill. With Chamberlain alongside him, Lansdowne stood a better chance of moving the Tory leadership away from exclusion.

Chamberlain and Lansdowne met for the first time on 23 October to coordinate their views before Chamberlain met Bonar Law the next day. Following the meeting he wrote to Lansdowne confirming, 'in my first conversation with Bonar Law last Friday morning (24th) he and I went over the ground which you had covered the evening before, with the amplifications which you invited me to seek from him'.[34] But it was Asquith's rather cryptic Ladybank speech, in which Chamberlain detected the seeds of an agreement with the government, that did most to galvanise their efforts. 'If there are to be conversations', he told Lansdowne, 'and if those conversations are to have any chance of a successful result, the best plan for both parties is to try to reach a *new solution* or in other words so to *change the issue* that each will be able to claim that they have substantially got not indeed all they desire but the essentials of their claim'. And the way to achieve this was to 'draw Asquith onto the lines of general devolution'.[35] Only devolution 'can fairly be represented to Asquith as the most advantageous to him', for exclusion would be 'the most difficult course for him' and although a 'victory for us [would be] a hollow victory'. Chamberlain rounded off this appeal for a settlement upon devolution by revealing the Grey–Carson letter on the feasibility of such an approach. 'Carson clearly indicates that he thinks that this is the right solution and expresses the hope that if there is a conference it may proceed on these broad lines'.[36] Clearly, for Chamberlain, Carson was a force to work *with* the drive for a devolutionary settlement and by omission, Bonar Law was not.

These observations were of great interest to Lansdowne, not least the disclosure of the Carson–Grey letter. For he too had detected 'a gleam of daylight' in the Ladybank speech 'indicated by the third of Asquith's "governing considerations" … that he recognised the importance of the extension of the principle of devolution in appropriate forms to other parts of the U.K.'.[37] Lansdowne even went further, offering a possible method for winning over the Nationalists to a scheme of devolution; 'might we not fasten on this and say that we are prepared to allow Ireland to be served first but only upon condition that whatever system of self-government is granted to her must be applicable to other parts of the U.K. ...?'[38] Thus by late October 1913, both Lansdowne and Chamberlain were not only acting in concert but had, so they believed, found a compromise formula that offered a real chance of success, and which avoided the exclusion of part of Ulster.

With Bonar Law to speak at Newcastle on 29 October, the Tory leader came in for much advice from his colleagues. Bob Cecil and Selborne implored Bonar Law to 'stress the Imperial danger quite apart from the Ulster opposition'.[39] Along similar lines Lansdowne pressed him to adopt the formula he had agreed with Chamberlain of devolution all round with Irish ambitions gratified first.[40] He realised that although Asquith evidently favoured a devolutionary settlement, two obstacles stood in the way of a successful arrangement: the need to deal with Ireland first and the opposition of the Ulstermen. These obstacles Lansdowne now challenged. 'I do not think that Asquith is altogether unreasonable in stipulating that, if there is to be devolution, Ireland should be served first.'[41] Furthermore, 'as Carson (I think) said to me the other day, it might be possible to set up some kind of an Irish Administration the existence of which would placate moderate Home Rulers without doing much harm'.[42] Before Bonar Law's Newcastle speech, influential Unionist leaders were pushing Bonar Law to ditch the extreme line he had pursued since late 1911 and his more recent 'flirtation' with exclusion, and move instead towards a viable basis for settlement, one which they believed Asquith himself desired and which Unionists would be able to accept.

Of course care must be taken not to exaggerate the strength of this initiative. For one, clear differences existed between Lansdowne and Chamberlain. Lansdowne still preferred a general election and only promoted devolution (something he saw as very different to federalism) under the threat of exclusion. 'We are, I suppose, in the abstract, all of us supporters of devolution ... but I hesitate to talk glibly about the adoption of the federal principle until I really know what I mean by the words'.[43] Chamberlain, on the other hand, saw a federal policy as the best long-term solution, realising that a common dislike of exclusion obscured their substantive differences. Nor was Chamberlain solely reliant upon Lansdowne.

The latter was useful support, but it was towards the more constructive elements in the party that Chamberlain looked, particularly to his old friends from 1910–11, Smith, Selborne and even Carson.

Despite intense pressure from Lansdowne, Chamberlain and others, Bonar Law's reply at Newcastle dashed their hopes by containing no coded devolutionary message. Chamberlain 'very much regret[ed] that B.L. after all said nothing of this side of the question and confined himself entirely to Ulster. I wonder whether it was accident or design?'[44] Indeed he even felt this evasion to be a personal slur. 'What B.L. said was well said but after all he omitted practically all reference to the Imperial question. He may have reverted deliberately to his original purpose after I saw him or having got his first sketch firmly in his mind felt unable to bring it in later.'[45] So annoyed was Chamberlain that in two speeches delivered at Newport and Cardiff during the first week of November, he challenged his leader's policy by offering a federal alternative.[46] 'Look at my Newport speech … I have said nothing I do not believe or mean, but if anyone is inclined to consider a federal solution, I have said enough to provide him with a text'.[47]

Anger at Bonar Law's Newcastle speech also moved Chamberlain to manoeuvre behind his back and open his own line of contact with certain Liberal leaders, notably Churchill, who invited him to dine on *The Enchantress* later that month. Churchill, picking up on the hints in Chamberlain's Newport speech, hoped they could have 'one of those frank, free and unfettered conversations which are so much in fashion now'.[48] Before the meeting, planned for 27 November, Oliver, who was intimate with proceedings, was actively stirring the federal pot. He informed Grey that 'there will be work to do early next week. Things have moved a good deal',[49] and urged Robinson to concentrate more upon Chamberlain's speeches, while flattering Lord Northcliffe, proprietor of *The Daily Mail*, that 'your legions have lent powerful aid' to the federal cause.[50] Oliver also arranged a private dinner for Chamberlain, Milner and Earl Grey to 'discuss things over claret'.[51] And as if that was not enough, Oliver published a pamphlet *The Alternative to Civil War*, a passionate appeal for a constructive solution to the present crisis, rather than a general election. The pamphlet attracted support amongst both Liberal and Unionist leaders. But leaving nothing to chance he enclosed a copy to Churchill; 'I imagine that in your mind, as in mine, the two things which loom the largest are (a) the need for securing our defenses … and (b) the disastrous consequences of threats of lawlessness … upon the authority of executive Government … I am only an advocate of putting heads together in a convention … If men could take responsibility and agree, it would be much better'.[52]

Aware of Chamberlain's enterprise, Lansdowne threw his weight behind the initiative. At Brighton on 18 November, he delivered a powerful pro-devolution speech,[53] that was received with great enthusiasm by federalists. 'Lansdowne has committed the Unionists to the consideration of the federal plan … (he) has waved the federal flag, the next step is for Asquith to act'.[54] As joint leader of the Unionist party, Lansdowne's public move against Bonar Law's stance was highly important, revealing strains within the Unionist leadership and injecting the Churchill–Chamberlain talks with a greater significance that they might otherwise have had. Yet he went further, for on 20 November, he unexpectedly and unofficially met Asquith at Windsor Castle, using the occasion to discuss the possible grounds for a devolutionary settlement. Chamberlain also raised the constructive banner with a strong federalist speech at Bromsgrove, a few days after Lansdowne. 'I have been scolded for the speech by my friends and praised by my enemies, so I ought to be ashamed of it, but I'm not.'[55] Scolded he certainly was, especially by the Tory right. 'If the party are now going to be asked to ground their arms', Willoughby de Broke told him, 'and consider a new instrument of Government for the whole of the U.K., I believe many of us will be bewildered and demoralised'.[56] But constructive elements were encouraged. Lansdowne agreed with Chamberlain's statements while Lord Avery 'particularly liked the notion that what is to be done for Ireland should only be what can presently (be done) for the other divisions of the U.K.'.[57] Churchill thought the Bromsgrove and Brighton speeches 'very important', telling Chamberlain a little later that they had been considered in cabinet.[58]

By the time Churchill and Chamberlain finally met, things had moved on a good deal. The meeting was more specific than the Bonar Law/ Asquith talks. Chamberlain argued against exclusion, seeing it as 'the worst and most humiliating solution for them and it did not satisfy us. The bill without Ulster was only one degree worse than the bill with Ulster. So we must change the issue',[59] and towards Home Rule all round, 'the old Liberal Unionist policy'.[60] If Asquith offered a 'federal settlement', Chamberlain continued, with powers reserved to the Imperial Parliament over customs, the Post Office, the Judiciary and 'all powers not specifically delegated', then 'I believe B.L. who doubtless would be in consultation with his colleagues *could not refuse* such an offer'[61] (my italics). Churchill was receptive to these ideas but uncertain of the timing, for 'leaders might be prepared but parties were not ... "a little red blood had got to flow" and then public opinion would wake up and then –'.[62] Chamberlain rejected any delay, 'if the House once meets the opportunity for peace will be gone. You will break the H of C in the process'.[63] The interview ended with agreement on the need for co-operation and even sympathy for a coalition government; 'the idea of fusion with an extreme wing left out on either side is obviously constantly in his mind and would be greatly liked by him'.[64]

The meeting is certainly of interest. A clear outline for settling the Home Rule crisis along devolutionary lines was made to the government via Churchill. Chamberlain implied it enjoyed strong support inside the Tory leadership, although the plan would have to originate with Asquith, a belief that seriously under-estimated the influence of the Nationalists. Chamberlain also admitted that Bonar Law could be forced into a federal scheme, an observation that suggested Carson could move the Ulstermen to accept devolution (a far from easy or automatic modification), and perhaps did harm to Bonar Law's negotiating position in future meetings with Asquith. Yet in making such bold claims and challenging Bonar Law's tactical line over Home Rule, it is hard not to see Chamberlain asserting his power. A federal scheme was the means for him to enhance his authority in the party and contest for the leadership, a prize taken from him by Bonar Law in 1911. Yet the high expectations raised before the meeting actually amounted to very little. That same day, 27 November, Asquith delivered an aggressive and uncompromising speech at Leeds in defence of the Home Rule bill. 'Asquith's speech has blown conciliation sky high', Austen bemoaned to Oliver,[65] and to Churchill he felt Asquith had 'slammed the door in our faces'.[66] It seemed to Chamberlain a clear step backwards after his Ladybank speech, an overly bleak interpretation heightened by an awareness of just how politically exposed he was in meeting Churchill in the first place. Lansdowne reassured Chamberlain the initiative still had momentum. 'I am inclined to think that Asquith probably believed himself to be doing exactly what Winston apparently thinks the leaders of both parties ought to do, viz: "to make speeches full of party claptrap and No surrender with a few sentences at the end for wise and discerning people to see and ponder".'[67]

Chamberlain accordingly replied to Asquith in measured tones. On 1 December 1913, he criticised the prime minister's Leeds outburst while keeping open the idea that a federal solution was desirable.[68] From elsewhere Chamberlain was assured the federal initiative was still on course. Lord Grey informed him that Haldane 'told me that Asquith had not withdrawn ... from the Ladybank position'.[69] Grey now sought to encourage Haldane by reaffirming that Unionists 'are prepared to swallow the federal plan in order to avert civil war'.[70] Churchill was also eager to convince Chamberlain that 'the P.M. has not withdrawn in the slightest degree from the Ladybank position', and confirmed he had such assurances from Asquith himself.[71] He also invited Chamberlain to another meeting, on 8 December 1913, with John Morley, another known sympathiser, and F.E. Smith to be present.

Oliver, perhaps aware of Chamberlain's cooling interest, kept up the pressure on him, stressing the immense dangers of the present situation spinning out of control if no-one imposed a federal settlement upon it. On 2 December, for example, he warned of the mutinous state of the army, faced with the prospect of coercing the Ulstermen under a Home Rule parliament at some future date. This was particularly relevant since Bonar Law's most recent speech in Dublin on 28 November, had raised the issue of possible army disobedience, if ever they were ordered against Ulster.[72] Two days later he again warned Chamberlain of developments within the Unionist leadership, this time Milner's latest idea for de-railing the Home Rule bill by amending the Army Annual Act, a ploy he already knew a little of from other Tory sources.[73] He saw federalism not only as a constructive step forward but as a means to prevent the crisis worsening. Oliver also tried to establish contact between Carson and Chamberlain. Having sent Carson a copy of his pamphlet, he received a positive response on 3 December: 'I do not know that I genuinely differ – so long as we Ulstermen are treated in the same way as other citizens of the U.K.'[74] Oliver passed this to Chamberlain as proof that his current initiative was worth pursuing and that a little more boldness now could well be the spark to wider changes. 'He [Carson] is very cordial and amplifies your point ... about the difference it would make to Ulster's feelings – all the difference in the world – if Wales, Scotland etc were being treated as an equal party with Ireland.'[75]

Despite the hiccup caused by Asquith's Leeds speech, the federal initiative still appeared to be moving forward by early December. Haldane, Morley, Churchill, Lloyd George and Edward Grey were enthusiastic, and even Asquith reaffirmed his good intentions at Manchester on 5 December. On the Unionist side, Lansdowne, Chamberlain, Selborne and Bob Cecil were sympathetic to a constructive settlement. Carson, though firmly tied to the Ulster cause and with no public latitude to offer a federal scheme his support, privately saw it as a long-term and viable solution. Smith would have jumped for any compromise project, as long as he was involved in its gestation and it threw in the added advantage of a possible coalition government afterwards. Balfour, though no federalist, also hankered after co-operation with moderate Liberals. While Walter Long, according to one historian, 'was beginning to think there might be something attractive in federalism'.[76] Furthermore, a clear basis of agreement had been outlined at the Churchill–Chamberlain meeting of 27 November, and relayed to various leaders on both front-benches. Much of the press, apart from the *Morning Post*, backed such a move and with parliament still in recess there was time to contain hostile attacks from within each party. If a federal settlement was to be constructed then now was the moment. 'If they [the Government] are anxious for a settlement', Oliver told Chamberlain, 'there is enough material to make a settlement … Things must be set a going forthwith (ie) certainly a going before Christmas.'[77]

In light of these considerations, the dinner between Chamberlain, Churchill, Morley and Smith on 8 December carried high hopes; 'perhaps Monday night's dinner is the foundation of it', Garvin speculated.[78] The conversations began with Morley and Churchill reassuring Chamberlain that their initiative still had legs. They also admitted to sharing his alarm at Asquith's delay in making a move. And they gave assurances that the government would never coerce Ulster into the bill, whatever the implications of Asquith's words concerning government authority being upheld, used to reply to Bonar Law's threat of army disobedience. Moving on, there was some discussion over various constructive solutions, where differences between them quickly became apparent. Churchill, Smith and Chamberlain shared a sympathy for a wider federal reconstruction, whereas Morley occupied a position almost indistinguishable from Lansdowne's in supporting a devolutionary system. Yet whatever settlement was agreed between them, they believed that Dillon and Redmond 'might sulk a bit but would not oppose'.[79] As with Chamberlain's earlier meeting with Churchill, the dinner proved useful for building bridges and understanding each other's position, but little concrete agreement emerged. Churchill suggested another dinner three days later, to which he also invited Robinson.[80]

What was also clear from these meetings was a hesitancy on both sides to commit themselves. Agreement needed a kick-start, to which Earl Grey wondered whether the king could not at this critical moment be what

Oliver called 'the flea ... to jog things'.[81] Meanwhile, Oliver continued to regard Chamberlain as the key to the situation but one in need of constant encouragement. Urging him to make ever more definite public statements in support of federalism, Oliver received an odd and rather chilly response, 'I have said all I have to say either publicly or privately'.[82] So the next day he sent Chamberlain two letters from the Liberal J.A. Spender, editor of *The Westminster Gazette* and a close friend of Asquith.[83] 'I thought and think the federal line as opened up by Oliver, Austen Chamberlain, Lansdowne and Carson, quite hopeful. It seemed to offer a basis for discussion which saved us all from coming straight up to an aye or no on the Ulster Question – total exclusion or total inclusion, on which at this stage we should certainly break.'[84]

Despite Oliver's brave attempts, by the second week of December interest in the federal movement was dwindling. Chamberlain tried to keep the movement going, entering into correspondence with Morley after 9 December and urging greater haste in matters;[85] 'Asquith has met Law three times I believe. This isn't business. If our leaders proceed in that leisurely way events will take the reins out of their hands.'[86] He also suggested to Morley that Asquith might hold direct conversations with Carson. 'He (Carson) has proved himself most moderate and deeply sensible of his heavy responsibility ... Make no mistake about Carson's object. He wants peace – on terms of course, but on terms which I believe the Government could accept'.[87] He even sketched out a possible basis upon which Carson could agree, namely 'the principle that Ulster was to be treated like the other parts of the U.K.'.[88] (The implications of these and earlier passages are highly significant, for Chamberlain, a federalist, recognised in Carson someone who could further his cause, while Bonar Law represented an implacable extremist to be sidelined.) Morley, though sceptical of Carson's moderation, conveyed Chamberlain's message to Asquith who subsequently invited Carson for an interview.[89] Asquith and Carson met on 16 December 1913, and again on 2 January 1914, but made little if any progress. Carson, against what Chamberlain had been led to believe, argued the same line as Bonar Law had at his first and second meetings with Asquith, namely permanent exclusion for a specified part of Ulster. Asquith, on the other hand, pursued a solution based upon Home Rule within Home Rule, an outline of which he sent to Carson several days later, in the form of suggestions. The wider federal basis to a settlement was not even raised. Carson, after consulting Bonar Law, returned Asquith's suggestions without encouragement. 'Mr Bonar Law is also of the opinion that for the same reason he does not think any useful purpose would be served in calling his colleagues together to consider them.'[90] In the failure of the Carson–Asquith meeting, moves within the Unionist leadership to find a federal solution dried up.

Several fundamental problems rendered such an outcome likely from the start. Supporters established no clear definition of federalism. Some like Chamberlain, Milner, Oliver, Churchill and Selborne thought in terms of a federated United Kingdom, whereas others such as Lansdowne, Morley, Derby, perhaps Carson (though he never clearly elucidated his thinking) and possibly Asquith, all preferred a devolutionary solution. Similar divisions centered on the timing of any constructive scheme, with Churchill calling for patience, while Chamberlain and Oliver argued for no delay. Tactics also proved a block to agreement. Selborne thought a 'settlement of the Irish Question before the general election will be no benefit to the Conservative party';[91] Oliver and Chamberlain viewed an election as a barrier to a subsequent settlement by consent. These rather basic problems were never overcome, and prevented discussions moving much beyond the level of general principles. Lansdowne lamented that he had 'always myself felt that no one has yet worked out a scheme for the establishment of such local legislatures'. This was echoed from the government side; 'Haldane ... insists and not without reason that none of the Unionist leaders have yet produced anything intelligible in the shape of a federal plan'.[92]

More fundamental to the failure of the federal initiative was the attitude of the key leaders. Bonar Law remained fixed in his hostility, as Lansdowne understated to Chamberlain; 'I do not think B.L. likes "these devilments of local parliaments"'.[93] Carson's position was more complex. At various points he revealed a sympathy for a federal settlement that, in the future, might well prove critical in agreeing such a structure. But in the short term, despite all the hopes invested in him by Chamberlain, his commitment to the Ulstermen and loyalty to Bonar Law restrained him. He therefore backed exclusion during his meetings with the prime minister. Asquith's attitude was equally ambiguous. He had shown an interest in the idea in his Ladybank and Manchester speeches, and had authorised Churchill's overtures to Chamberlain. Yet he never fully committed himself while his Leeds speech had thrown doubt on the whole process. By the time of his third and final meeting with Bonar Law on 9 December, Asquith had clearly retreated from any desire to reach a settlement, much to Bonar Law's relief but the alarm of others. 'My reading of the situation', Chamberlain wrote on the 10th, 'is that some members of the Govt are fully alive to the danger of delay and are doing their best to see that no time is wasted, but that the P.M. himself has been, and still is, inclined to take the "wait and see" line.'[94] Oliver was less reserved; 'the aged one [Asquith], if not yet hibernating will do so by nature'. His 'habit is that of the vampire, he sucks the blood out of his opponents by … blandishments, and then curls up like a dormouse and goes to sleep'.[95]

By this stage many Unionists (and a few of his own colleagues) believed Asquith was dragging his feet. Lansdowne wondered whether the prime minister was not stringing them along and in terms of any future entanglements could 'see nothing ahead but rocks-reefs upon reefs of them'.[96] On 16 December he sent Bonar Law a deeply pessimistic memorandum on the talks,[97] registering his altered opinion of Asquith's intentions. Little light could now be detected in Asquith's approach, describing the prime minister's tactics as 'procrastination on our party … Whenever the P.M. has spoken with any attempt at precision his suggestions are of a kind that fill me with alarm … One of the few things which Mr Asquith has said distinctly is that he means to press forward with the Home Rule bill under the Parliament Act.'[98] Asquith should now be challenged on what changes he would contemplate and if these proved unsatisfactory, as was likely, then 'negotiations should not be continued'.[99] It may well have been, as suggested by one eminent historian, that Asquith's tactics at this point were designed 'to keep the opposition guessing as to his ultimate policy, while perhaps also demonstrating to the Nationalist leadership that he was prepared to pursue their strategic objective in so far as it was possible'.[100] Whether left guessing or not, Asquith's tactics certainly produced a hardening of opinion amongst Unionists against any further contact. 'Asquith is simply playing with us', wrote Selborne on the 21st,[101] while Balfour found that 'it is tolerably clear now … that the Govt think they will get into the least trouble by letting things slide.'[102] Chamberlain gave the clearest indication of this reaction, 'I am doing no politics at present … I suspect Asquith has missed his mark and lost all chance of a settlement by consent.'[103] By the middle of December, it was clear the federal initiative had dried up.

UNEASE ON THE RIGHT

The strongest opposition to the attempt by the Unionist leadership to reach a compromise settlement with the government came from the Tory right. Their suspicions of a sell-out by their own leaders had surfaced during the Agar-Robartes amendment back in June 1912 and again in January 1913, with Carson's exclusion amendment. Public overtures from Loreburn and Churchill, and rumours of secret meetings with Asquith, signalled another die-hard resurgence by the autumn. Bonar Law realised that even to meet with Asquith was sufficient to provoke a storm of protest. During his first interview with the prime minister he admitted that a 'strong survival ... of the Diehard movement' existed within the party,[104] and to Croal he spoke of a 'violent echo in England'.[105]

One of those most alarmed on the right was Lord Milner, who on 24 October sent his concerns to Bonar Law. He was worried that recent mutterings of a deal with the government merely diverted attention from their strong attack upon the issue of Ulster. 'Ulster holds the field and if only Unionists can succeed in keeping public attention concentrated on that subject as our supreme injury, they must win the game'.[106] Moreover, he believed government overtures to search for a settlement were bogus; 'all these vague expressions of sympathy are merely playing with the question'.[107] It was far better, he recommended, for the party to avoid all thought of a compromise and government traps and re-double their efforts behind Ulster. 'That is the weak spot in the enemy's line, where they are already beginning to run, and against that point all the attacking forces should be directed'.[108] Milner's comments suggest he was either unaware of the support for exclusion coming from the Ulstermen or, more likely, he saw it as a defensive reaction to weakening support from the Conservative party: a duck for cover when your ally got cold feet. To close friends Milner was less guarded. 'We are, of course, extinguished as a political force', he lamented to Colonel Denison, 'We were perhaps bound to be extinguished any way. The choice was between a painless, gradual but inglorious extinction and a sharp fierce struggle, in which there was just a chance of victory and in any case an honourable death.'[109] That chance of victory lay with Ulster.

> It seems to me very probable that the Ulstermen, if they are real Diehards and not sham ones, like our noble selves, will bring about an impasse. And a deadlock is just now, in my opinion, the one thing that can save us. The party game is for the moment played out – its old rules are all broken to pieces and if we are to have constitutional Govt at all, we simply must put our heads together and agree to some rules that everybody will respect. Of course if Ulster collapses, this log-rolling business may go on for a while longer. But I don't think Ulster will collapse.[110]

The message was clear, Ulster was the key to the events, the means to repair the Constitution and, more implicitly, to save the existing social order. Yet there is also an element here of the constructive coalitionist that Milner would become after 1916, Ulster to drive politics to a halt and from the stalemate rebuild the political system: behind the life and death struggle, the ghost of 1910 still swooned. Everything hinged on the Ulster campaign succeeding, as he told Oliver on the 23rd, 'there is only one word of salvation for Unionists just now and it is to shout "Ulster, Ulster" all the time'.[111] Ensuring the Ulster campaign succeeded was the crux of the matter, and on this Milner was evidently thinking beyond his polite entreaties to Bonar Law.

> If the Govt do ultimately go through with their scheme un-modified, and war results, I for one, shall not feel satisfied to wave my arms importantly in the air and cry 'how dreadful', and I fancy there are a great many people on this side of the water in like case. And I think the government ought to be made to realise the determination of Ulster. Moreover, if anything effective is to be done six months hence it will have to be thought-out beforehand. You may hope the worst will not happen but if it does happen it ought not to find us unprepared.[112]

With these thoughts in mind, from late October Milner began to sound opinion amongst Unionists and draw around him like-thinking men. This included many of the up-and-coming Tories, such as Amery, Winterton and Comyn Platt, angered by their leaders' rumoured willingness to compromise. It also included men with specific skills, useful to any future Ulster campaign. One such man was Lord Roberts, who held enormous influence within the British army, and who would be able, so Milner imagined, to prevent the army ever moving against Ulster. Milner explored with Roberts the consequences of a military crackdown in Ulster, come the imposition of Home Rule. 'If they tried to do so, I really don't know what we over here, who think the Ulstermen are perfectly right, would do. One thing is evident to me and that is that we could not allow them to be coerced without doing something to help them more than talking.'[113] Roberts agreed; 'you are quite right, we could not allow the Ulstermen to be coerced without doing something to help them …'.[114] Keen to move matters on, Milner invited him to lunch and 'by that time I hope I may have consulted some other *serious* people and found out what they are prepared to do, if the Government pushes things to extremes'.[115]

In addition to Milner, others on the right showed nerves at the unfolding circumstances of October–November 1913. Willoughby de Broke was sufficiently alarmed to press on with his die-hard campaign. Since the creation of the BLSUU back in March, over 7,000 volunteers from all over the UK had joined his movement.[116] However, it still lacked influence within the Unionist leadership, as was apparent by their favourable reception to Asquith's Ladybank speech. Against this 'weakening' and to bolster BLSUU support at the top of the party, Willoughby de Broke invited Lord Salisbury to 'join our committee? A little help from men like you would be invaluable'.[117] Salisbury's help would certainly have been significant in stiffening the leadership against exclusion. But perhaps of more value, Salisbury's support would aid de Broke in rallying opinion within the Lords against a compromise deal, knowing such a plan would have to pass through their house. De Broke forecast a replay of events of 1911 but this time he would not be thwarted. And in the massed ranks of the Southern Unionist peers he had the support for his future rebellion.

Southern Unionists had railed against the idea of Ulster's exclusion as long ago as 1912. Rumours of such a plan again roused them into action. Lord Arran protested that 'this idea of compromise on the Home Rule bill on the basis of exclusion of Ulster ... cannot be accepted by Covenanters except by breaking their oath'.[118] He sent his views to Carson, Craig and Londonderry, to which 'Carson has not replied and I do not expect him to do so either'.[119] Along similar lines, Lord Midleton, unnerved at recent murmurings of a compromise, pressed Bonar Law to establish a body made up of Unionists from the three Southern Irish Provinces, to coordinate tactics with Carson.[120] As with Lord Arran, Midleton clearly mistrusted Carson and his evident willingness to accept Ulster's exclusion from the bill. The gulf between Ulster and Irish Unionists had widened considerably, revealing a growing Southern Unionist unhappiness with their leader. Yet even amongst more mainstream English Peers, Southern Unionist sympathies were strong. Salisbury warned against the 'abandonment of our friends in the West and South' of Ireland, after Asquith's Ladybank speech and Bonar Law's speech at Newcastle.[121] 'I do not think we must ever use language implying that we believe that any solution on these lines [exclusion] can in fact be found and I am inclined to think that we should not promise even if it can be found, to abandon our Parliamentary opposition to the bill.'[122]

Following Bonar Law's second meeting with Asquith on 7 November, the Tory right became more vocal in its opposition. This emerged from a growing recognition that Asquith was simply maneouvering for position with talk of a compromise deal, wasting time rather than attempting to solve the crisis, while extracting from him recognition of the principle of Home Rule. Opposition was also encouraged by victories in the by-elections at Linlithgow and Reading on 7 and 8 November, interpreted by Unionists as a popular rejection of Liberal Home Rule.[123] Leslie Wilson saw them as proof 'that the country will not have this Home Rule bill',[124] and Long thought the results 'will show them [the Tory leaders] the feeling against any agreement. The general view seems to be "give them no quarter and drive them out".'[125]

As a result of these circumstances Tories rallied against the very idea of a compromise. Balfour perceived the added pressure this placed on Bonar Law; 'if the bye-elections continue to bring unpleasant results to the Government it will of course make it yet more difficult for the Unionist leaders to assent to the Ulster compromise'.[126] And as if to prove Balfour's point, Hugh Cecil now felt sufficiently emboldened to offer Bonar Law his 'very earnest hope that you will not and that Carson will not be tempted into making any positive proposal for a settlement. I am sorry Carson went as far as he did.'[127] Much of the die-hard sentiment sprang from a feeling that if they compromised now they were giving up a strong hand that, despite some nerves, was actually moving the government to an election. 'Most of the men I speak to on our side', Sandars noted, 'think there will be no compromise but a great many expect a January election.'[128] Given these sentiments, for Tory leaders to go ahead and compromise seemed not only foolish but dangerous. 'Long, who reflects the "grip" of the Carlton, tells me that a lot of our people are ready to become diehards and to send us, if we entertain any proposals for a settlement based on the exclusion of Ulster.'[129] Nor would the political fall-out from an arrangement be limited to Westminster, for 'any compromise made at the expense of the Union ... will completely take the heart out of the Unionist party in the constituencies'.[130] Bonar Law recognised the problems ahead, confiding to Balfour that in response to a compromise 'there might easily be an active movement against it'.[131] His words had a prophetic ring for that same day, *The Morning Post* published a 'Call for Service', on behalf of the BLSUU. 'We call on our able-bodied fellow countrymen who think that the Ulstermen are arming in a righteous cause to enroll themselves.'[132] It continued, 'those who rely on the belief that the crisis can be relieved by a process of bargaining ... are building on a very slender chance and indeed are helping the fatal policy of drift'.[133]

These were warnings to Bonar Law that the party would not accept an agreement with Asquith. But they also suggest that Bonar Law was unable to constrain the political conflict within the boundaries of established parliamentary behaviour. Of course with much of what was said on the right, there was an element of bluff in their fiery rhetoric: 'some of us are convinced that *the best way to prevent a civil war* is to back Ulster in deed as in word'[134] (my italics). Some commentators were even rather dismissive of them; 'to get their horses ready and practise with firearms ... I rather suspect that nothing serious is really being done at all'.[135] Intimidation rather than insurrection, the very tactic Bonar Law was using against the government, was their stock-in-trade. And if this is the case then, as with Bonar Law, the die-hards were still playing the parliamentary game and looking to alter things at the centre. As de Broke let slip to Salisbury, 'the enrolling of men in Ulster *has brought the Radicals to their senses*'.[136]

Whatever lay behind the tough rhetoric, the growing anger on the right drew many of the more uncommitted out against a settlement. Of most significance in this respect was Walter Long. Previously undecided at moves towards a compromise upon exclusion, Long had been more concerned with Lloyd George's Land Campaign.[137] However, after 7 November his interest altered. 'I have seen a great many of our most reliable men and their unanimous opinion is that if Asquith makes any overtures and we accept them the result would be absolutely fatal to our party.'[138] Two days later he reiterated his concern, 'if we come to any arrangement with the Government we shall run grave risks of splitting even smashing our party'.[139] Long had been shocked by Bonar Law's willingness to discuss exclusion while, apparently, ignoring the signs of Nationalist hostility to it. These were extremely poor tactics, for 'if Asquith offers exclusion of Ulster and we accept, of course Redmond will turn him out and the consequences will be that both English parties will be irretrievably dammed as intriguers'.[140] It was far better to let the compromise initiative founder on the back of Nationalist obduracy. The irony was that Bonar Law's understanding of the situation was remarkably similar to Long's, though he was far less sensitive to their tactical consequences and to questions of public perception than Bonar Law. Unable to perceive the subtlety of Bonar Law's game, Long continued to warn him away from a compromise, culminating in a strongly worded memorandum.[141] The memorandum was a thinly veiled threat of rebellion, if

Bonar Law agreed to an accommodation with the government. '*In all probability* any attempted compromise will be followed by a schism, even greater and more deep seated than that which occurred at the time of the passing of the Parliament Act.'[142] It was a direct warning against exclusion;'how then can we possibly agree to force Home Rule upon the other three provinces, more especially as we believe that this bill is the very worst and most unworkable form of devolution ... The great object we all have now is to get the Government out, is it not.'[143] The last sentence reveals the extent to which Long had gravitated to a more die-hard position: Home Rule was not just a danger to Ireland but a means of removing the government itself.

This stance reflected pressure on Long from prominent Southern Unionists and leading right-wing Tories. But in so shifting Long, the possibility of co-operation with Lansdowne now opened up in an alignment of traditional Unionists against clever tinkering with the Union. 'I am alarmed at the prospect of some compromise being arrived at. The language used by Lord Lansdowne at Brighton exactly expresses my feeling in regard to the exclusion of Ulster. The proposal has no attractions for me; it is a clumsy expedient at best'.[144] Cooperation between the two was firmly based. Like Lansdowne, Long was a devolutionist rather than a federalist and preferred their present commitment to an election rather than finding a settlement. Also, by mid-November, Lansdowne was himself beginning to migrate rightwards, back towards the more hard-line position he had occupied in September. Along with the support of Chamberlain, the positioning of Long behind Lansdowne represented a formidable block within the Unionist leadership against the idea of exclusion.

And yet, any likelihood of the party accepting exclusion at the time of Bonar Law's first meeting with Asquith, had, by their final meeting on 9 December, all but disappeared. The prime minister did not move beyond the terms he had hinted at during their first discussion, of a form of temporary exclusion for Ulster, ignoring completely the more optimistic tone of his Ladybank address. The talks shattered the impression of Asquith as a force for compromise. Curzon despaired that it was 'going back from what Asquith had previously led you to think'.[145] Similarly, Lansdowne felt 'he must have known when he proposed to you that Ulster should come in automatically after a certain number of years, that his proposal would not be looked at'.[146] A week after the meeting Lansdowne sent a memorandum of the situation to Bonar Law. In it he accused

Asquith of being 'desultory and tentative' (compare this to his reception of the Ladybank speech),[147] and doubted whether a meeting would have occurred at all 'had it not been for the feeling of consternation with which the Prime Minister's Leeds speech had … been received'.[148] By early December much of the Unionist leadership including one-time optimists such as Lansdowne, Curzon, Selborne and Balfour now saw Asquith's approaches not designed to reach a solution but simply to delay. 'All the evidence goes to show that the latter means to sit tight and do nothing for some time to come,'[149] or as Selborne said, he 'is simply playing with us'.[150] The suspicions of the right had finally infused most of the Unionist leadership.

Such an assessment of Asquith raised serious questions, with significant tactical consequences. In particular, why had the prime minister engaged in talks in the first place? Why had he authorised the Churchill initiative? And with the return of the political stalemate, how was he going to extricate his government from the crisis looming on the horizon? What, in other words, was he up to? Clues to this emerged during Chamberlain's dinner with Churchill and Morley. 'There is a real danger', Chamberlain told Lansdowne the next day, 'of the Government trying to solve the difficulty by the mere excision of Ulster and attempting to cast on the House of Lords the onus of rejecting this by not accepting the Second Reading of the bill. This idea smiles on Winston more than it does on Morley.'[151] A similar assessment came from Bonar Law's memorandum on his third meeting. He suspected that Asquith might offer exclusion, 'which probably would not satisfy Ulster … (but) which people in England will consider reasonable … (and thus) if they were rejected there would be less sympathy in England with Ulster resistance'.[152] Selborne came to a similar conclusion:

> it looks as if he means to allow his communications with you to drag on indefinitely … Then when the session is in full swing he will make suggestions for alterations in the Government of Ireland Bill, for the acceptance of the Lords but which will be quite unacceptable to our Ulster friends and to us. He will then try and turn the National disappointment that there has been no settlement by consent against us.[153]

In effect, Asquith would present the Unionists with a *fait accompli*, daring them to reject his 'unacceptable' compromise offer in the Lords and suffer the onerous responsibility if they did so. And from such a sequence of events, if the Government then had a snap dissolution on the acceptance of their offer, they would be given 'a greater chance of winning the election'.[154]

Two things made this a plausible scenario. First was the knowledge that under the terms of the Parliament Act, any amendment to a Bill not made during the first Parliamentary circuit could only be accepted by agreement with the House of Lords. This placed the Unionist leadership, which dominated the Upper House, in a very delicate position. On the one hand, if they were to reject Asquith's compromise proposal to Home Rule, as seemed likely given the 'unacceptable' terms suggested by Asquith in his meetings with Bonar Law, then they would suffer the public odium of having rejected a settlement to the Home Rule crisis. If, on the other hand, they accepted the compromise proposal, then Lansdowne faced the prospect of a mutiny against his leadership in the Lords, far greater than in 1911 and, in all probability, splitting the Unionist party in the process:

> I have *grave misgivings* as to the attitude of the House of Lords. We should be offered a measure which is fundamentally wrong in principle and which is tolerated by Mr Asquith's Irish supporters only because it is from our point of view fundamentally wrong ... If ... it is found impossible to obtain the acquiescence of Irish Unionists outside Ulster, *our difficulties will be immensely increased*.[155]

The situation was all the more problematic given what Selborne observed as the government's 'running the press very carefully over the matter'.[156] Robert Cecil noticed a similar manipulation of public opinion; 'the Ministers who have always managed the press very skillfully are spreading abroad the impression that all is peace – a compromise in the air'.[157] To reject a compromise deal against a backdrop of mounting public expectation of a political settlement, would seriously endanger public support for the Unionist position.

Second was an awareness of Asquith's tactics during the 1910 conference, which had sought, unsuccessfully, to find a solution to the question of the veto powers of the Lords. During these negotiations, Asquith had prepared the ground well for the eventual passage of his parliament bill. First by dragging out the talks in order to delay the inevitable general election. This was a development that improved Asquith's standing with the electorate, by fostering the impression of him as conciliatory. He also 'exited' from the talks in such a way that the Tories were labelled unreasonable and even seen as responsible for the collapse of conference, for refusing to contemplate Irish reform. Thus when the election came in

December 1910, Asquith had manoeuvred the Liberals into a far better standing with the public and so reaped the electoral benefits with a third election victory. For Unionists, circumstances by December 1913 looked suspiciously like 'an attempt to repeat the tactics of the Constitutional Conference'.[158] Lansdowne even warned Bonar Law to keep a detailed record of his conversations with the prime minister, for 'you will remember the unscrupulous manner in which our opponents took advantage of the absence of records in the case of the Conference of 1910'.[159] The vulnerability of the Lords and the experience of 1910 convinced many Unionist leaders that Asquith was again trying to wrongfoot them.

To counter this move, Lansdowne pressed Bonar Law to demand a statement of intent from Asquith and, if none was forthcoming, to break off talks. 'Invite (Asquith), if he still desires a settlement by consent, to state definitely in writing what changes in the bill he has in contemplation. If as I anticipate the changes which he would be in a position to offer prove to be ... wholly inadmissible, we shall have to decide whether negotiations should not be discontinued.'[160] Long also saw little point in meeting Asquith again, 'unless there was evidence to show that they could be continued with some prospect of success'.[161] Asking Asquith to declare his intentions was a means to bring talks to a speedy end but without it reflecting badly upon the Tories: after all, requesting details of his compromise plan could not be represented by Asquith as unreasonable. In addition, ending talks would reduce the growing pressure from the right. 'W. Long is here and tells me that he learns from many sources that any settlement based on the acceptance of H.R. with special treatment for Ulster, would be bitterly resented by our supporters.'[162] Bob Cecil also warned Bonar Law that 'some of your colleagues on the front benches are getting a little anxious to know what exactly is going on'.[163] While his brother Hugh rounded on Bonar Law, it is 'for Home Rulers to make Home Rule workable not for us',[164] and that '[Asquith] should not be allowed to forget that on the Govt of the day the responsibility rests of governing the country and we must clear ourselves, before the country, of all share in a policy of drift'.[165] In addition, inviting Asquith to offer detailed proposals, and thus take the initiative for a settlement, threw upon on him the impossible burden of agreeing a compromise scheme with his Nationalist partners. This, in turn, ensured that any scheme he then advanced would be so limited in scope that the Unionists might easily reject it on the grounds of being unreasonable without angering, so they imagined, public opinion.

The pressure on Bonar Law to end the secret talks was not helped by discussions between Asquith and Carson. Asquith on 10 December 1913 suggested he meet Carson, a switch of negotiators which Bonar Law found 'a little strange', but given his close contact with Carson, one he was not seriously alarmed by,[166] although Lansdowne, Long and the other leaders saw it as further delay by the prime minister. Carson and Asquith met on 16 December, at which Carson offered terms little different to those suggested by Bonar Law at his second meeting, namely that 'specified' Ulster counties be permanently excluded until they decide otherwise. Asquith made no attempt to negotiate, but instead promised to send Carson his own ideas ('a few rough suggestions'), which arrived on the 23rd.[167] As with Bonar Law's third meeting, Asquith did not advance anything more serious than a form of Home Rule within Home Rule, a plan Bonar Law and Carson had already rejected. Indeed the seeming pointlessness of this meeting suggests that Asquith's real intention was, according to P. Jalland, disinformation, a smokescreen for a long-term strategy which by this stage much of the Unionist leadership had guessed.[168] After consulting with Bonar Law, Carson refused Asquith's terms.[169] This refusal Asquith used, at a second meeting on 2 January 1914, to suggest responsibility for the present situation lay with the Unionists and outlined the public hostility that would fall upon them as a result. Asquith also invited Carson to 'present in black and white' his own proposals, but Carson refused, mistrusting how he might use them. Instead, he followed the line that Bonar Law had taken in requesting the principle of exclusion be accepted before any proposal came from him, effectively placing on Asquith the onus of agreeing a compromise formula with the Nationalists before they made any further movement.

And there the talks ended, inconclusive and having more to do with manoeuvring by both sides, with an eye on a future appeal to the people, than with any serious attempt to find a settlement by consent. Bonar Law now formally brought them to an end, asking Asquith if he could announce their termination during his speech at Bristol on 15 January, to which Asquith agreed.

BONAR LAW AND PARTY POLITICS, OCTOBER 1913 TO JANUARY 1914

Bonar Law's meeting with Asquith on 15 October had achieved several important things: it convinced the prime minister of his reasonableness and receptiveness to finding a compromise. He also steered their discussions away from a devolutionary or federal experiment, and towards the idea of excluding all or part of Ulster. Moreover, Bonar Law had discovered what he believed to be the furthest most point Asquith would (or could) go in a compromise; 'it is evident to me that he had in his mind only the four counties remain[ing] in the Union and as regards the two counties a plebiscite should be taken'.[170] Bonar Law realised that if this were offered to him, it would appear 'so reasonable that we would be in a very bad position if we had to refuse it'.[171] But he regarded such a position as unlikely because 'Redmond *cannot* agree to the solution of excluding Ulster', and certainly not on anything but a short, temporary basis, a qualification that undermined the original reasonableness of the compromise offer.[172] It was immaterial whether Asquith offered nine-, six- or even four-county exclusion, since the Nationalists apparently rejected the very 'principle' of it. This judgement was reinforced by Redmond, who in Limerick on 12 October declared, 'Mr Churchill in his speech in Scotland alluded to a possible exclusion of a part of Ulster … Now I have to say here that the suggestion is a totally impractical and unworkable one.'[173]

Bonar Law's close advisors endorsed his belief that Redmond would not accept exclusion. 'Mr Short tells me', Balfour wrote, 'that the Westminster declares, in emphatic terms, against the exclusion of any fraction of Ireland, from the Home Rule bill. If Redmond says this as representing the Nationalists and the Westminster says it as representing the ordinary moderate Liberal, I presume the last chance of the Govt making a proposal *even about the four counties* has vanished.'[174] For Strachey also, '[exclusion] will … I am convinced, act as a measure which will wreck both the bill and the Govt if they can be got to adopt it … Do nail the Government to exclusion and so smash them.'[175] From a different angle, Edmund Talbort, the Unionist chief whip, wondered whether the existing bill could absorb an exclusionary amendment without changing it entirely, and so warranting a completely new bill.[176] What all shared, including Bonar Law, was the notion that exclusion was a tactical loophole, support for which displayed Bonar Law's moderation but which as a basis for a settlement was unworkable.

Despite this optimism, Bonar Law's approach still faced many dangers and complications. One was the sudden rise of the Land Question, following Lloyd George's speech at Swindon on 21 October. The prospect of a Land Campaign had troubled both Lansdowne and Long, who saw it distracting public attention from the subject of the Irish Question and thus undercutting the Tories 'trump' electoral card. Where they were less prescient was the degree to which it threw the Tory party into immediate disarray. 'I am afraid', Pretyman observed, 'there are great differences in the party about Land policy.'[177] Differences over land were inevitable, with the land-owning section still so strongly represented.[178] Speaking for this section, Long advocated safe, conservative and gradual reform, with no attempt to out-radicalise Lloyd George. Others in the party, such as Joynson-Hicks, Steel-Maitland, Maurice Woods, Henry Bentick and a young Stanley Baldwin looked to meet Lloyd George's challenge with a bold, progressive and attractive policy. And in not a few of the reformers' minds was a desire to be rid of the futile struggle over Ireland: land reform, for them, was the more important issue and the ground upon which the next election would be won or lost.

A second problem for Bonar Law – and a the result of his meeting with Asquith – was an altered perception of the prime minister as a far stronger politician than he had once thought, willing to meet Bonar Law's intimidation with a cold, steely resolution.

> If [Asquith] is compelled to have an election before the bill becomes law and if he were beaten in that election, then his position will be the most humiliating it is possible to conceive. He and his party have staked everything on the Parliament Act and in that case their whole action in the last three years would have been simply futile. He must realise this, and therefore *nothing but compulsion of the most extreme kind* would make him to submit to an election before his bills are carried; and there is a great danger that rather than face that risk he will go straight on and land the country in something like disaster.[179] (my italics)

This was a major concern to Bonar Law, who had been working from the assumption that Asquith was a timid leader who would capitulate at the first whiff of civil war (a view shared by Carson and the Ulstermen). It now seemed that Asquith might be playing the same high-risk game as himself,[180] taking the crisis as far as it could go to create divisions amongst Unionists[181] or even to push them into submission. Bonar Law would need to go much further in his threats and browbeating, as he himself admitted to Croal, a prospect likely to intensify party anxieties and splits. The conflict over Home Rule was fast becoming a game of 'chicken' – a battle of nerves to see whose political support and position caved in first.

But perhaps the greatest danger to manifest itself more clearly in the days after his first meeting with Asquith stemmed from Bonar Law's tactical line. Underpinning his whole approach was a set of assumptions that were at risk of being proven unfounded or wrong. Perhaps Asquith would square the Nationalists? Perhaps Carson and the Ulster Unionists would agree to temporary exclusion for just four Ulster counties? Perhaps Belfast would not remain calm and in the process provide the government with excellent grounds for destroying the resistance of the Ulstermen by imposing martial law? And perhaps Asquith, in the end, would prefer civil war in Ulster to submission? Though confident in the quality of his own power of political foresight, Bonar Law was never wholly sure, throughout the autumn of 1913, that one or more of these scenarios would not materialise. Furthermore, Bonar Law's tactics created problems in his party. His policy, since September, had been one of showing reasonableness for public opinion, in anticipation of the irresistible logic of the government's irresolvable predicament coming crashing down upon it. It was a waiting game, requiring patience and audacity rather than bold moves and initiatives. It also meant Bonar Law had to go through the motions of appearing to support a compromise move and responding positively to Asquith's overtures, even though he saw (and hoped for) no chance of success. Could Bonar Law execute these manoeurvings and yet still maintain his hold over the party, with many alarmed by his apparent support for exclusion? Appearing moderate had already led many on the right to assume Bonar Law was beginning to get cold feet, if not preparing for a sell-out.[182]

These misgivings amongst Unionists were exacerbated by Asquith's speech at Ladybank on 26 October 1913. The speech certainly contained much partisan rhetoric, what Stamfordham called 'high pitch music'.[183] Asquith talked of 'a complete Constitutional case for proceeding … in regard to the Irish Government bill' and scotched any idea of a formal conference between leaders.[184] However, towards the end he threw out an offer; 'if there is a genuine disposition in all quarters, by an interchange of views and suggestions, free, frank, and without prejudice … I invite that interchange and both I and my colleagues are perfectly ready to take part in it'.[185] This apparent offer to negotiate drew a variety of responses from Unionist leaders. Salisbury and others on the right were deeply suspicious, dismissing the need for any such 'interchange' and attacking the idea of a compromise on exclusion.[186] From higher quarters came more moderate advice, 'The King … feels certain that you will continue to try and cultivate the ground which has already been broken.'[187] Lansdowne and Chamberlain also read it as conciliatory, and were encouraged to believe Asquith might be converted to a devolutionary measure.[188] Along with Selborne and Bob Cecil, they urged Bonar Law in his reply at Newcastle to move away from his extreme tactics and concentration upon the Ulster problem, by emphasising the all-Irish, rather than the solely Ulster, nature of their opposition to the bill. They hoped this would give Asquith a clear signal that only a devolutionary plan could remove their objections.[189] Along different lines Steel-Maitland and Oliver saw an opportunity to wrongfoot Asquith by 'making an assumption on the statement', namely that he refused the idea of exclusion in speech and then wait for him to challenge this.[190] If he did not reject this interpretation, Asquith would undermine his own public standing while simultaneously reinforcing Bonar Law's moderation. But if he did reject it, then he ran the risk of aggravating the Nationalists.

Bonar Law's speech at Newcastle on 29 October, his first since meeting Asquith, was delivered against a backdrop of these competing party positions. In tone it was typically venomous ('[Asquith] can always be trusted to speak like a statesman; but to act like a statesman – well, that is different').[191] He threw scorn and ridicule on recent Liberal references to the land question. 'What is the meaning of their wonderful Land campaign? What is the meaning of springing it on the country now, just when the Home Rule question is becoming critical?',[192] warning colleagues not to chase Lloyd George's 'hares' at this moment. More dispiriting for Lansdowne and Chamberlain, Bonar Law stuck firmly to the Ulster problem and repeated that if a solution was to arise then exclusion, not devolution, was his desired path. 'I happened to read a few weeks ago … the first duty of the Unionist party was to express its disapproval of "Carsonism" in Ulster. This meeting at which Sir Edward Carson and I speak from the same platform, is the best answer I can give to that suggestion.'[193] This is not to say that he simply rejected Asquith's tentative offer. Bonar Law was most careful not to repulse it outright but instead threw the initiative for settling the issue decisively back onto the government. 'If he does mean to extend to us an invitation … then we shall not decline to respond to it and we shall carefully consider any proposals he may make to us and consider them with a real desire to find a solution, if a solution be possible.'[194] By such means, his reasonableness was demonstrated without making a conditional promise. And in placing the burden of locating a solution back onto Asquith, Bonar Law hoped to aggravate tensions between the government and its Nationalist allies over the basis of a settlement. Yet, most fundamentally, Bonar Law reaffirmed the stance he had taken up since 1912, that an election was the best way to prevent civil war and if none was forthcoming then 'the pledge which I made at Blenheim still holds good … If the Government try to drive the people of Ulster out of the Union … before they obtain the sanction of the electors … the whole Unionist party will support her in her resistance.'[195] This reveals the Tory leader as a very tough-minded politician indeed, dramatically raising the stakes on the issue and supremely confident that he had Asquith in a position from which there was no escape. If the prime minister was looking for a softer approach and a more conciliatory tone, in deference to his Ladybank speech, then he was sorely disappointed by Bonar Law's oration, which could explain his bad-tempered reply at Leeds a month later.

The Newcastle speech also reveals that, despite the intense federalist and devolutionary pressure he was under from colleagues, Bonar Law was quite willing to go against the advice of a majority of the Unionist leaders. Lansdowne, in particular, was deeply irritated by Bonar Law's concentration on Ulster, fearing it would ensnare them in a conference on exclusion and lamenting to Chamberlain that 'we shall make nothing of this plan [devolution] so long as the Ulster red-herring is being trailed backwards and forwards across the track'.[196] Bonar Law's resistance to devolutionary pressure was designed to convince Asquith that the *only* way out of this crisis was by excluding Ulster, something Bonar Law was by this stage convinced would never happen. It was also the product of a better 'feel' for the mood on the Tory backbenches and a recognition of the growing threat from the right of the party. George Younger spoke for many in the party when he wrote, 'your speech last night has given the greatest possible satisfaction … it is most certainly up to them and not to us to formulate proposals for a settlement'.[197] And Salisbury, rarely supportive of anything Bonar Law did, admitted he 'admired' it,[198] a line shared by Long. Newcastle went far in restoring the shaken nerves of the right, though some remained unconvinced, and perhaps always would. Lord Ashtown was angry that the speech said nothing for the Southern Irish Unionists and reminded Bonar Law, 'there is a very bitter feeling amongst the Unionists here'.[199] This may have been a slip, although a central intention of the speech had been to reassure Carson and the Ulstermen of his support, at a moment when certain Unionist leaders were pressing for a settlement along lines that, for the Ulstermen, ran counter to their interests.

Somewhat ironically, given the vehemence of his speech, the day after

Newcastle Asquith invited Bonar Law for another conversation.[200] Again he had little option but to go along with the request, despite misgivings about the purpose, finally meeting the prime minister on 6 November. Once talks were under way, Bonar Law showed no such apprehension. Indeed at first glance he seems to have been unusually frank, indicating to Asquith that Carson would *probably* accept a six-county exclusion scheme, with a plebiscite at the end of ten years.[201] He also implied that Home Rule for the rest of Ireland would be acceptable, as long as the Post Office and Customs duties were omitted and a Land Conference convened, along the lines of the 1902 experiment, all of which Asquith agreed. However, these seemingly bold statements and generous promises must be placed in the context of Bonar Law's overall tactical position. He already realised that the exclusion of four Ulster counties, with plebiscites in a further two, was Asquith's maximum. Thus his proposal for the exclusion of six counties suggests he was out-bidding a known position, pitching his terms just beyond what he believed Asquith would accept. In any case, his offer never moved away from permanent exclusion, an arrangement he described as 'only to be terminable by a plebiscite by the people of Ulster in favour of joining the Irish Parliament'.[202] And permanent exclusion of any part of Ulster was, he understood, something the Nationalists would never agree to.

Far from representing a mistake, as Lansdowne described it, Bonar Law's candidness was deliberately intended to advertise his apparent moderation. Appearing reasonable was a vital consideration for Bonar Law. No leeway could be given to Asquith to exhibit the Tories as intransigent. Strachey pointed out the danger of this; 'what Asquith would probably like best of all would be to be able to say that he had made the most frank and free offer to exclude Protestant Ulster but that the Ulster people and English Unionists would not accept it and that therefore he had no option but to go on with the bill, the whole bill and nothing but the bill. I am afraid that if he could get apparently good ground for saying this a good many "wobblers" would go with him.'[203] Immoderation, then, threatened party divisions. But it also, offered Asquith two possible methods for outmanoeurving Bonar Law. One was to seek a separate agreement with the more malleable Ulstermen, who, through Carson, had already expressed their acceptance of exclusion; a move that at a stroke would undercut Bonar Law's justification for further resistance. Second, and as Bonar Law had earlier speculated, Tory rejection of attempts to find a compromise would give Asquith the opportunity for a snap election on the compromise proposals themselves rather than the issue of Home Rule, with every possibility of success. Only, then, by discussing various exclusion plans, showing sympathy for a settlement and stressing his closeness to Carson, could Bonar Law reduce the likelihood of these developments occurring.[204] Bonar Law gave Asquith no room to paint the Tories as unbending, leaving the only way to ensure they rejected the compromise (and thus unveil themselves as obdurate) by making the proposal so unreasonable that it would not be seen as a genuine basis for settlement by the public.

More assertively, Bonar Law's second meeting with Asquith saw him throw the initiative for a compromise arrangement back onto the Government. This was evident in his firm rejection of Asquith's demand for cross-bench support on third reading, to ensure passage of any future amendment to the Home Rule bill. 'In the House of Commons the position was different, that we might think it was possible the bill would be defeated … and that therefore we should like to be free to vote against the third reading. As I expected he did not agree to this.'[205] Already Balfour had seen the necessity of Unionists agreeing to this, while Chamberlain, Lansdowne and others probably saw it as inevitable if a devolutionary amendment was to succeed. But Bonar Law was not going to implicate himself in such a front-bench, 'pro-order' stitch-up simply to help the government out of a sticky situation. Refusing to help steer a reconstituted Home Rule bill through parliament meant Asquith would have to rely on Nationalist support in the Commons for any amendment, a most unlikely prospect unless the amendment were so watered down as to be meaningless. Thus the government were once again reliant upon their unyielding allies; 'it is obvious that any settlement of this kind is out of the question if the Nationalists are determined not to have it; for the Unionists do not wish it and you cannot impose a settlement which nobody wants'.[206] Two days later Bonar Law could confirm to an anxious Long that 'so far we are committed to nothing'.[207]

Finally, some controversy surrounds an assumption made by Bonar Law in his account of the second meeting, that Asquith would put the scheme of six-county exclusion to his cabinet,[208] and if no agreement was reached go to an election. '[Asquith] replied … "I shall definitely make this proposal to my Cabinet on Tuesday and I think I can carry my Cabinet with me … As soon as I have got the agreement of my Cabinet Birrell will approach the Nationalists … my impression is, that he has definitely made up his mind that a settlement on these lines is the only alternative to a general election".'[209] Patricia Jalland has suggested this shows a naïveté on Bonar Law's part in accepting such a statement, if ever actually made,[210] and is further evidence of the Tory leader's inexperience and lack of negotiating skill. But it might be that Bonar Law was manipulating events, knowing that other Unionist leaders would examine his account of the meeting. Indeed we might detect at work here the same tactic recommended earlier by Oliver and Steel-Maitland, of wrongfooting Asquith by making an assumption on his words and deeds then waiting for a response. Thus by emphasising Asquith's readiness to agree to six-county permanent exclusion and even go to an election, Bonar Law could paint the prime minister as duplicitous when little of this subsequently transpired, as seemed most likely. He could not be blamed if these did not materialise, it was merely Asquith again breaking his promise, while extracting something tangible from Asquith did his credibility amongst other Unionists little harm. What was more dangerous for Asquith was the possibility of an idea circulating that he had agreed to put a formal offer before cabinet and hold an election if rejected. Rather tantalisingly, Bonar Law wrote to Balfour (himself no stranger to such tactics) the day after he met Asquith, '*of course we could never make any use of the knowledge of his intentions communicated to me* yet if the proposal is definitely made to the Cabinet it really cannot be secret; and they would be in a hopeless position if they fight an election on proposals which they themselves tried to alter'[211] (my italics). We might speculate on the consequences for Asquith. Ministers would have been incensed at such a promise to Bonar Law, without their prior agreement. The Liberal party would be demoralised that their leader had wilted so dramatically in the face of Ulster threats, and in the process, broken his word. Nationalists, not for the first time, would have felt betrayed by their historic allies, causing their resolve to win the full Home Rule bill, to stiffen even more. Thus as a piece of party political distortion, it had very few drawbacks for Bonar Law.

Bonar Law's second meeting with Asquith had on balance been a success. He mollified the growing apprehension on the right of the party and yet gave Asquith no opportunity to smear him as irreconcilable. He avoided any devolutionary entanglement and stuck firmly to his tough approach. And he had thrown the initiative for finding a compromise back onto the government and their Nationalist allies, in which the chances of success were, he believed, low. This was a central element of Bonar Law's entire strategy, one of the principle assumptions he was operating upon, namely that the prime minister would be unable to reconcile the

Nationalists to a compromise settlement that public opinion would regard as reasonable. Confiding to Long, 'from a party point of view I hope the Nationalists will not agree, for if they do our best card for an election will have been lost'.[212] A week later he was convinced they could not agree; 'it looks now as if the Nationalists would not have the exclusion of Ulster at any price, and if so that will greatly simplify our position'.[213] And again, three days later, 'it seems to me as if there were no chance of the Nationalists even considering the exclusion of Ulster; and if so our course is plain and indeed I think there must be an early election'.[214]

This attitude was reinforced by his third meeting with Asquith. 'I really do not understand why he took the trouble of seeing me at all. The only explanation I can give is that he is in a funk about the whole position and thought that a meeting might keep the thing open at least.'[215] Bonar Law saw little chance of a compromise, and given he believed Asquith would do everything to avoid civil war, he could triumphantly declare on 1 December that 'there is so much likelihood of an early election'.[216]

Problems remained, notably party hostility to the very idea of compromise, which stood at variance to Bonar Law's current need to appear moderate and statesmanlike. This dichotomy between party opinion and his public stance, stretched him and created the potential for serious party divisions. Another concern was that some leaders were pressing him to change course. Lansdowne, Selborne and Chamberlain were demanding all talk of exclusion be dropped for a devolutionary solution, while Balfour and Smith called for a pro-order coalition. Steel-Maitland, Hills and others, sought to drop Home Rule altogether and focus on Tariff Reform and Land policy. The threat from Lansdowne and Chamberlain was particularly serious, having established contact with leading ministers and attracted influential support within Unionist circles. They also had the private sympathy of Carson and sections of the press, notably *The Times*, *Observer* and *Daily Mail*. Bonar Law reacted by giving scope to their activities, allowing them freedom to agitate and not criticising their speeches at Bromsgrove and Brighton, despite the different line they took. He watched the Chamberlain–Churchill conversations without alarm, even commenting rather curiously, 'I agree with every word of it', after reading the transcript.[217] Yet Bonar Law had the feel of the party. He knew that federalism or devolution was unacceptable to the vast majority of them, at a moment when they had the government in such a difficulties. Moreover, to have applied a heavy hand would have been self-defeating, forcing them into a more independent line and a direct attack to his leadership. At the same time Bonar Law remained resolute, fixed to a line that offered Asquith the choice of civil war or an election. His Newcastle speech on 29 October, stuck firmly to this basic option, to the annoyance of Chamberlain and Selborne. Nor, in private, did he move from Ulster and exclusion as his negotiating base. This was evident after his third meeting with Asquith. 'The end of our interview was a statement by him [Asquith] that he understood that nothing could be considered by us except the exclusion of Ulster and he would carefully consider whether a settlement on that basis was possible.'[218]

Bonar Law's resolve to cling to his existing tactical approach was a serious obstacle to any federal or devolutionary agreement between the front-benches. Without his support, the federal initiative was not well placed to succeed. Carson, though sympathetic and even eager for a settlement along these lines, could not talk compromise to Asquith without destroying his and Ulster's credibility. Nor could Balfour, Lansdowne or Chamberlain rally the party against its leader, for on this cause Bonar Law clearly echoed party sentiment. His position was far stronger than others realised, and this strength flowed from his understanding of where backbenchers stood. More serious threats came from the right. Long warned Bonar Law that any agreement on exclusion would foster rebellion, likely as not with him at its head. Around Long had grouped like-thinking Tories and Southern Unionists, worried about throwing away an electoral advantage by agreeing a settlement. Ironically, resistance to exclusion brought contact between Long and the pro-devolutionists Lansdowne, Selborne and Chamberlain. In other words, while a devolutionary solution was never a serious threat to Bonar Law, his willingness to discuss exclusion united much of the Tory leadership against him.

Yet Bonar Law had no choice but to keep meeting Asquith and appearing moderate, a dilemma he was at pains to spell out to Long: 'They [the party] probably do not realise, however, that by refusing to negotiate with the government we should only make our position worse; for undoubtedly if Asquith can square Redmond and we refuse to assist him in making arrangements with the exclusion of Ulster, they would do it on their own account and go to the country on that issue. In that case we should equally lose our best card for the election and worse than that we should seem, at least I think so, to the majority of people unreasonable in the attitude we take.'[219] This passage, though designed to reassure Long and forestall agitation on the right, also reveals several interesting elements about Bonar Law's tactical line. First, Bonar Law was still wedded to

Constitutional methods; his tactics were to secure power through electoral means. There was a point beyond which he would not go in resisting Home Rule, namely, if Asquith squared the Nationalists and Ulstermen over exclusion, the same benchmark he had explained to J.P. Croal after his first meeting.[220] Second, Bonar Law was relying on Nationalists and Liberals falling out with each other to undermine attempts at compromise, so preserving public sympathy for the Tories. It was a course that required patience and fortitude, a waiting game, though one beyond the grasp of Long. 'One of our best, ablest ... supporters told me yesterday, that he realised the difficulty of offering a simple negative to any reasonable offer but he added, "the great mass of the people will not understand it, they will think our leaders have sold the pass and our party will be smashed for twenty years".'[221] In reply Bonar Law disclosed his hand more clearly; 'I really do not think I differ in any way from the views you express and as far as I can judge the situation is developing quite satisfactorily for us. I think so because it seems to me as if there were no chance of the Nationalists even considering the exclusion of Ulster; and if so our course is plain and indeed I think there must be an early election.'[222] Implicit here was an appeal for trust and restraint, holding back the right from constant attacks which simply gave Asquith cause to believe a compromise plan would be rejected by the Tories and would certainly divide their forces.

Despite this, Long maintained his pressure, demanding his meetings with Asquith be made public,[223] a clear rejection of the waiting game and designed to rally party opinion behind him. Again Bonar Law urged delay and asked for patience and understanding: 'as regards making the meeting public I do not think that would be wise. If I saw any chance of a settlement then there would be no harm ... but I see none; and my impression is, to have it known that I was meeting Asquith would only tend to diminish the fighting spirit among our people, which would be very undesirable.'[224] In reply Long admitted to be 'delighted to hear what you tell me of the prospect. This quite alters the case.'[225] Yet by the 31st he was still pestering Bonar Law with memoranda and threats.[226]

Threats from the Right did not push Bonar Law into a tougher approach. He continued with moderation, appearing willing to meet Asquith and negotiate on exclusion. In this sense accusations that he was weak and mesmerised by Asquith were unfounded; he simply realised how vital it was to present an image of reasonableness to the public and to Asquith. Arguably he showed much the most perceptive grasp of the situation, stemming from an awareness that exclusion was not possible. His only concern was to preserve party unity while he was posturing. Hence he took Long into his confidence and coloured public speeches with tough rhetoric. His address at Dublin on 28 November was an 'uncompromising' and 'impassioned outburst', in reply to Asquith's hostile Leeds speech the day before.[227] Bonar Law was also in regular contact with Carson. Great sympathy existed between them, based on Bonar Law's unshakable advocacy of Ulster's position; and with Carson behind him he had a cushion against right-wing attacks. In addition, the possibility that an election was imminent served to dampen potential unrest on the right. They would champ at the bit and foam at the mouth but would not bolt from the stable.

Bonar Law achieved a delicate balance between party animosity and political necessity. The meetings formally ended after Bonar Law's Bristol speech, on reasonably favourable terms for the Tories. Certainly they could not be viewed as unreasonable or as a force against compromise, as they had been stigmatised in 1910. Party unity was strained but not broken; indeed it was Liberal splits that became more pronounced while Asquith's difficulties in squaring the Nationalists were widely acknowledged.

CHAPTER SEVEN

Meetings, mutinies and Tory resistance, 1914

INTRODUCTION

BY EARLY January 1914, the secret conversations between Asquith, Law and Carson, which had begun in October, ground to a halt without success. Unionist concerns now focused on Asquith's intentions. These became a little clearer with the start of the new parliamentary session on 9 February, when he announced he would soon introduce fresh 'suggestions' for a settlement. This fuelled deep unease amongst Unionists. What if, for example, Asquith had managed after all to square the Nationalists to the permanent exclusion of six Ulster counties? Or, more likely, what if Asquith's suggestions still fell far short of this basic minimum? Could Law afford to reject them, fearing, as he did, the adverse public reaction and the likelihood Asquith would capitalise on this with an immediate dissolution, upon the platform that his proposals were the only solution capable of settling the Irish problem once and for all? The possibility of such a manoeuvre led some Unionists, including Law, to go to the extraordinary length of planning to amend the Army Annual Act, in order to force an immediate dissolution.

Asquith finally introduced his compromise scheme on 9 March 1914, although its outline had been leaked to *The Daily News* five days earlier. It advocated a plebiscite in all nine Ulster counties to see which ones desired to contract out of the Home Rule bill but with the proviso that the excluded areas would automatically come in after six years. Unionists responded to the terms, which had already been offered and rejected by Law at their second meeting, with derision. 'We do not want a sentence of death with a stay of execution for six years', was Carson's damning phrase.[1] Law, more sensitive to public sentiment, greeted it with an alternative demand for a referendum on the entire bill, thus neatly deflecting Asquith's offer without endangering public sympathy. The Liberal party was incensed by this rebuttal of what they regarded as a genuine and far-reaching compromise. So angry was Churchill that he was moved to bloodthirsty threats and dire prophecies during a speech at Bradford. In his and other ministers' exasperation lay the seeds to the bungled government attempt to reinforce troop emplacements around Belfast from 18 March, the so-called 'Ulster Plot', events that themselves provided the spark to what has become known as the Curragh 'mutiny'.

Events at the Curragh radicalised the situation, most famously with the landing of arms by the Ulstermen at Larne on the evening of 24–5 April 1914. In this tense atmosphere, the political leaders stood far apart. Undeterred, an increasingly desperate Asquith tried to impose a settlement on events by introducing his compromise scheme as an amending bill in the House of Lords, to be passed in conjunction with the Home Rule bill. Somewhat inevitably the Lords repudiated them, but avoided outright rejection by amending the amending bill in June 1914, to now permanently exclude all nine Ulster counties, aware that neither Asquith nor the Nationalists were likely to accept these terms. The ensuing stalemate again threw politics into confusion. As a last desperate effort to break the impasse, with the amended amending bill scheduled to re-enter the Commons on 20 July where the government presumably would reject it, the king invited all the main political leaders to a conference at Buckingham Palace over the period 21–4 July 1914. Here for the first time Asquith, Lloyd George, Bonar Law, Lansdowne, Redmond, Dillon, Carson and Craig were brought together, but still without success. Nationalists dug in their heels over Asquith's March suggestions, as the furthest they would go, aware how close the Home Rule bill was to becoming law. The Ulstermen did not shift from the permanent exclusion of six counties of Ulster. And Bonar Law remained convinced that without an agreed compromise, Asquith would retreat to an election rather than face civil war in Ireland. But there events were to stand, for circumstances across the broader European canvas intervened to temporarily suspend the struggle over the Home Rule bill. Britain entered the Great War on 3 August 1914 accompanied, rather ironically, by a huge sigh of relief from most political quarters. The unexpected cabinet unity on entering the war represented a collective belief that a path (at least a temporary one) out of the Irish quandary had been found.

ONE LAST HEAVE: CHAMBERLAIN, LANSDOWNE AND DEVOLUTION

For those Unionists keen on a settlement, the New Year brought few signs of hope and a great deal of despair. Talks between Law, Asquith and Carson had made little progress, despite intense pressure from Lansdowne, Chamberlain, Selborne (and even private sympathy from Carson) to move in a devolutionary direction. 'If you want agreement', Oliver reminded Chamberlain, 'you must employ "agreers" … No good employing "disagreers" for the job'.[2] Garvin similarly 'feared our business is making little progress and more grave warnings are required'.[3] None were graver than Law's speech in Bristol on 15 January 1914, where he signalled the end of his conversations with Asquith by repeating his threat to support armed insurrection in Ulster if no election was forthcoming. 'The Opposition front-bench has no intention of coming to terms', Spender accused Oliver, 'and that any further overtures beyond what the P.M. will make … will simply be used to trip them up. This they infer from Bonar Law's speeches and the tone and temper of the opposition generally'.[4] *The Westminster* wondered whether the Tory party 'has learned sufficient wisdom to reject the heated advice tended to it to smash all the crockery if it cannot get its own way'.[5] Even amongst the more fainthearted on his own side, Law's speech was criticised as too extreme. For Lord Hythe, 'I know the government are reasonable' whereas the Unionist party, in 'go[ing] the whole hog on the Ulster ticket is unreasonable'.[6] In such an atmosphere, federalists dispersed, Churchill accompanying Asquith to Cannes, while Chamberlain sulked in Folkestone where he 'did not want to talk politics'.[7]

Unionist concerns were heightened over January 1914 by a growing conviction that Asquith was planning to offer them a compromise scheme 'more or less on the lines already indicated' during his second conversation with Law, namely Home Rule within Home Rule or 'veiled exclusion'.[8] Law and Carson had already flatly rejected this in private and would have had little choice but to reject it publicly, despite the grievous tactical position this would place them in. Yet Tory federalists also had serious reservations, despite being generally more positive and recognising in it terms that could be extended and worked upon. For one, Home Rule within Home Rule offered no real solution if the Ulstermen would not accept it, as Carson had already made clear. It also diverted the initiative away from a wider constructive arrangement for all the United Kingdom, while abandoning Unionists in the south and west of Ireland, something

Lansdowne and Carson were acutely aware of. And in providing Asquith with a favourable electoral position (enabling him to go to the country on his compromise proposals and likely to win public support for them), many suspected that party concerns were his prime motive rather than finding a lasting settlement to the problem.

Political developments during January reinforced this reading of Asquith's tactics. Bridgeman noted in his diary a changed attitude on the government benches, 'it was clear that they had realised at last the gravity of the situation. Instead of laughing … they listened with extraordinary attention'.[9] More worrying was a speech by Birrell on 26 January in Bristol, during the course of which he spoke of 'generous terms having already been made to the Ulstermen', a slip that appeared to confirm that Home Rule within Home Rule was uppermost in the government's thinking.[10] *The Times* noted that 'the government and their supporters are assiduously disseminating impressions which are intended to depict their own attitude in a singularly favourable light'.[11] In other words, creating an atmosphere of hope and compromise, and of generous concessions already made, which, Asquith felt 'would do a great deal to influence public opinion and to meet the objections felt by moderate people in the country – in fact, he (Asquith) intimated that they would put public opinion on his side'.[12]

Unionist fears came to ahead at the shadow cabinet meeting of 5 February 1914, four days before parliament reassembled.[13] Here Law and Carson outlined to their colleagues the details of the various meetings with Asquith during the Autumn recess, and concluded that Asquith would not move beyond the offer of 'veiled exclusion'. This, they believed, he would introduce as soon as parliament met, against a backdrop of a well-prepared public opinion, eager for any way out of the Irish imbroglio and so willing to accept Asquith's inadequate proposals. Both Law and Carson could see no chance of accepting these terms, a line backed by all there, though the leadership failed to elaborate upon how Asquith's offer would be satisfactorily rebuffed. The best they could manage was for Long to move the amendment to the address demanding an election before Home Rule proceeded any further, with Law to follow him with a strong assault on the government. The meeting thus ended without a very clear idea of future developments and with, according to Salisbury, 'a feeling of considerable uneasiness' at their position.[14] For the likes of Chamberlain, Selborne and other supporters of federalism, circumstances looked bleak indeed: Asquith was evidently unwilling (or unable given his reliance upon the Nationalists) to take the bold step and re-formulate the problem along devolutionary or federal lines.[15]

When parliament finally opened on 9 February 1914, federalists were therefore in a state of great apprehension at what Asquith was likely to say. The next day the prime minister rose to speak during the debate on the address. 'We were all convinced that Asquith would announce the proposals for dealing with the Ulster difficulty on which the government had decided. He did nothing of the kind'.[16] Instead, Asquith declared he would 'use no last words and would exclude no possible solution',[17] an extremely vague passage that Unionists took to mean that he would bring forward *new* suggestions and submit them to the House. The result of this ambiguous rhetoric was to throw the Unionist leadership into disarray, 'every tongue was set wagging and every head speculating as to what was the meaning of the speech they had just heard'.[18] Having expected Home Rule within Home Rule, it now appeared that Asquith might after all have squeezed (or been in the process of squeezing) a viable compromise from the Nationalists. So taken aback was Law that he refused to reply to Asquith, much to the annoyance of Chamberlain who felt he should have pushed for clarification on this point,[19] while Carson chose to wait till the next day before replying.

Over the next few days the impression spread amongst Unionists that 'the Government will be forced to adopt exclusion, that the coercion of Ulster has now been made impossible and that the bill cannot pass in its present form'.[20] The evident unhappiness of the Nationalists at Asquith's speech (observers thought they 'were very sick',[21] believing a deal with the Unionists had already been done) and dissatisfaction amongst more militant Liberals seemed to reinforce this impression. In addition, Chamberlain had received intelligence from Walter Long that Sir David Harrel, the ex-Under-Secretary at Dublin Castle, had visited Asquith to inform him that the police were incapable of dealing with resistance from the Ulstermen. The conclusion Chamberlain drew was that the government 'cannot now attempt the coercion of Ulster and that they must propose its exclusion'.[22] Though the exclusion of Ulster remained an anathema to federalists, they were clearly encouraged by what appeared to be Asquith's attempt to find a genuine solution. Accordingly, Lord Selborne and Chamberlain began to shift their federal appeal, adjusting their stance to recent developments and signalling to Asquith that cross-bench help could be on offer in his difficult job of reaching agreement with the Nationalists. They now admitted that the exclusion of Ulster might be a *necessary* but *temporary* measure to remove the immediate threat of civil unrest in Ulster, with the federation of the UK following shortly on behind it. It was an alteration in the timing of the federal project – exclusion in advance of Home Rule all round. Writing to Lord Charnwood, Selborne admitted that 'civil war in Ireland can quite certainly be averted by taking Ulster out of the Government of Ireland Bill ... by leaving it attached for all purposes to G.B., or, by giving it the machinery of a subordinate Government in Belfast'.[23] This shift had the added advantage of marrying the Ulstermen's demand for exclusion with Southern Unionist concerns to maintain a viable link with Britain. It also offered Carson a creditable all-Ireland line to pursue, in light of his consensual reply to Asquith on 12 February and his privately expressed sympathy for Home Rule all round as a long-term solution. Such a manoeuvre 'would fulfil Carson's conditions and, indeed, has been privately favoured by him'.[24]

Like Selborne, Chamberlain realised that actual rather than veiled exclusion had to form the starting point of any agreement if it was to win over Carson. Ten days after Asquith's speech Chamberlain now admitted to Oliver that 'the present exclusion of Ulster as absolutely essential',[25] but as a precursor to the long-term federation of the UK. In this he recognised that if the government were indeed preparing to exclude Ulster, then they might find it an easier pill to swallow (or at least provide them with more negotiating leverage with the Nationalists) if exclusion was smothered into a wider structure of devolved government across Britain. After all, 'by itself [exclusion] was a most humiliating surrender for the Government',[26] whereas 'federalism makes the exclusion of Ulster easy'.[27] 'Lansdowne, Selborne and I have given in our public speeches some favour to the idea, for it would be absolutely destructive of the separatist features of the present bill', the key, Chamberlain assumed, to Nationalist obstructionism.[28] Thus Chamberlain saw in events great hope. If Asquith went for Home Rule All Round, he would find a sympathetic echo inside the Tory leadership. The combined forces of Chamberlain, Carson, Lansdowne, Balfour, Selborne and Curzon would have been more than enough to convince Law of the need to accept it.

Yet, despite his optimistic reading of the situation, doubts remained in Chamberlain's mind about what Asquith might be up to. What if the prime minister were simply playing with them, as many on the right believed, and only offered four-county exclusion, a settlement Carson could not agree to. More politically damaging for the Tory devolutionists, what if Asquith offered to exclude six counties of Ulster with no time limit, but rejecting the wider federal reconstruction by leaving the rest of the bill intact. Carson would surely have been forced to accept this by the Ulster Unionist leadership, regardless of the impact upon the Tory party or Southern Unionists, both being most unlikely, as Jalland suggests, 'to end their resistance to Home Rule for the rest of Ireland, if Ulster was excluded'.[29] And even if a compromise agreement was thrashed out, the problem remained of how any alterations to the bill would be carried through parliament. To absorb them into the original bill would necessitate the Lords helping to pass it, an impossible task for Lansdowne facing, as he undoubtedly would, a solid phalanx of increasingly rigid Tory peers grouped around Lords Willoughby de Broke, Milner and Midleton. It would have been 1911 all over again, with the prospect of deeply acrimonious divisions in the party. A way around this was, as Chamberlain suggested, to incorporate alterations into an amending bill that would accompany the Home Rule bill through the last stages of the parliamentary process. The Lords could then pass the amending bill while still rejecting Home Rule, aware that it would pass automatically through the upper house under the parliament Act. 'Thus they would take no responsibility for the passage of Home Rule but would provide the means by which … an amending bill embodying the concessions would take effect'.[30] For Chamberlain, then, the situation as it unfolded early in 1914 was one of great possibilities for federalists and of great dangers, 'this strange situation … the most anxious and at the same time in some ways the most hopeful I have ever known'.[31]

As ever it was Oliver who looked to dispel Chamberlain's fears and doubts, urging him to move more boldly towards a federal solution.[32] To impress upon him the seriousness of the situation he sent him a thirty-eight-page memorandum pleading that the Tory party take up the federal cause immediately rather than wait on the government.[33] As with the federal initiative in the autumn of 1910, Oliver visualised a broad-bottomed coalition, a theme he pursued in his covering letter: 'I see no way out of national danger except a Government which omits Squiff, W. Long, Haldane, Curzon, Grey, Lord Halsbury, Runciman etc, etc and Leo Maxse etc and which contains yourself, Lloyd George, Carson, Winston and possibly one or two more, Milner … Crewe, Jameson, Bob Cecil'.[34] Such speculations of national government were fuelled by a lunch in the middle of February between Oliver, Astor and Lloyd George. The chancellor voiced great enthusiasm for a federal scheme 'but unless we agreed to this in principle beforehand Asquith could not possibly put it forward as it would wreck the Govt if we refused his offer if made publicly'.[35] The episode again showed Oliver that the 'right' people were thinking along the right lines, if only they could be persuaded to work with each other.

And of great significance in this respect was Carson, who responded positively to the change in direction by leading federalists early in 1914. Home Rule All Round was something he had earlier recognised as a possible way out of the crisis, as long as it was preceded by the exclusion of Ulster. Like Chamberlain he recognised that this offered Asquith something more than the straightforward partition of Ireland with which to bargain with the Nationalists. It was also a means of marrying Southern Unionist concerns with the immediate interests of Ulster. More especially, Carson was only too aware, by early 1914, of the weakness of the UVF and its inability to stand up to concerted government action or even to keep its more 'hooligan' fringe under control.[36] Carson thus faced growing pressure, a consequence of which was his agreement in January to large-scale gun-running into the province. Another was to pursue, with eagerness, the grounds for a compromise with the government. Early in the New Year he had discussed such ideas with Garvin,[37] who then relayed Carson's views to Oliver as 'exclusion pending federation ... If he seemed to take anything less than ... (this) ... his people would sling him aside'.[38] That same day in a speech at Belfast Hall, Carson suggested that his terms could well encompass Home Rule all round. It was no use talking unless 'they give us, as a basis, the preservation under an Imperial Parliament of those rights which our ancestors won for us'.[39]

Asquith's vague statement of 10 February 1914 seemed to suggest to Carson that he was now beginning to search for a 'real' solution. Keen to keep up this momentum he replied in a very measured, calm and moderate tone. While confirming 'that nothing short of exclusion of Ulster would induce her to lay aside her purpose', he then pleaded with all sides, and even to his Nationalist 'fellow countrymen', to find a peaceful and consensual settlement to the present crisis. 'Carson's speech last night had powerfully contributed to an accommodation'.[40] Indeed so temperate had his speech been that ministers 'professed to find in the debate and especially in Carson's speech, a new situation which offered a prospect of a friendly solution';[41] an interpretation shared by Stamfordham.[42] In private Carson continued to cultivate influential publicists, confiding to Oliver his support for Home Rule All Round. 'If we were being treated similarly to all other elements of the UK we could hardly assert the right to resist by force something which was equally being given to all members of the community in which we live'.[43] It seems clear, then, that Carson was pursuing a compromise upon the basis of exclusion pending federation. It was a line capable of drawing support from Chamberlain, Lansdowne, and Southern Unionists, all of whom who were hostile to the simple exclusion of Ulster from the bill.

Thus primed by the likes of Chamberlain, Carson, Oliver and Garvin, those sections of the press sympathetic to federalism went into overdrive. Dunraven published eulogies to Home Rule all round in *The Nineteenth Century* and in *The Times*.[44] Both *The Times* and the *Observer* ran sympathetic articles, and even the strongly pro-Government *Westminster Gazette* expressed support. Spender admitted to Oliver that although there were obstacles to federalism, 'there are so many people well-disposed in high quarters on both sides' that a solution was possible.[45] Lord Charnwood and Murray Macdonald added to the general federalist ferment by publishing a pamphlet in the middle of February, called *The Federal Solution*. And not to be out-'penned' Oliver made a similarly forceful attack on veiled exclusion in a pamphlet issued later that month, *What Federalism is not*.[46] From higher quarters, Lord Stamfordham wrote in support of the current initiative. 'I have never swerved from the total exclusion of Ulster as the sole expedient in the difficulty; but better still if she could be left out until the federal system has been applied to Ireland'.[47]

By early March, however, things again retreated. The impression grew that Asquith might not go as far as many had assumed from his statement in February. Both Sanders and Bridgeman noted a hardening in the prime minister's attitude,[48] while Chamberlain understood 'from secret information ... that the present intention ... is to propose a very wide scheme of safeguards giving to Ulster Home Rule within Home Rule'.[49] These fears were strengthened by what appeared to be a leak to the lobby correspondent of *The Daily News* that Asquith would only offer temporary exclusion for those counties opting out after a plebiscite, namely four-county exclusion.[50] Chamberlain, his hopes apparently dashed yet again, was furious; 'the Government have finally and deliberately shut the door on any federal solution ... If Asquith had acted on the hints thrown out by Lansdowne, Carson and myself and had confronted us with a definite proposal to cooperate in that solution, I think it might have been carried'.[51] If indeed these were Asquith's intentions then the outlook for a devolutionary compromise was grim.

Asquith announced his proposals in parliament on 9 March 1914. As predicted, they offered the temporary exclusion for six years of those counties which, following a plebiscite, demanded it. The rest of the bill remained intact and would apply to the remainder of Ireland. After six years the excluded counties would rejoin the rest. The government pointed out that at least two general elections would occur before the excluded counties were to rejoin the south, allowing the Tories, if they could win an election, to alter this to a permanent status. This was of small comfort to the Unionists and to Law in particular for whom the Home Rule crisis was the means of winning an election. Carson flung the offer back at the government with words that even F.E. Smith felt went too far,[52] though he added that if the proposal was modified to the permanent exclusion of all nine counties he would present it to the Ulster convention, thus retreating from his private support for Home Rule All Round. Law was more cautious, aware of the battle for public opinion in which he and Asquith were engaged. Instead of outright rejection, he demanded more details about the plan and proposed an alternative way forward of a referendum on the entire Home Rule bill. From the government side both Lloyd George and Churchill were outraged at the Tory response. Churchill was particularly bitter, lashing out at Bradford on 14 March where he frankly admitted that if the opposition could only offer refusal then 'let us go forward together and put these grave matters to the proof'.[53] Coming from a moderate and known supporter of federalism, the speech depressed constructive Unionists. Chamberlain, slumping back into his natural pessimism, now believed that 'conciliation vanishes and the forces are once more drawn up in battle array'.[54] The federal initiative seemed lost beneath growing political acrimony. The 'unbridgeable gulf' which separated the two sides seemed as wide as ever. 'The fact is neither the Nationalists nor the Ulstermen want to compromise … the feeling in our party now is stronger against compromise than it was'.[55]

It is clear, then, that the parties were already drifting apart before news of the events at the Curragh broke in London on 20 March. Tales of mutiny, mass resignations and officers being allowed to 'absent' themselves injected renewed bitterness into politics. The various revelations and rumours shocked moderates on all sides and in so doing encouraged another last surge towards a federal compromise. On 23 March the roundtablers, Craik, Curtis and Grigg, circulated a 'biggish document damning both parties and saying that it is time to quit the present mess and start making a new one of the Constitution'.[56] A week later they were invited onto *The Enchantress* to discuss their proposals with Churchill. These embodied the exclusion of six Ulster counties for an indefinite period or until parliament decided otherwise, with an all-Irish assembly convened simultaneously 'to consider the terms on which Ireland might be constituted a single self-governing unit in a scheme of devolution embracing the whole U.K.'.[57] Following their meeting with Churchill, Grigg and Curtis sent their scheme to other leaders and to Bonham-Carter, Asquith's private secretary. These efforts slowly repaired relations between the front-benches, for by April Sanders was able to note that 'everyone is talking again about conciliation',[58] while Dicey sensed that 'the air is full of cant about compromise'.[59] This groundswell of support for a federal settlement registered itself on 2 April 1914, in a joint appeal to MPs by F.E. Smith and Churchill, which suggested that 'a solution of a federal character for the U.K. offers the best prospect of a settlement'.[60] The appeal greatly alarmed the Nationalists and die-hard Tories alike, but won the support of seventy-eight Liberals and fifty-six Unionists. An excited Chamberlain interpreted it as 'a growing feeling of sympathy with this idea in our party and among the Liberals, say something like eighty men on each side of the House who openly avow their wish for it besides many who would accept it or any other course advised by their leaders and there is a large body of opinion outside Parliament which is increasingly favourable to it'.[61]

Encouraged by circumstances Chamberlain sent Carson a copy of the Grigg/Curtis memorandum, recognising he was the key to any compromise deal. 'They have suggestions to make which are worth consideration at any rate and on some points ... your opinion would be decisive'.[62] Selborne, who had played a role in devising the memorandum, also put pressure on Carson. 'I believe you and I think much alike on the question of devolution',[63] while there 'really would be very little difficulty in setting the proper division of functions between a Parliament for the U.K. and an English Parliament or council'.[64] Carson reacted positively and, dining a little later with Selborne, assured him that if such ideas were brought forward he 'would bring them before his friends'.[65] Carson sent the plan to Law recommending he meet Grigg, Brand and Curtis,[66] though Law failed to do so. By the middle of April it appeared opinion within sections of the Tory leadership had, again, swung in a constructive direction.

The initiative received an added boost on the night of the 24/25 April 1914, when the Ulstermen landed some 25,000 rifles and three million rounds of ammunition at various points along the coast of Co. Antrim – the so-called Larne Gun-running episode.[67] 'It has given an immense momentum to the pacifists', wrote Sir Almeric Fitzroy,[68] while Chamberlain believed that 'once again the more responsible people seem overwhelmed by the imminence and the greatness of the danger which confronts us'.[69] The more immediate result of these developments was to undermine the Tory censure motion on events at the Curragh, timetabled for 28 and 29 April. Larne took 'all the edge off the attempt to prove the existence of the plot', and instead gave added momentum to federalist attempts to find a constructive way out of the increasingly dangerous mess.[70] With Chamberlain set to open the censure debate, Oliver urged him to build bridges rather than to rake over the past; 'it is one of those occasions on which the life of the country ... is literally hanging in the balance'.[71] The next day Oliver openly denied that events of the 17 to 21 March amounted to a plot, hoping Chamberlain would now be measured and limited in his attack and even throw out some conciliatory overtures.[72] Feeling the great responsibility that now lay upon him, Chamberlain's speech was mildly critical but punctuated with sufficient appeals to find a devolutionary solution. His efforts, however, were over-shadowed by Churchill.

Churchill, in rather dramatic fashion, had asked the opposition front-bench, and Carson in particular, during the same censure debate whether they would be willing to accept a federal solution: 'Winston has taken the first step towards re-opening the paths of peace'.[73] Carson responded favourably, agreeing to support any constructive arrangement as long as the six Protestant counties of Ulster were first excluded, terms already proposed in the Grigg/Curtis plan and mentioned privately by Churchill and Smith. Carson 'went very far towards conciliation', according to one junior whip, and Chamberlain thought his speech 'hardly less remarkable. Its frankness and its obvious sincerity made a great appeal to the House'.[74] Chamberlain had already noticed a change in Carson's tone; 'he feels ... that we have been on the very brink of civil war and there is no time to be lost if the danger is to be averted. He is perhaps not less impressed with the impossibility ... of simply reverting to the old Unionist policy in the South and West'.[75] Recognising Carson's sympathy for a wider devolutionary settlement, Chamberlain gave strong encouragement to a federal solution in a speech at Wolverhampton.[76] Thus from a low point in early March, momentum for a federal alternative had slowly built up through April, in reaction to the growth of extremism and the very real threat of civil war. 'There is now in all quarters an impression that a settlement must somehow be made', wrote Chamberlain a little over-sanguinely.[77]

Certainly the pressure was strong enough to push Asquith and Law, accompanied by Carson, into yet another meeting, this time at Edwin Montagu's house on 5 May 1914.

As on previous occasions, Chamberlain greeted these developments with a mixture of optimism and fear. Notwithstanding the hopeful signs, he continued to fret that the sympathy for a constructive settlement would be diverted into 'some form of compromise [exclusion] which we shall be unable effectively to resist and which will be hardly less bad than the original bill'.[78] He despaired that despite all the 'loose talk of federalism, nobody attempts to concentrate opinion on the changes, which must be made in the Home Rule bill'.[79] In fact, Chamberlain and others suspected that the threat of exclusion was all the greater by April. For the refusal by officers at the Curragh to march north, making the coercion of the Ulstermen all but impossible, meant little could now stop exclusion. And the RIC had no desire to engage with the Ulstermen, given the largely Catholic basis to their recruitment. But as Ulster strengthened and exclusion became a reality, so Unionists in the south and west of Ireland grew more vocal and active (in fact their resistance increasingly moved beyond the purely vocal). Lord Midleton informed Law that he and Lord Barrymore had established a committee of about thirty peers ready to agitate inside the Upper House in defense of all-Ireland, Unionism.[80] Lansdowne also sensed, by April, that Southern Unionism was on the march with another die-hard campaign clearly in the offing,[81] an assumption corroborated by Midleton's letter to *The Times* on 15 April entitled *The Duty of Unionists*.[82]

Chamberlain and Lansdowne used these rumblings to try and foist a federal alternative onto the other Tory leaders. At a shadow cabinet meeting on the 5th of May, just before Law and Carson were to meet Asquith, they vocalised Southern Unionist anxieties that they would be forced into 'acceptance of the bill as a condition of the exclusion of Ulster'.[83] In other words in agreeing to save all or part of Ulster, the Unionist leadership would have to agree to sacrifice Unionists in the rest of Ireland. Sensing the 'dig' at his all-Irish credentials, Carson snapped back that he would never accept the rest of the bill, whether Ulster was excluded or not, though he was forced to concede it would inevitably pass under the terms of the Parliament Act. Lansdowne then pressed forcefully for 'some scheme of devolution' as the only viable solution capable of preventing the automatic passage of the bill under the Parliament Act.[84] In support, Chamberlain urged both Law and Carson to link the exclusion of Ulster as a temporary remedy to an eventual federal recasting the bill; 'to play what I call the "great game" and to make that suggestion themselves to Asquith'.[85] Both Law and Carson could not agree to this option (itself somewhat revealing about Carson and the degree to which he had shifted from his earlier devolutionary sympathies). It was clear by early May that wide and bitter differences of opinion existed within the Tory leadership.

Given Lansdowne and Chamberlain's failure to convert Law and Carson to a federal alternative, the talks were of little significance. Though inspired by growing federal support, the meeting brought together two leaders who lacked any kind of sympathy for the idea; 'Asquith by temperament is unfitted for agreement. Equally so is Bonar Law. And obviously each makes the other worse the more they come into contact'.[86] Only Carson had ever shown private support, but even that now seemed to have disappeared. Under these conditions, there was little chance of constructing a federal solution and the meeting limited itself to discussion of the principle of exclusion over which there was still no basis for agreement. And here the federal movement finished, the end of an extended attempt, begun back in 1910, to reach an agreed settlement to the Irish question along the lines of devolving power to regional assemblies throughout the UK. Both sides were to meet again, at Buckingham Palace between the 21 and 24 of July, but the discussions did not originate from a federalist initiative and stuck firmly to finding the elusive formula for exclusion, for which few of the participants had any faith.

We can speculate on the failure of the federal project throughout the years from 1910 to 1914. One key problem that was never overcome were the differences over what federalism and/or devolution actually meant, a definitional weakness that worked to separate rather than unify its sympathisers. Most critically, Chamberlain and Lansdowne spoke with slightly different emphasis on the issue.[87] For the federalist cause this was unfortunate for it seems plausible that if the two had been closer in their aims, they might have exerted more influence over Tory policy towards the Home Rule bill, forcing Law to play what Chamberlain called 'the great game', and even giving encouragement to Carson to offer more public support for devolution. A second obstacle to the success of federalism was the lack of sympathy it drew from both Asquith and Law, despite powerful bodies of support amongst the leaders and on the backbenches of each party. Asquith and Law remained determined opponents of federalism, born largely of (different) tactical considerations. For many historians, Asquith *used* federalism as a method of delaying events to divide the opposition[88] and as a pretence to keep his Scottish and Welsh MPs in line, while remaining fixed to orthodox Home Rule.[89] Conversely, Law regarded Federalism as a threat to his political strategy of forcing an election, and thus was something to be avoided at all costs. It also seems clear that support for Federalism weakened amongst Unionists as a result of the mounting extremism of the period from March 1914 onwards and from the wider drift to the right by sections of the party. A good illustration of this was Milner and Amery, both of whom could be counted amongst the enthusiasts of federalism through 1912 and 1913, but who, by 1914, increasingly saw the scheme as unachievable in the present climate and so committed themselves instead to organising the British Covenant. In other words, far from raising the likelihood of a federal compromise, as the likes of Chamberlain and Oliver hoped, events at the Curragh, the continued prevarication of Asquith and the Larne Gun-running episode undermined any foundation for a compromise. This lack of a base upon which federalism could be built was critical. For at the root of the crisis during this period was the incompatibility of Ulstermen and Nationalists, the former who would not go lower than Home Rule All Round, the latter envisaging Home Rule within Home Rule as their absolute maximum. A federal settlement could *only* come at the expense of one or both of these groups, via party cooperation or even a coalition. But after the events of March 1914 too little trust existed between the front benches to effect this degree of collaboration.

TORIES, THE ARMY AND A NEW DIE-HARD REVOLT

Early 1914 witnessed the militant spirit spread within the party. The secret meetings, between Asquith and Law led many on the right to believe that a compromise was being hatched or perhaps had already been agreed, as many Nationalists thought. Asquith's statement of 10 February and Law's refusal to reply to him appeared for many Unionists like collusion between the front-benches,[90] in the words of Lord Arran they were 'sure the pass had been sold'.[91] Such anxiety was enhanced by the intense federal activity in the press and by some of their leaders effecting a softer tone in debate, notably Carson and Chamberlain. Earl Crawford observed 'a feeling that our leaders will go too far',[92] while Lord Leconfield believed 'we must not give way but I do not trust our leaders a yard and they will do so for certain, unless we can stop them'.[93] These suspicions drew upon a deep-seated sense of mistrust, born of the events of 1911, that their leaders would surrender when the situation became critical. They also grew out of a concern that Asquith was delaying matters in the hope that Ulster would explode or the Unionist coalition split apart.[94] Even more worrying, many Unionists in the Upper House suspected that he was waiting for the right moment to introduce an amending bill of limited scope, placing onto the Lords the odium of rejection or acceptance, civil war or peace.[95] Against this backdrop of rumours, speculations and anxieties, the Tory right believed only nerve and the refusal of all attempts at compromise would call Asquith's bluff and destroy the bill.

To avoid the Lords once again becoming the arena of Tory capitulation, die-hards began to organise. 'Yes I think it worth while to tout our brother Peers', Lord Stanhope told Willoughby de Broke, 'I think it is necessary to dot the i's and cross the t's as to the possible move of the Government in again trying to corner us'.[96] Stanhope recommended to de Broke that Lord Crawford would be one who could effectively mobilise the peers against compromise. Throughout January, discreet soundings were taken amongst peers as to the strength of numbers. Then on 4 February the four ringleaders of this new die-hard revolt – Stanhope, Ampthill, Arran and Willoughby de Broke – issued a *Letter to Peers*.[97] The ostensible reason for the circular was to rally support for an amendment on the Address in the Lords, calling for an election, a new departure for the Upper House and designed to advertise their intense feeling on this issue.[98] But the letter was also intended to galvanise support against exclusion. 'It is hardly necessary to point out to your Lordship that to vote for the exclusion of Ulster from a Dublin Parliament is to accept the principle of Home Rule for Ireland … It is impossible so to alter the present Bill as to make it acceptable to all parties in Ireland as well as to the Unionist party as a whole. We submit that if Unionist Peers abandon the Union by passing a Home Rule bill before a general election is held it would be an act of betrayal'.[99]

A concerned Lansdowne pre-empted this independent action by die-hard peers by giving notice on 5 February that the Tory leadership had decided to move just such an amendment on the address;[100] 'the same idea has occurred to our leaders', Selborne wrote to Willoughby de Broke.[101] Rebellion was therefore avoided and face saved by the leadership but it left bitterness and recriminations within the party in the Lords. Lansdowne sent a curt letter to de Broke, 'I should have thought you might have held your hand, say for twenty-four hours, until you had ascertained the intentions of the party leaders ... we should have avoided an appearance of disunion, which, at such a moment as this is surely to be regretted'.[102] More worrying for the leadership, such independent activity by the die-hards was beginning to overlap with a similarly assertive Southern Unionist movement within the Lords. Lord Midleton was quick to stress the nature of their cooperation to Willoughby de Broke.[103] Both Southern Unionists and die-hards recognised that the Ulstermen were increasingly focused upon the cause of Ulster rather than preserving the Union with all of Ireland, an observation hinted at by Lord Arran in a letter to Willoughby de Broke: 'the Ulster party will never agree to the paragraph in our whip explaining that to accept Ulster exclusion is also to accept the principle of Home Rule'.[104] This growing collaboration was a powerful block within the Unionist party to accepting exclusion and would become central to the leadership's tactical calculations by June/July 1914. But even in the circumstances of early 1914 it explains Lansdowne's refusal to agree to the excision of Ulster from the bill during discussions amongst the leadership and his pressure to take-up an all-Ireland devolution scheme instead.

The Tory right were also active in other quarters. By the start of 1914 the BLSUU reputedly had over 400 agents nationwide and up to 10,000 men organised through local squads and companies ready to fight for the cause of Union.[105] Never one to stand still, and worried by the current atmosphere of party politics, Willoughby de Broke was eager to expand the movement. On 6 January he invited Lord Milner onto the League's council, to which he initially declined.[106] According to his biographer, Milner's role in the crisis up to this point had been minimal, his attention having been focused upon the issue of tariff reform.[107] However by late 1913 Milner began to show greater interest. On 3 December 1913 he had enquired of Carson 'whether there is not something which men like myself, who disbelieve in mere talk at this juncture, can do to help you'.[108] A month later his diary records, 'spent the morning in my rooms thinking out some plan for the support of Ulster'.[109] The next day, 12 January, Milner, on Willoughby de Broke's invitation, agreed to take charge of the BLSUU. At about the same time he began working closely with the UDL, who on 19 February placed at his disposal the entire staff and organisation of the UDL, which included its ruling council, comprised of Lords Harrowby, Oranmore, Crawford and Westmeath, and with Ian Malcolmson as secretary.[110] Milner now absorbed the UDL into the British League, creating one large movement, able to galvanise support for the cause and organise the network of local units and branches into a nation-wide structure. The basis for constructing such a movement was to be through a British Covenant, to mirror the Ulster one of 1912.

The Covenant would advertise the strength of popular support for the Union and provide willing recruits who could fight for the cause. Thus it would be a stepping stone to a more military organisation 'analogous to the signing of the Ulster Covenant which was the first step in the organisation of Ulster for resistance'.[111] A memorandum in the Milner papers points to another role he envisaged for the movement. 'In the last resort the same organisation which has been created for the purpose of demonstration could be used to furnish a really effective resistance to the action of the Government … [and] … an organised and immediately successful national uprising'.[112] Of course, Milner like Willoughby de Broke, was quick to stress that 'the main object … is to avert civil war if it can possibly be averted'.[113] It seems likely their talk of national uprisings were merely bluff to 'frighten the Government and its supporters' in order, as he told Oliver, 'to make them realise that persistence in their present policy … would meet with inflexible resistance'.[114] But extreme words and threatening the Government also suggest, as with the Ulster Covenant, that the British Covenant was a controlling mechanism, to 'help to keep Ulster confident and steady and prevent the danger of precipitate action'.[115] An anxiety still lingered that Ulster might break out into sporadic violence and spoil her case.

Once in charge, Milner began to 'strengthen and transform' the League, creating a new ruling body 'by the accession of a number of influential people'.[116] These included F.E. Smith, Basil Peto, McNeill and Bedford, all existing members of the BLSUU council, alongside Long, Hugh Cecil, Amery, Lord Lovat, Mark Sykes and, most importantly, with Lord Roberts as president. Milner was clearly drawing around him the old band of 1911 in preparation for another die-hard campaign. 'I want the stalwarts', he told Selborne, 'to begin to have some sort of rudimentary organisation, not to leave everything to the last moment'.[117] This time they would not be caught napping, as in July 1911. These connections overlapped with individuals in groups such as the National Service League and in the Army, particularly through Sir Charles Hunter. Hunter was a member of the UDL council and close to Earl Roberts, with contacts at the War Office who, in the past, had been a go-between to Sir Henry Wilson. Milner exploited these military contacts, having been informed of a disturbing trend, by Ian Malcolm secretary of the UDL, of 'territorial objections to signing (a British Covenant) are even more widespread than I thought among the officers ... I need hardly say they are all ready to be persuaded by a good argument'.[118] On 5 February 1914 he informed Lord Roberts of his plans, persuading him to involve himself.[119] Milner recognised the value of Roberts as a man who would assuage the officer corps if he gave his support to the Covenant. Roberts agreed by signing an appeal in the press on 3 March. Milner's plans were also boosted by Law. The two men were close and shared a similar understanding of the Home Rule crisis. On 13 January 1914 they had discussed the situation in Ulster at Law's home, a treat bestowed on few colleagues.[120] Law's speech at Bristol was received with favour by Milner and his circle, and interpreted as a green light to their plans for a British Covenant. It 'practically appeals to the Unionist party to strengthen the hands of its leaders', Leo Amery told Robert Cecil,[121] assuring him that Law was willing to give the Covenant his official blessing and the financial and organising help of Central Office.[122] A few days later Law suggested to Lansdowne that such a development if 'started by the right people and on the right scale ... would be decisive';[123] but he added, showing his acute sensitivity to public opinion, that 'it would be worse than useless unless it received an overwhelming response'.[124]

After a month of planning, the British Covenant was finally launched in the press on 3 March 1914. It called upon young men to sign a declaration against Home Rule and to offer their services for use in 'any action which may be effective to prevent it being put into operation'.[125] The Covenant marked the beginning of Milner's attempt to galvanise the BLSUU into a nationwide organisation. To that end, on 3 April, a month after the Covenant appeared, a new League of British Covenanters was launched at a meeting in Caxton Hall, London. The very next day the new League orchestrated a huge demonstration in Hyde Park, where members of the shadow cabinet spoke to an estimated crowd of nearly half a million. The Covenanters were also active in the by-election at Ipswich on 23 May which resulted in a Liberal candidate being ousted by a Unionist, although the contest was not a straightforward endorsement of the Unionist candidate, having been complicated by the intervention of a Labour candidate.[126] The Covenanter organisation also raised money to channel behind the Ulstermen, who by early 1914 were running increasingly short. An impressive list of possible contributors was drawn up,[127] many of whom went on to make substantial contributions. A list of donations, found in the Milner papers, reads like a seating plan at a society ball:

£30,000 from Lord Astor, £25,000 from Sam McCaughly, £10,000 from Lords Rothschild, Bedford and Iveagh, £5,000 from Lord Portland and a mere £4,500 from E. Cassell.[128] Whatever active role many Unionists were prepared to take in defence of Ulster and the Union, it was clear many were willing to help in a financial capacity. A great deal of money was flowing from various Tory sources into Ulster via the Covenanter movement, the UDL and the BLSUU.

Despite this, the initial public response to the Covenant is difficult to gauge accurately. In February, just over a month before the launch, the state of de Broke's BLSUU stood at 15,000 volunteers, drilled, armed and ready to fight in Ulster, according to an advert in *The Morning Post*.[129] Six months later, according to Walter Long, the figure stood at two million signatories, collected through ten thousand agencies, which seems a wildly exaggerated number of recruits by the person who Milner had put in charge of collecting signatories.[130] Yet even Milner was not short on exaggeration, informing Selborne that the movement was 'assuming enormous proportions' and 'the response to our appeal has been so strong that I think it only needs a little more support to become decisive'.[131] Yet in the same letter he complained of an 'absence of certain leading names'.[132] The May edition of *The Covenanter* referred to 'an enormous number who are prepared to make real sacrifices',[133] but the day before, Milner had grumbled to Oliver about 'those blessed Unionists what a crowd and *The Times* and everybody and everything have gone absolutely limp'.[134] It is also important to bear in mind the distinction between verbal or even written support, and agreeing to fight for and in Ulster. Aware of this distinction the wording of the Covenant was watered down after intense hostility from key Unionist leaders, in order to provide signatories with an escape clause. Organisers were even forced to affix to the pledge the proviso that 'by signing that declaration no man will pledge himself to take any particular action of which at a given moment his conscience and judgement do not approve'.[135]

More damagingly, apart from Law, the British Covenant attracted little support from within the Tory leadership. Lansdowne was lukewarm; 'I agree with you in thinking that such a movement could only succeed if started by the right people … and I am inclined to add at the right moment – I do not think the right moment has arrived yet'.[136] Crawford, someone Willoughby de Broke had initially looked to organise the die-hard peers against exclusion, declined outright to sign the British Covenant on the (rather sensible) grounds that he did not trust the judgement of Amery or Milner.[137] Chamberlain was uneasy with the wording and in any case saw little purpose to petitions, informing Amery that 'they count for little or nothing'.[138] Bob Cecil refused, declaring that 'the English hate illegality' and that he himself had too many 'scruples' to sign such a document.[139] He only later signed after Amery had substantially changed the wording, to the point of neutralising any firm commitment by the signatory, and only then after a great deal of pressure. Even Selborne was far from comfortable with the pledge. Milner complained to Carson that it was hard to persuade many people to sign such a pledge; so 'the thing must go on without them'.[140] Not for the first time, Law stood apart from the rest of the Tory leadership upon an initiative that was both more extreme and constitutionally more suspect.

In other words, the more immediate significance of the British Covenant was that it tended to raise serious questions over what Gollin describes as 'the moral frontier', and thus stood to actually divide Unionists rather than unite them.[141] Upon what basis would British Tories fight or offer practical resistance? Was it a fight for the Union as a whole or just Ulster or even just part of Ulster? If Ulster was excluded on a basis acceptable to the Ulstermen, would they still be committed to resisting Home Rule for the rest of Ireland, by force if necessary? These questions never achieved satisfactory agreement within the Tory leadership or across the breadth of the party or even amongst the more assertive forces of the right. Some, for example Lords Willoughby de Broke, Milner, Bedford, Stanhope, Arran and other Southern Unionists, wanted to fight for the whole Union. Others, including Law, Carson, Smith, Hugh Cecil, Selborne, Amery and Midleton – all supporters of the BLSUU and all politicians rather than ideologues – would not have fought for the rest of Ireland if Ulster was saved. The Tory right was a more fragile and splintered coalition of groups than the image they projected through the press: a group more reliant on bluff than a united movement of devoted volunteers.[142]

More ominously, the organisation of the Covenant (and Lord Robert's acceptance as president of the League) brought about a strengthening of the ties between Tories and sections of the army, both at the War Office and with serving officers. Questions about the position, role and duty of the army with regard to Ulster had arisen at various points during the political crisis. Leading Tories, including Law, Carson, Smith and Hugh Cecil had all publicly speculated upon whether British troops would obey orders if commanded to act against Ulster. During the second reading of the Home Rule bill, Law asked the house, 'do Hon Members believe that any Prime Minister could give orders to shoot down men whose only crime is that they refuse to be driven out of our community and deprived of the privilege of British citizenship'.[143] More sensationally, events surrounding Captain Wilfred Bliss Spender, during the summer of 1913, and his attempt to retire from the army to join the Ulstermen rather than be forced into resignation by the War Office, raised serious questions about the possible resignation of other officers.[144] However, such developments and comments had been relatively isolated, given the Unionist awareness that playing the 'Army card' was a most ambivalent course for them to pursue, exposing them to the cry of 'tampering' with the army which many on the Radical and Labour benches were only too keen to exploit. This danger was brought home to the leadership during the Spender affair when Carson became the focus of radical attempts to prove he had encouraged the young captain to give up his promising career for purely political reasons. Fiddling with the loyalty of the army also upset the ingrained sensitivities of many Tories, what Law described as 'the instinctive feeling that nothing ought to be done to bring the Army into party politics'.[145]

Despite such apprehensions, connections between the Tories and the army, if still a little shadowy, grew closer during 1913. Law, Carson and Milner were in regular touch with Lord Roberts and Sir Henry Wilson, DMO at the War Office. It had been through the efforts of Roberts and Colonel Hickman, a Tory MP, that General Richardson had been recruited in July 1913 as head of the UVF. In addition, the king, who shared some of the Tory concerns about the Home Rule bill, regularly met with officers. Thus, many channels existed down which the anxieties of the military at the possible predicament they faced over Ulster could be relayed to the very highest political levels. By early January 1914, as suspicion of Asquith's intentions mounted, sections of the Tory right began to focus upon the question of how the army might play a role in events. In particular, interest revived in the idea of amending the Army Annual Act when it came up for renewal in the Lords in the spring.[146] This stratagem had first been aired by Garvin and Goulding, in 1911, as a method of forestalling the Parliament bill.[147] It resurfaced, briefly, in June 1913 when discussions amongst the Tory leadership over the role of the king prompted Hugh Cecil to explore the viability of such a venture.[148] By 1914 the idea was again discussed, this time at the very top of the party, as a means of forcing an immediate dissolution, and so avoiding the type of watered-down compromise scheme being hatched by Asquith to win over a bored public opinion to his side.

On 13 January 1914 Law informed Lansdowne that he had asked Sir Robert Finlay, a former Unionist attorney-general, 'to look into this matter' of amending the Annual Army Act.[149] By 30 January, Law was now in a position to fully recommend it to Lansdowne and Balfour: 'it is indeed a very serious step; but after all it is not so serious as allowing the Government to drift into a position where force is used in Ulster', to which he received a grudging agreement from both.[150] By 2 February 1914 the movement, in addition to Law and more tentatively Lansdowne and Balfour, could claim the hesitant support of Curzon, 'the three Cecils, Selborne, Austen Chamberlain and Carson'.[151] Law asked Finlay to prepare a memorandum on the feasibility of such a tactic;[152] this was presented to the shadow cabinet on 5 February. Finlay's memorandum supported the move, provided great care was taken in its wording and over precisely what it intended to amend, enabling Law to press for the adoption of the course with his colleagues. However, sufficient doubts remained, particularly with Curzon, Balfour and Lansdowne, for the whole process to be delayed by establishing a small committee of lawyers. Under the direction of Sir George Cave and including Robert Cecil, Carson, Finlay and Lord Halsbury, the committee were 'to go into the whole subject and after they have done we shall have another meeting and decide upon our action'.[153]

It is important to understand what precisely was being contemplated by the small committee, rather than to accept the Liberal understanding of it as a wild and hazardous course.[154] One suggestion was to reduce the operation of the Act to just three months, while another plan was to limit its area of operation to exclude Ulster.[155] What all the schemes endorsed was the idea of *amending* the Act, not *repealing* it, and to amend it specifically to prevent the Army coercing Ulster, and only then if no general election was held beforehand. It was not intended to paralyse the entire British army or inhibit the army's freedom to respond to any foreign threat. Moreover, the plan was aimed at restoring army morale, given the anxiety felt within all ranks about their possible role in Ireland. 'It seems to me', Law informed Craik, 'that this is the best and perhaps the only chance of saving the Army'.[156] And the Tory actions fit snugly behind the original purpose of the Act:

> The Army Act is an annual bill which was voted originally … as an annual bill in order that Parliament might have the opportunity of preventing the crown or executive of the day using the standing

army to the injury of the liberties of the subject. As a matter of constitutional law … no case could be clearer than ours'.[157]

Whatever the constitutional justifications for such a move, the likely political impact would surely have been to harm the Unionist cause. Indeed once the rumour spread of what was being considered, resistance to the plan grew quickly. Strachey of *The Spectator* rallied against it, spurred on by Curzon who, as in 1911, saw himself as the guardian of moderate Toryism, only this time he was able to draw much support from the Tory back benches.[158] Other pro-Unionist editors, such as Croal of *The Scotsman* and Robinson of *The Times*, also rejected the idea. Oliver pleaded with Milner and Chamberlain to drop the scheme,[159] as did Dicey: 'I am certain that the English public will never tolerate the dictation of the Army. I think the public are in this right'.[160] These apprehensions were mirrored in the Liberal press. Spender, writing to Oliver, assured him that 'the threats of violent action by your Diehards are heartily welcomed by those who call themselves "fighting politicians" on our side and that they see many advantages in another election forced by the House of Lords'.[161] Such anxieties were reflected in the shadow cabinet, where the doubts registered early in February now grew in intensity. At a shadow cabinet meeting on 12 March Curzon, Derby, Selborne, Acland-Hood, Midleton and Devonshire all expressed dissent, while Carson for the first time admitted to some concern.[162] Opinion had clearly shifted against the idea. Yet Law was determined to keep the option open and again carried the day: 'Decision: provisionally to agree to amendment of army act but to leave details and decision as to moment of acting to Lansdowne and B.L. (This I fancy was against the general desire of those present)'.[163]

Unfortunately for Law, the shadow cabinet decision of the 12th was not reflected in wider party opinion which was increasingly hostile. Ian Malcolm, secretary of the UDL, was typical of this sentiment, telling Robinson that if the party touched the Army Act, 'he (Malcolm) would leave the Unionist party'.[164] Others, such as Carson, became less convinced of the manoeuvre, expressing to Milner on 18 March disbelief that the party would now tolerate such a step.[165] And even Law by 19 March was less convinced than he once had been, telling Strachey that 'he could not honestly say he thought there was much chance of the bill being amended'.[166] In the end the decision of whether to amend the Army Act or not was overtaken by events at the Curragh on 20 March 1914. The incident at the Curragh, in which sixty[167] British Army officers voluntarily accepted dismissal (or threatened resignation) rather than 'march on Ulster', nullified at a stroke any plans the government might have been laying to use the army in Ulster. The government could no longer rely on the Army to implement its Home Rule Act onto Ulster, if and when it passed, although it is important to remember that Asquith had already on several occasions let slip that he would never contemplate such a move. 'It has had a magical effect', Colonel Repington wrote to Lady Craigavon, 'for whereas a good part of the army might have marched before, I do not believe that wild horses will drag the army into Ulster now. The feeling against the Government is intense in the army'.[168]

The Curragh incident originated in the decision by a small cabinet committee, headed by Sir John Seely and Winston Churchill, to reinforce military depots in and around Belfast and to send the 3rd Battle squadron from its base at Gibraltar to 'exercise' off the Isle of Arran.[169] Both the War office and Sir Arthur Paget, the Commander-in-Chief in Ireland feared the effect these precautionary actions would have on those officers and troops who came from Ulster. An agreement was somehow reached that men with connections to Ulster would be offered the 'option of disappearing',[170] but all others who refused to move north would be dismissed. Translating this formula into clear instructions for his officers, when Paget addressed them at the Curragh barracks near Dublin on the morning of 20 March, proved problematic. For Paget left his officers with the impression that they had been given the choice between moving north for 'active operations of an offensive and aggressive character' or being dismissed.[171] To his horror sixty officers led by Brigadier-General Hubert Gough preferred dismissal. Gough was ordered to the War Office where he was interviewed on 22 and 23 March, although by the 21st news of the so-called 'mutiny' had already electrified London.

The story of events at the Curragh has been told elsewhere.[172] What perhaps requires analysis is the role Unionist leaders took in the episode. The government's decision to secure depots in and around Belfast was no surprise to the Tory leadership. Since the Royal Proclamation on 1 December 1913, banning the importation of arms into Ireland, depots were viewed as an obvious target against which the Ulstermen would move, given the latter's continuing shortage of arms and ammunition. Indeed, rumours of a possible raid by the UVF had first surfaced back in November 1913.[173] Their reinforcement in the tense atmosphere of early 1914 was therefore to be expected. In addition, since the beginning of the year, troop movements had received wide coverage in the press and were closely followed by Unionist leaders. On 3 January 1914 *The Times* noted detachments of the 1st Dorset Regiment moving into Carrickfergus Castle, provoking 'much comment in Belfast'.[174] Intelligence from BLSUU agents in February detailed unusual army manoeuvrings in the province. Hugh Ridgeway, secretary of the League, received 'reports … from honorary agents to the effect that the Government is beginning to take steps as regards the Ulster movement'.[175] He confirmed that muster notices had been sent out to regiments and that 'military concentration is to take place at Glasgow'.[176] Churchill's belligerent speech at Bradford on 14 March also indicated that some sort of military response was afoot. Craig certainly thought so, returning immediately to Ulster.[177] While Milner's War Office contact, Sir Henry Wilson, was most assiduous in passing on any relevant information to Milner and Sir Charles Hunter.[178] By 16 March rumours were beginning to circulate about the imminent arrest of Carson and Craig, and the deployment of army detachments in Ulster. These were sufficiently worrying for Carson to declare during the Tory censure debate on the 19th, 'your army is welcome there (Ulster) as is your fleet … Ulster is on the best of terms with the Army.[179] In other words, before 20 March when Paget offered his officers at the Curragh his extraordinary choice, there were enough straws in the wind to indicate that some sort of military reinforcement might well be attempted in Ulster.

Against this background, leading Unionists did all they could to shape and condition the actions of many army officers; 'to make certain that the officers did not make up their minds in a political vacuum, isolated from the opinions of those who were anxious for them to disobey the orders of the Liberal Government'.[180] In this respect the close social and political contacts between the army and the Tory party, and the frequent Tory assertions that any attempt to coerce Ulster would see the army refuse, became self-fulfilling prophecies. But more concrete evidence of undermining army loyalty can be found. Towards the end of January, Law wrote to Lord Roberts suggesting that he might sign a letter to *The Times*, which Law composed, defending an officer's right to disobey orders under certain conditions and in present circumstances if and when ordered to move against Ulster.[181] The letter was never published, but Roberts' willingness to sign would have been widely known within the officer corps and provides 'vivid evidence of the lines upon which the leading Unionists were thinking in the early months of 1914', prepared to challenge the sanctity of army obedience for their own ends.[182] A similar line of thinking can be detected in a memorandum in the Milner papers written in January

1914. Concerned with the aims of the Covenanter movement, it noted that 'there should be no attempt to do anything *at this stage* which could in anyway impair its (army) efficiency or that of the territorial force',[183] the inference being that at a later stage it might be necessary. This, again, reveals that interference with the decision-making processes of officers was part of the Unionist strategy, if at some undefined moment in the future. Moreover, the idea of a guarantee fund to support officers who resigned and lost their pensions, rather than move against Ulster, had been mentioned in Unionist circles and with Sir Henry Wilson in particular, as far back as November 1913.[184] By March 1914 the idea of an indemnity fund was picked up by Carson who passed the suggestion on to Milner, and with some success having been pledged £10,000 by Sir Marcus Samuel.[185] In addition to financial assistance a plan for reinstating officers who resigned over Ulster was also widely discussed at top political levels at this time. Such ideas were not new. Long reminded Law that they talked of this 'some months ago … and you approved the policy'.[186] What was so attractive about guarantee funds and reinstatement policies was that they made resignation far less hazardous for doubtful officers than it might have otherwise have been. They provided a financial cushion to ease the moral dilemma of resigning. Claims that the Opposition were tampering with the army had some foundation to them, however subtly and indirectly it was done. And although much of the blame for events at the Curragh falls squarely on the shoulders of Sir Arthur Paget, and his 'error in appearing to offer a choice to his subordinates',[187] it was Tory speeches, innuendo, influence and promises that helped shape the 'mind-frames' of those officers who decided to hand in their commissions.

After the initial resignation of Gough and fifty-nine fellow officers, events moved to London. Gough was summoned to the War Office for interviews on the 22 and 23 March. At the meeting on the 22nd, Paget's actions were countermanded by General Ewart, the Adjutant General, General French, Chief of the Imperial General Staff, and Seely, who told Gough he and his officers would be reinstated and should quietly return to their regiments. Gough demanded a written pledge that the army would not be used to coerce Ulster (surely an extraordinary request for an officer to place before his commanders). Worried by the state of the army, Seely and Ewart agreed to his request on the 23rd, drawing up a memorandum to that effect but which Gough rejected until, without cabinet approval, Seely agreed to Gough's commands: the army would not be used to crush political opposition to Home Rule. Gough's actions after the

21st are open to much doubt. He and his fellow officers had resigned as a result of a choice foolishly offered by Paget. His actions at meetings on the 22nd and 23rd, in pressing for a written pledge, are more difficult to explain. Perhaps it was a genuine concern for the state of the army. Yet equally plausible is the possibility that Gough was 'steeled' in his determination to squeeze a watertight guarantee from the government by the hothouse atmosphere he encountered when in London. And in this respect Tory leaders were an important ingredient in fostering crisis.

In London General Gough immediately made contact with Sir Henry Wilson who wasted little time in pointing out to him the political possibilities of the situation. Wilson was already in daily contact with Tory leaders. On 19 March he dined with Milner, Carson and Lovat, where he informed them of the orders to reinforce points around Belfast. The following evening (20th) Wilson learnt of the resignations from General John Gough, Hugh's brother, stationed at Aldershot, who had received telegrams that evening from the Curragh (in fact it was through John Gough that the news broke in London).[188] Early next morning Wilson briefed Tory leaders at Lansdowne House on the situation and was present at the War Office when Gough was interviewed on the 22nd.[189] That same day (22nd) Wilson spoke to Seely on the best way of restoring army unity: 'General Wilson had replied "the reinstatement of the dismissed officers and a declaration that the army would not be asked to coerce Ulster to submit to Home Rule"'.[190] Given his role up to this point and desire to extract from Seely a pledge not to use the army against Ulster, it seems clear that Wilson influenced Gough to push for the same type of pledge. Writing to Law on 26 March, Carson recounted that Gough 'refused to go until they got it in writing ... General Wilson at the W.O. kept whispering to them "get it in writing" ... at last Sir J. French and Col Seely drew up a declaration full of words and some flattery'.[191] And as if that was not enough, it was through Wilson and John Gough that the murmurings of sympathy-resignations began to spread to Aldershot (where John Gough was stationed), developments that placed Seely under even greater pressure. Sir Henry Wilson, a dedicated Unionist and in close, regular contact with leading Tories, was a key influence on events.

Gough's attitude was hardened on the 22nd and 23rd by his brother John, who was also in communication with certain well-placed Tories. On receiving news from his brother on the evening of the 20th, John Gough called at Lord Salisbury's house, where he informed Chamberlain of events.[192] The next day (the 21st) Chamberlain met John Gough, advising him to see Lord Roberts, another far from impartial source.[193] On the 22nd, Chamberlain was visited twice by Mrs Gough, Hugh's mother, and informed of the substance of the War Office meetings with her son,[194] though he probably knew what was occurring from Wilson. Here was another direct line to Hugh, along which the political benefits of squeezing from the government a declaration never to coerce Ulster could be channelled. Jalland has observed that 'the Curragh officers did not mutiny or refuse to obey orders. However, their own behaviour became questionable once they took advantage of the situation to demand pledges limiting the Government's policy'.[195] In the process by which he demanded such pledges, the influence of Tory leaders in suggesting, hinting and priming Gough was of great importance.

Whatever their precise role in the events of 17–23 March, the Tory leadership now sought to exploit them for political advantage. Though little more than a bungled affair to reinforce certain military installations, Tories portrayed the government, with some success, as carrying out an 'Ulster pogrom', with the purpose of placing Ulster under martial law and intent on arresting Carson, Craig and the other leaders of Ulster. Scenting their opportunity, Unionists prepared their attack. Fierce attacks in the Unionist press, especially from *The Morning Post*, *Daily Mail* and *The Times*, sapped government morale. The day before the house met, Law informed Asquith that 'I propose to ask you … that a statement can be made by the government upon the serious position which has arisen in the army and that this statement can at once be discussed'.[196] The next day in an electric Commons' atmosphere, Tories launched a bitter assault on ministers, and particularly Churchill who many believed, with some force, was the ringleader behind all the military and naval manoeuvrings following his Bradford outburst. The debate lasted several days and initially went very badly for the government. Instead of making a clear, frank statement of events at the start, Asquith tried to pass the episode off as a 'misunderstanding',[197] as did Seely, whose attempt to reassure the House that all was now well and the officers would be reinstated, fell flat. For most observers it looked like the government did have something to hide: 'what they are concealing we do not know, but we do know they are ashamed of it'.[198] Even Liberal backbenchers were angered at what seemed to be the government's overly dismissive response. Under sustained pressure from the opposition, Asquith was forced to publish a white paper two days later, contradicting much of what Seely had said and publicly repudiating the Minister of War's promise to Gough that the army would never be used in Ulster, what Balfour termed the 'peccant paragraphs'. Sir John French and Sir John Ewart, the Adjutant-General, resigned immediately, followed a few days later by Seely, developments that left the government visibly tottering. Dismay spread amongst Liberal backbenchers, not only at the chaos the government had got itself into but at, what for many, was their democratically-elected government's very public submission to the Unionist-infested Army. 'The radicals are furious at Asquith', noted a junior Tory whip.[199] By Friday 27 March the government appeared on the verge of collapse.

However, the Tories failed to press home their advantage. Ministers slowly regained their confidence, led by Churchill, who on 30 March delivered a tough exoneration of the government's position, flatly denying the existence of a plot and defending their right to restore law and order, through force if necessary.[200] The same day, Asquith declared that he would take over the War Office, a shrewd political move that restored the confidence of the army and the Liberal party. In addition, Tories came under mounting fire for their tampering with army loyalty, especially from Labour members John Ward and Will Crooks. Indeed, Law himself gave the government the opportunity to counter-attack on this line by inadvertently making 'a reference to the right of soldiers under certain circumstances to disobey, which was not approved by our side and gave the other side an opening'.[201] The speeches of Carson, Bonar Law and Smith now came back to haunt them: 'Winston certainly got hold of a number of quotations rather damaging to our side'.[202] Under such fire, Tories grew uneasy about their close connections with army officers, so dampening their attacks. The moral ascendancy they had won during the early debates now dissipated as suspicion rose as to the nature of relations some Tories had with the army. And as damaging, in electoral terms, the issue of tampering with army loyalty pushed Liberals and Labour members back into the informal political compact that had sustained the Progressive Alliance since 1903 and had proven so effective at the 1910 general elections.

Events at the Curragh did not, then, result in the fall of the government or bring about an election, as the Tory leadership had clearly hoped for during the week of 23–7 March. They did, however, have serious political consequences for both parties. The breach between the government and opposition was substantially widened, undermining any idea of a compromise, much to the satisfaction of Law and the Tory right. The Irish Nationalists became more intractable in their demand for all-Irish Home

Rule. For them the Curragh incident revealed government weakness and connivance between Tories and the army, both suggesting they could never get fair treatment at Westminster. This served Law's purpose well, for it made Asquith's ability to move the Nationalists to a reasonable compromise far more difficult. In addition, the Curragh episode rendered the army a doubtful tool to use in the coercion of Ulster into Home Rule. Taken together, it now seemed clear that Asquith not only lacked the means to forcefully place Ulster under a Dublin parliament but was severely limited in how far he could compromise by obdurate Nationalists. The one course of action left to him, so Law believed, was an election. In this respect, events of 17–27 March might have worked to Law's benefit, tightening the tactical straightjacket around the prime minister.

Events at the Curragh were also a great test for Carson and Ulster. Carson's reputation was enhanced. He left for Belfast on the 19th, in typically dramatic fashion ('I am off to Belfast ... I go to my people'),[203] against a backdrop of rumours concerning his imminent arrest. Once in Belfast he brought self-restraint to the Ulstermen, advancing his image as a strong leader in full control of the situation. Behind the scenes he was a lot less confident, for the position of the Ulstermen was precarious by early 1914. Since January they had suffered severe shortages of cash and arms. As a result Belfast was becoming increasingly nervous as the bill entered its last circuit and with the government delaying and manoeuvring for position. The League of British Covenanters was developed partly to assuage these deficiencies, channelling much-needed finance to the Ulstermen, rallying support and, if need be, augmenting the UVF with volunteers. It was this same nervousness for the future that persuaded the Central Committee of the UUC, which included Carson, to endorse General Richardson's and F.H. Crawford's plan for a huge shipment of arms into Belfast.[204] The Larne Gun-Running episode of the evening of 24/25 April 1914, like the Curragh incident, reinforced the Ulstermen's bargaining position. Anything short of a 'clean-cut' was now unacceptable, given they could realistically look to their own protection. Events at Larne were also well received by the Tory right. Although they rejected the whole idea of partition, clean-cut or not, by making Ulster less tractable, the right believed that compromise actually became less likely. All the party had to do was hold its nerve and await Asquith's surrender. On the other hand, encouraging sections of the Ulstermen and indeed public opinion in Ulster to be less tractable increased the pressure on those within Ulster Unionism, such as Carson, who eagerly desired a political solution and the avoidance of unconstitutional activity. Events at Curragh and Larne might actually have fostered greater tensions and divisions within the movement.[205]

LAW, LEADERSHIP AND THE POLITICS OF TORY REBELLION

Law greeted the New Year with a mixture of satisfaction and growing unease. Tactically, the situation was far from hopeless. His negotiations with Asquith had revealed that a real measure of exclusion was, at present, beyond the prime minister's grasp: permanent six-county exclusion was the absolute minimum concession to the Ulstermen, yet this was clearly something the prime minister was finding difficult to accept. Law also firmly believed that Asquith would never coerce Ulster under a Dublin parliament, an impression that was to strengthen over the coming months. Accordingly, Law's perception of the government was that they were 'hesitating between the dread of armed resistance and the fear of losing the Irish vote'.[206] If both conclusions were correct then there was, Law believed, a good and growing chance Asquith would opt for an election as the best way out of his difficulties. Against this optimism stood increased sectarian tensions in Ulster, as their day of reckoning loomed ever closer, which weakened their appeal in the eyes of public opinion and sapped the moral righteousness of their cause. There was also evidence of mounting unease on the Tory right and amongst Southern Unionists, fuelled by an innate mistrust that their leaders would 'sell out' and, more acutely, by a growing suspicion of the means by which Asquith was planning to extricate his government from the delicate political position it was in. It was the latter consideration, of what Asquith was likely to do, that weighed most heavily with Law during the first few weeks of 1914.

On 7 January 1914 Law wrote to Balfour outlining what he imagined to be Asquith's future course. 'What probably he has already made up his mind is to happen is that at the right time they will make public some proposals, such as those suggested to Carson, which they think will improve their position in G.B. by giving the impression that under such an arrangement Ulster will have no real grievance and then they will have an election'.[207] In other words, Law feared Asquith was intent on introducing a 'dummy' compromise offer, one he realised was unacceptable to Unionists and Ulstermen but sufficiently attractive to buy off public hostility and perhaps even go to the people over. Evidence for such a course of action came from a variety of sources. In addition to Birrell's speech at Bristol on 26 March (as mentioned earlier in the chapter) *The Times* editorial of 27 January noticed that 'the government are assiduously disseminating impressions which are intended to depict their own attitude in a singularly favourable light'.[208] Two days later, 'they hint, nod and whisper that they alone are righteous ... The way is being deftly prepared'.[209] If this was the direction the government were travelling in, then Law faced grave tactical difficulties. To accept such a compromise would risk alienating the Ulstermen. It would almost certainly split his party and, crucially, it would neutralise a central element of his strategy, namely an appeal to the people on the Home Rule bill. But to reject it, as he clearly had to, brought just as many problems. For rejection, however valid, would allow the Liberals to brand the Tories as extremist and so endanger their public standing, and thus would 'advertise [Asquith's] own reasonableness, and the bigotry of the Unionist party in general and Ulster in particular'.[210] Losing public support carried an additional danger. With the public behind him, Asquith, under cover of restoring law and order in the wake of an outbreak of (presumably engineered) sectarian violence, might have been tempted to exploit the circumstances by sending in troops to restore social order and crush the Ulster rebellion. This scenario was taken very seriously by Unionist leaders. On 14 January Carson received information from inside the household of a junior minister that the government were intent on 'procrastinating until the patience of the hooligan element in Belfast is exhausted and they begin to riot. This is the moment when troops ... will step in and crush the riot'.[211]

Law sought to meet these threats head on. In a tough speech at Bristol, he tried to expose the government's plans. He began by warning his audience in Bristol that 'the government ... are looking forward to the possibility of the seething passions of Ulster boiling over, of their doing something which will put them in the wrong and that then they may be able without alienating the sympathy of this country, to put them down by force'.[212] He then attacked the idea of a 'dummy' compromise scheme, which might improve the prime minister's tactical position but would still leave him facing civil war in Ulster, and with the Ulstermen supported by the Tory party.[213] The struggle now went beyond mere parliamentary tactics. 'We shall not be beaten in that kind of game for this reason that we shall play no game ... In my belief we are drifting rapidly to civil war which will shatter to its foundation the whole fabric of our National existence'.[214] And as if this was not dramatic and hard-hitting enough he issued a blunt warning, 'we must now assume that it is their [the government's] present intention to carry out their policy to the bitter end and on that assumption it becomes our duty ... by every means in our power to prevent them from committing what ... we believe would be a great crime'.[215]

Amery interpreted the speech as 'marching orders' for the party.[216] It certainly gave impetus to plans for a British Covenant. Willoughby de Broke thought it 'was the best, the very best you have ever made'.[217] At the same time it was a warning to moderates, like Chamberlain, who sought a compromise with the government. And any hopes that Asquith might have had of cooperation with the Tory leader were quickly dashed. In extreme rhetoric it sits alongside his 1912 Blenheim speech, as an assault on parliamentary government, though similarly justified on the constitutional grounds that an election should be held before any further progress was made. Importantly, the speech hardened the attitude of the more radical Liberals and Irish Nationalists against making concessions; after such dramatic and public threats, concession would appear like surrender to aggression. Thus Law's 'more strident note finds an echo' in Nationalist intransigence, which in turn lessened Asquith's room to manoeuvre the Nationalists towards a viable compromise package, let alone one which public opinion would regard as reasonable.[218]

And yet Law was not satisfied with tough speaking alone: after all he had been doing that since 1912, without any tangible success. Alongside his extreme words, he now came to believe that Asquith's clever tactics could be countered by amending the Army Annual Act. This was no impulsive scheme, as historians once thought, plucked from the pages of *The Observer*.[219] Indeed he had suggested such a course as far back as 26 July 1911 during the parliament bill struggle, in a letter to *The Times*.[220] His allusion in Bristol to 'every means in our power' indicated that he was thinking seriously of such ideas.[221] Having made inquiries with Finlay, Law formally advocated the idea to Lansdowne and Balfour on 30 January.[222] This decision certainly appears to have been a 'desperate throw',[223] and could easily have backfired, losing Tories public support while taking the heat off the government. But for Law these risks were outweighed by the opportunity the manoeuvre presented to thwart an election on Asquith's forthcoming (and what he believed to be 'dummy') compromise proposals. 'The government will have an election', he told Lansdowne:

> selected at their own time, after they have made in the most elaborate way the proposals for the protection of Ulster which were suggested

> to Carson. Such an election would seem to me to be as bad for us as anything could be under present circumstances, for I am afraid that a great many people would think that these proposals were so reasonable that Ulster would not be justified in resisting and that it would settle the Irish Question'.[224]

In place of an election on these terms, amending the Army Annual Act could facilitate a contest on far more favourable terms for Tories, namely whether Ulster could or should be coerced out of her British citizenship and under a Dublin parliament. It was a choice he put to Lansdowne between 'an election more or less forced by us on what we will try to represent as the plain issue; shall the army be used to coerce Ulster without the consent of the electors **or** on proposals for Home Rule which to moderate men will not appear unreasonable'.[225] More triumphantly he told Craik that 'here is a method which is strictly constitutional, for nothing is clearer than that the method in which the army is maintained has been adhered to for the express purpose of putting a check on the executive government and preventing it from using their army against the will of the people'.[226]

In private, then, Law pursued his plan of amending the Army Annual Act through January and February 1914. Yet his public position remained, as it had since September 1913, one of reasonableness and appearing open to any attempt at finding a solution: even in his recent Bristol speech he had expressed his willingness to search for a 'real' settlement to the crisis. Asquith's statement to the House on 10 February, to bring forward new suggestions, in raising the hopes of those who actively sought a compromise, forced him to respond in equally conciliatory tones. He reiterated his demand for an election and warned against inadequate compromise plans, while confirming exclusion was the best (only) way to avoid civil war. In fact so conciliatory was he that some thought he had concocted a secret deal with the prime minister.[227] Law was only too aware of the strength of feeling amongst many leaders, notably Chamberlain, Selborne, Smith, Lansdowne and Carson, to reach a settlement with the government. Pulled between compromisers and the Tory right, Law trod a difficult and dangerous path.

When Asquith finally introduced his scheme for Home Rule within Home Rule on 9 March, Law quickly saw that 'from his merely party point of view clever. He apparently has squared the Nationalists. He has a fair chance of dividing the Unionists'.[228] The dangers he had sensed back in the autumn were now clear and bright. Public opinion, wearied by two years of intense struggle would look with favour on it, and with displeasure on those who now stood in its way. The compromisers in the Tory party could also look on it with favour, as the first step towards a real settlement. The right would reject it outright, as perhaps would Carson and the Ulstermen. And it threatened the basis of his entire strategy of the last three years. The dilemma Law faced was the same as in the autumn – how to defeat a compromise offer while preserving a public face of reasonableness. With the spotlight now squarely upon him, Law replied in very measured terms to Asquith. He sensibly avoided rejecting the proposal completely and was careful to stress that he did not rule out (indeed he favoured) exclusion, thanking Asquith rather mischievously for finally accepting the principle of exclusion. But alongside this reasonableness, he attacked the plan on the basis of its six-year time limit and demanded Asquith flesh out the details of his plan. This he hoped would reveal the hollowness of Asquith's proposals and perhaps undermine the lustre they might have held for any moderate Tories. Asquith refused to be drawn on the details, enabling Law to depict him as unreasonable and insincere in his attempt to reach a settlement. To advertise this, Law called for a censure motion for 19 March and challenged Asquith to put the whole question of Ulster's exclusion to a referendum, declaring his willingness to stand by the verdict of the people. Asquith again refused, again to the benefit of Law. These were shrewd counter-attacks by the Tory leader, preserving public sympathy and party unity, yet blocking the advance of concessions. His speech, though overshadowed by Carson's dramatic oration, certainly helped focus public opinion back onto the basic Tory demand that an appeal to the people was the best path out of the crisis.

Law's demand for a referendum had the additional benefit of laying the groundwork for a future amendment to the Army Annual Act: it was, after designed to provoke just such an appeal to the people. Law had remained fully committed to the manoeuvre through February and into March. By the time of the shadow cabinet meeting of 12 March, a sharp movement of opinion away from the scheme was now more apparent.[229] And two days later his good friend Craik reported 'the rumours are creating disquietude amongst many and I confess I share it … Mutiny and rebellion may at times be justified … but if we begin to impose limitations on discipline by law where are we to end.'[230] Law recognised the mounting resistance and altered his position accordingly, telling Croal a few days later that 'there is a sufficient amount of that feeling at the present to make it impossible to do it'.[231] By the time the Curragh incident rendered the plan obsolete, the force of party opinion had convinced Law against any interference with the Army Act.

The Curragh incident brought many advantages for Law. It removed the possibility of the army coercing Ulster into the bill and without this the government had no means of implementing Home Rule in the north. The episode made for good propaganda, undermining Asquith's hope of appearing reasonable to the public: a government which talked of compromise but plotted coercion. But the Curragh episode also brought serious problems. Would events backfire against the Tory party? Would public opinion be alienated by Liberal claims that Tories were meddling with the army? The incident also removed the means for provoking an immediate election on a favourable basis. And perhaps more seriously, in denying Asquith the ability to fall back on coercion, politics were brought back to where they had stood at the start of March, namely with compromise high on the political agenda. Scenting a panic-stricken government, Tory moderates and federalists began to organise. Carson's conciliatory tones suggested he was keen for a way out, if only Asquith would take the leap towards Home Rule All Round. And Law forecast that despite the current atmosphere, fresh compromise initiatives were in the air and that 'some further offer will be made and very likely the exclusion of the six counties'.[232]

The efforts of those seeking a settlement crystallised in the meeting between Asquith, Law and Carson on the 5th of May. Little chance of a settlement on exclusion existed. Both the Ulstermen and Nationalists were becoming more rather than less intransigent. After the Curragh and the Larne Gun-running, Ulster felt that she could stand out for her maximum demands (the permanent exclusion of at least six counties). The Nationalists, with the bill about to pass the Commons for the last time on 25 May 1914, believed they could hold out for the whole bill, and avoid any type of 'amputation' and the creation of, what Redmond called a separate 'Orange Free State'.[233] For Law the implications were clear: 'we said also to Mr Asquith is not the position really this. That you have only three possible alternatives, first to coerce Ulster, second to exclude Ulster and third to have a general election'.[234] If the first option was now impossible and the second almost as unlikely (remembering Law told Hugh Montgomery the same day of the meeting, 'it does not seem to be probable that the Nationalists can be brought to agree to the real exclusion of Ulster; and if they do not then there can be no question of compromise'),[235] then only the latter option loomed large. Law's major problem in the closing months of the struggle was not what Asquith was up to but how he was going to keep his party's nerve and hold them together.

Holding the party together proved extremely difficult as the bill reached the end of its journey in the Commons, by May 1914, (according to the Parliament Act the bill would again go up to the Lords where, if rejected for a third time, it would be automatically presented to the king for royal assent). These difficulties were enflamed by Asquith, who confirmed at the meeting on 5 May that he would continue with the Home Rule Bill and then introduce a separate amending bill in the Lords, enshrining some form of separate treatment for Ulster, presumably along the lines of his 9 March proposals. Both bills would then be presented at the same time for royal assent. This plan he subsequently announced to the Commons on 12 May, though he failed to elaborate on the details of his amending bill when pressed by Law. It was a subtle last effort by Asquith to place the Tories in a precarious position: by incorporating the compromise measures into a separate amending bill, Asquith threw onto the Lords the burden of rejecting his compromise proposals. The scheme had definite echoes of earlier struggles in the Lords.

Southern Unionist and die-hard forces feared their leadership would accept the compromise if it satisfied Ulster, allowing the other three provinces to 'go to the wolves'. Accordingly, they began to organise the Lords to reject the amending bill, irrespective of the line taken by the Tory leadership in the Lords. Such independent activity (and suspicion for their own leaders) had already surfaced back in February when Lords Willoughby de Broke, Arran, Stanhope and Ampthill moved a separate amendment to the address. By May things had moved on a great deal. A Committee of Peers 'connected with the three provinces outside Ulster',[236] was established by Midleton and Lord Barrymore. The committee passed a resolution in the Lords declaring the amending bill could only be accepted if it included a clause for an immediate election.[237] Midleton assured Law 'that the view expressed herein is supported by a strong mass of opinion' and that 'we are in danger of a serious split in the party, if by any manoeuvring we shall find ourselves forced to support the amending bill without the promise of a G.E.'.[238] He also on behalf of the committee, published their resolutions in the press on 25 May.[239] Midleton's canvassing of peers converged with other right-wing attacks. Amery criticised the idea of helping the government out of their hole,[240] while Gwynne of *The*

Morning Post rallied opinion against any compromise or clever tactics over the amending bill.[241]

During the course of May, Midleton's Southern Unionist group in the Upper House came to overlap with Willoughby de Broke's knot of extreme right-wing Peers. Together, they sought to reject the government's compromise offer, regardless of what it offered, and to take their stand upon the necessity of an election. Willoughby de Broke urged Lansdowne to give a lead to this line; 'we do not think it right to agree to repeal of the Union in any shape or form or to the promotion in Parliament of any new scheme which has not been submitted to the electorate'.[242] Events bore an eerie similarity to those of 1911, with the wild men trying to stiffen the Lords against a sell-out and against the official leadership. Lansdowne certainly interpreted events in this light, 'he (Midleton) and others have been actively organising a "die-hard" movement which might become formidable'.[243]

Law regarded these developments as a threat to his line of public moderation and private resistance. For the die-hard scheme of rejecting the amending Bill simply played into Asquith's hands, enabling him to blame the Lords for the slide into civil war and 'turn the election cry against the Lords: "Lords have forced civil war" … it would pay in some constituencies and might seriously injure our majority'.[244] It would destroy the party's image of reasonableness, undermining public sympathy and consequently their ability to win an election. And such a manoeuvre was all the more pointless, since Law was convinced after 5 May, Asquith could never agree to 'real' exclusion. His amending Bill would not be a settlement but a decoy, designed to provoke rejection. 'The House of Lords must not fall into the trap and enable the coalition to say they have killed conciliation'.[245] Nor would inserting a demand for a general election help much, since Asquith could represent it as a wrecking tactic not a solution, given the Ulstermen would not stand by the result. The die-hard revival of May/June 1914 placed Law's entire strategy of previous two years in jeopardy. Worse still, his ability to control events had diminished after 25 May since Home Rule had finally passed the Commons. This left him reliant upon Lansdowne's ability to control the upper house, a far from comforting thought if recent history was any indication.

Lansdowne agreed with Law's assessment of the situation. 'Midleton and co fail to see that we desire not only to have a general election but to win it and that we shall probably lose it if we allow Asquith and his friends to out-manoeuvre us'.[246] Both saw the need to play a waiting game, to see what Asquith's amending bill had to offer, then act accordingly. The danger inherent in this line was that it suggested passivity for the re-grouping die-hards and thus encouraged them, as in 1911, to redouble their efforts. Lansdowne had to work hard behind the scenes to extend and impose his authority in the Lords. In this he was fortunate to have royal support behind him. The possibility of the Lords rejecting the amending bill filled the king with horror, confronting him with the awful choice between giving his assent to a bill he knew would provoke civil war or vetoing it and provoking a constitutional crisis that would see a 'people versus king' cry from the government at the subsequent election. Through Stamfordham, the king pressed for the amending bill not to be rejected.[247] In an audience with the king at the end of May, Lord Salisbury learnt of His Majesty's anxieties: 'It was he said everyone's duty to do their utmost to prevent civil war. Moreover it would help him very much – "it will save me"'.[248] Protecting the king was an effective plea with which Lansdowne could rally the Lords against rejection. It also would keep the king on their side for any future eventuality, as Salisbury clearly implied in his letter. Oddly, given his work with the British Covenant, Milner seems to have concurred in this argument, writing to Willoughby de Broke on 3 June: 'what to do on the amending bill and on which both bills depends the possibility of our being able to ultimately appeal to [the King] with effect. Tactics are very important at this juncture'.[249] In addition to exploiting royal pressure, Lansdowne sought to galvanise more general support amongst the peers. He contacted Salisbury, a prime mover in the 1911 episode, to draw him closer and to 'rope in Milner ... he may not know much about procedure but his mind is acute and the more we can associate him with ourselves the better'.[250] Milner had been another force behind the 1911 crisis; drawing his sting early on was vital. Lansdowne also moved to bring Curzon, Balcarres, Derby and Devonshire behind him: leaders with great influence in the Lords. They all met at Curzon's house on 8 June and again on 11 June to talk tactics.[251]

Overall, the leadership's position in 1914 remained far stronger than in 1911. They were not hopelessly split, and in the Commons they had the active support of the main spokesmen. But all was not well within the party; the last few weeks before the amending bill was presented to the Lords on 23 June saw intense manoeuvring. As in 1911, the main difference was tactical. Law and Lansdowne argued that they should wait to see what was offered on the 23rd before deciding their course of action, especially since they expected it to fall far short of anything they or Ulster could agree. If this transpired (which it did), it was tactically better to amend the amending bill to one Ulster might accept, in other words to nine-county permanent exclusion. This course would prevent Asquith from branding the Lords' action as extreme and an incitement to civil war. Yet such an amendment would never be accepted by the Nationalists, when the Bill arrived back in the Commons for re-consideration. 'If you stick to "Ulster as a whole and no time limit" I think we are safe as I feel sure that Asquith will never consent to this *or rather he won't be let*'.[252] In addition, the onus for rejection would be thrown back upon the government. These were essentially the same tactics that Law had used during his secret meetings with Asquith: to outbid him on terms which he could never accept, but which would preserve the Tory image of reasonableness. If, on the other hand, Asquith did the unthinkable and satisfied Ulster, then they would have had little choice but to accept it in any case:

> I have no doubt that a general election would result in our favour; but so far as I can judge the alteration in public opinion has been brought about simply by the position of Ulster and if we ... were to take an attitude which the country thought unreasonable on that question then I am by no means sure that the result of an election might not be quite different.[253]

Alternatively, the die-hards viewed tinkering with definitions of exclusions as playing with fire; Asquith and Redmond might very well agree to the revisions the Lords made, so allowing the south and west of Ireland to leave the Union. Unionists in the country would lose heart at the Lords' amending rather than rejecting a compromise package at this stage. Thus the only straightforward and clear-cut approach was to insist upon an election. It was a small but vital gulf between two wings of the party. Long, a known supporter of Southern Unionism, worked hard to convince them of the safety and sense of the line taken by the leadership. On 29 May he wrote to Midleton, pleading with him not to split the party,[254] and again on 10 June: 'In this matter I think the principle of our policy is perfectly plain and that there is no difference of opinion about it amongst us'.[255] With a similar intention of bridging the differences in the party, Lansdowne called a meeting of leaders in the Upper House to thrash out their differences, although no record survives of how successful this proved.

When, therefore, the amending bill was finally introduced on 23 June, Asquith had not moved beyond his 9 March position, confirming all Law's assumptions about the constraints upon him. For the die-hards, their fears proved unfounded; Asquith, after all, was restricted by the Nationalists. At a shadow cabinet meeting the next day, the Tory leadership agreed to read the amending bill a second time and then to amend it on third reading to nine-country permanent exclusion, a line which still provoked dissension from Midleton.[256] Southern Unionists remained alarmed and Carson, in particular, was bitterly attacked for agreeing to the plan. Midleton and Barrymore sent Law a memorandum critical of the decision and published in the press a resolution by their Committee of Peers which demanded that the Amending Bill be rejected.[257]

Lansdowne's authority, however, held, and on 14 July 1914 the amending bill was duly altered to nine-county, permanent exclusion, and sent back to the Commons for consideration. There was little chance of the new terms being accepted by the Nationalists, or by many on the Liberal backbenches. Asquith's only real chance was to patch an agreement on the amending bill before the Commons debated it on 20 July. He, therefore, accepted a royal invitation to convene a conference of party leaders at Buckingham Palace on 21 July. But there was no basis for agreement. All sides had drifted further apart since March. The Ulstermen felt that they could hold out for all nine counties; Redmond would not accept permanent exclusion, and probably would have faced difficulties (especially from Devlin who sat for West Belfast) if he agreed to anything above four counties for a temporary period. It was not simply a difference of the 'muddy highways and by-ways of Tyrone and Fermanagh',[258] as Churchill memorably described it; there were unbridgeable gulfs between both Irish parties. If Asquith could not secure a compromise, without the ability to coerce Ulster and without Unionist support for the imposition of a settlement onto Ireland (as Churchill had suggested on 22 July) he had little else to fall back on, so the Tory leadership imagined, but a general election.

CONCLUSION

It was at this point that the Irish issue which had dominated the minds and tactics of politicians since January 1914, and in many cases since 1911, was eclipsed by the outbreak of World War. On hearing rumours of war in Europe, Law and Carson contacted Asquith on 31 July offering to suspend the 'cut and thrust' of party politics as a pre-requisite for Britain moving quickly to support France. Asquith agreed and with surprisingly little

Cabinet dissension entered the war on 4 August 1914. Unfortunately for Law and Carson, Asquith appreciating the opportunity which the party truce gave him proceeded with the Home Rule bill into law, along with the exclusion amendment as revised by the Lords on 14 July, and with the proviso that all would be suspended for the duration of the war. Unionists reacted with anger at the apparent duplicity of Asquith but in the face of Britain's imminent entry into the war their protest was limited. A few stormy meetings with Asquith and a silent mass exodus from the Commons chamber on 15 September, after yet another powerful speech from Law, was all the party could offer. Thus in the sense of blocking Home Rule for Ireland the Unionists had clearly failed; Home Rule had reached the statute books, albeit suspended for the duration.

But Law's struggle had never been to defeat the bill but rather to force a general election and but for the war (and this was something very few could have predicted) there are grounds for crediting Law's tactics with some degree of success. If we hypothesize that war did not come in August (and clearly Law's tactics made no contingency for this development) several interesting scenarios suggest themselves. Precisely when and how Asquith would have dissolved is unclear. He still needed the king's assent, which would be by no means automatic, especially if he did not simultaneously submit the amending bill. There was a strong possibility that the king might have insisted on a dissolution before he put his signature to the bill, particularly as he was coming under increased pressure from Unionist sympathisers to do so. Asquith might have gone to the country on his original amending bill of 23 June, though little advantage can be seen in this course. He might even, supposing the king gave his assent, have carried on with Home Rule without the amended bill, allowing Ulster to set up its provisional government and hoping it would, in time, collapse. But to fight the election due by 1915 at the latest, having allowed a provisional government to establish itself within the British Isles, would have alienated many Liberal supporters from such an act of irresolute leadership and given the Tories an electoral advantage, contrasting the state of harmony and prosperity in Ireland in 1906 compared to the present. It also presupposed that he could keep the South in order and prevent conflict between Ulster Volunteers and National Volunteers. Perhaps the most likely course would have been to carry the bill onto the statute books, and then to dissolve immediately on a platform of removing the Irish Question from British politics. Yet the Tories would still have campaigned hard on the issue that Ulster should not be coerced, and they had probably done enough by that stage to remove the Liberals from government. From any point of view, by July 1914 the Liberal Government was in a hopeless position.[259]

Hypotheticals aside, events between 1911–14 shed much light upon the Tory party and Tory politics generally, as well as upon the leadership and reputation of Bonar Law. For the Tory party their resistance to the Liberal Home Rule bill reached an unusually high level of extremism, unusual, that is, for a party so closely identified with maintenance of the constitution. Nor was it extremism on the margins of the party but mainstream to many of its members at Westminster and to sections of the leadership. Much of this extremism was rooted in a deepening anxiety amongst Tories for the survival of British society and empire (or at least their vision of both) in a period of acute economic, social and imperial pressure and stress. Such anxiety was heightened by the intensifying political struggle over the constitution, which had begun in 1906 as the Tory party under Balfour and Lansdowne tried to 'check' the massive Liberal majority in the Commons by exploiting the veto powers of the Lords. The issue of Home Rule, coming as it did at the end of a series of conflicts over the constitution, as with the Budget in 1909 and the Lord's veto between 1910–11, served to bring into sharp focus (and indeed to heighten) the constitutional struggle between the two parties. Thus by 1912, both Tories and Liberals were operating in politics along different and conflicting understandings of the constitution. For Liberals and the Labour party the growing (but far from complete) assumptions and convictions of democracy were moving them steadily towards a vision of the British constitution in which the will of the Commons (as the Peoples' chamber) should not be frustrated, and the government's decisions (as the chosen leaders of the peoples' assembly) had to be carried out. On the other hand the Tory party clung to the ideal (and largely fictitious belief) in a balanced constitution, where no one part of the constitution could wield unlimited power, and where institutional mechanisms were vital to restrain a strong government, and especially to prevent that government altering the constitution itself. With no set body of constitutional 'rules' to guide the politicians[260] and in the tense atmosphere of 1912–14, such conflicting perceptions of the constitution made for a potentially explosive situation. In this sense the analogy with the seventeenth century is not far fetched, for the main political actors were similarly operating according to different perceptions of the constitution, with the result, by 1642, that civil war broke out.

Given this variety of dangers and pressures, the surprise was not that sections of the Unionist coalition were so extreme but rather that it managed to avoid any serious split or division. Such unity was all the more remarkable if it is remembered that after the creation of one-chamber rule in 1911, with the abolition of the Lords veto, the Liberals introduced, in addition to Home Rule, bills to disestablish the Welsh Church, abolish plural voting and pay MPs; all changes to the constitution which, if passed, would have done so without being first put to the British electorate. That the Tory party survived these challenges owes a great deal to Law. Thus, whether championing extremism was wise leadership or not, or even was the best course or not for constitutional government, it undoubtedly maintained the unity of the Conservative party in a way that Balfour's leadership surely would never have done, if he had remained leader after 1911. Thus before the Great War could return the Tory party to what they believed to be their natural role as the party of government, from 1915, Law insured the party survived the most testing period in its history. In addition we must be careful with terms like 'extremism'. For Law and many others regarded their actions as rooted in a clear-cut reading of the constitution, that the government were abusing the 'constituent' powers, which every British government clearly had. In the circumstances demanding an election or even a referendum on the question, before proceeding with the legislation, was perhaps not as unreasonable as has been seen. Similarly historians have been slow to question the efficacy or even the constitutionality of Asquith undertaking so many changes to the constitution in so short a time and in a political atmosphere, after 1911, so dangerously charged. Of course, before we begin to imagine Law as a dedicated and close student of constitutional practice, we must not lose sight of the fact that over Home Rule, and the Ulster question in particular, constitutional theory and party political tactics neatly combined. It was this combination which allowed him to go to any length to achieve an election and to believe that his party could then win it.

While the struggle over Home Rule had clearly been good for Law's standing in the party (as it had been for Carson), the consequences of the bitter struggle in Ireland were less advantageous. Ulster Unionists were armed, organised and prepared to assume political control of their region (however they defined that region). They had split from southern Unionists, a vein of Unionism that perhaps had worked to soften previous Ulster militancy and had kept an all-Ireland vision alive. With their rupture, and with the stengthening of Ulster, so the partition of Ireland increasingly became a reality. Moreover, in organising themselves against Home Rule and exposing British governmental weakness, they encouraged Nationalists to emulate their example. If Ireland's freedom was now to be won (or even the promised Home Rule bill guaranteed to pass into Law), guns were revealed to be a far safer option than the word of British Liberal politicians. 'The Orangeman who can fire a gun', Patrick Pearse wrote in 1913, 'will certainly count for more in the end than the Nationalist who can do nothing cleverer than make a pun'.[261] The seeds to events in Ireland over the following decade were clearly planted in the pre-war period.

References

NOTES TO INTRODUCTION

1. I. Gilmour, *Inside Right: A Study of Conservatism* (London, 1977), pp. 32–3.
2. R. Blake, *The Unknown Prime Minister: The Life and Times of Andrew Bonar Law 1858–1923* (London, 1955), chs 7–13; also *The Conservative Party from Peel to Churchill* (London, 1970); J. Ramsden, *The Age of Balfour and Baldwin 1902–1940* (London, 1978), pp. 77–86; D. Dutton, *His Majesty's Loyal Opposition: The Unionist party in Opposition 1905–1915* (Liverpool, 1992), ch. 9; D.G. Boyce, 'British Conservative Opinion, the Ulster Question and the Partition of Ireland 1912–1921', *Irish Historical Studies (IHS)*, xvii (1970).
3. B. Coleman, *Conservatism and the Conservative Party in Nineteenth Century Britain* (London, 1988), pp. 3–8.
4. M. Pugh, *The Making of Modern British Politics 1867–1939* (London, 1982).
5. J. Ramsden, *The Age of* ..., pp. 65–8 and 77–86.
6. Ibid., p. 67.
7. Blake, *The Unknown* ..., R. Blake, *A History of the Conservative Party from Peel to Churchill* (London, 1970); J. Ramsden, *The Age of Balfour* ...; J.D. Fair, *British Inter-party Conferences: A Study of the Procedure of Conciliation in British Politics, 1867–1921* (Oxford, 1980), ch. V.
8. B. Coleman, *Conservatism and the Conservative Party in the Nineteenth Century* (London, 1988).
9. C.C. Weston, 'Salisbury and the Lords, 1868–1895', *Historical Journal (HJ)*, XXV (1982), p. 106; P. Marsh, *The Discipline of Popular Government: Lord Salisbury's Domestic Statecraft, 1881–1902* (London, 1978), pp. 35–47; J. Ridley, 'The Unionist Opposition and the House of Lords', *Parliamentary History*, 11, pt 2 (1992), pp. 235–53; B. Lenman, *The Eclipse of Parliament: Appearance and Reality in British Politics Since 1914* (London, 1992).
10. J.D. Fair, *British Interparty Conferences: A study of the Procedure of Conciliation in British Politics, 1867–1921* (Oxford, 1980), p. 104.
11. A uni-cameral assembly has one chamber whereas a bi-cameral one has two chambers.
12. P. Norton, *The British Polity* (London, 1994); B. Lenman, *The Eclipse of Parliament* ..., intro.
13. Blake, *The Unknown* ..., p. 531.

14. A.T.Q. Stewart, *The Ulster Crisis: Resistance to Home Rule 1912–1914* (London,1969); A. Jackson, *The Ulster Party: Irish Unionists in the House of Commons, 1884–1911* (Oxford, 1988); P. Bew, *Ideology and the Irish Question: Ulster Unionism and Irish Nationalism 1912–1916* (Oxford, 1994).
15. P. Buckland, 'The Southern Irish Unionists, the Irish Question and British Politics 1906–1914', *IHS*, 15 (1967); also *Irish Unionism: The Anglo-Irish and the New Ireland 1885–1922* (Dublin, 1972); *Irish Unionism: Ulster Unionism and the Origins of Northern Ireland 1885–1922* (Dublin 1973).
16. G. Phillips, *The Diehards* (Harvard, 1979); G. Phillips, 'Lord Willoughby de Broke and the Politics of Radical Toryism, 1909–1914', *Journal of British Studies*, 20 (1980), 203–24; A. Sykes, 'The Radical Right and the Crisis of Conservatism before the First World War', *HJ*, 26 (1983), 661–76.
17. D.G. Boyce and J.O. Stubbs, 'F.S. Oliver, Lord Selborne and Federalism', *Journal of Imperial and Commonwealth History*, 5, 1 (1976), 53–81; P. Jalland, 'United Kingdom Devolution, 1910–14: Political Panacea or Tactical Diversion', *English Historical Review*, 94, 373 (1979), 757–85; J.E. Kendle, *Ireland and the Federal Solution: The Debate over the United Kingdom Constitution, 1870–1921* (Toronto, 1989).
18. G. Stedman-Jones, *'Re-Thinking Chartism' in Languages of Class* (Cambridge, 1983); J. Vernon, *Politics and the People* (Cambridge, 1993); J. Vernon, 'Who's afraid of the Linguistic Turn?', *Social History*, 19, 1 (1994); J. Vernon, *Re-Reading the Constitution* (Cambridge, 1996); D. Wahrman, *Imagining the Middle Class* (Cambridge, 1995).
19. Sir J. Ervine, *Sir Edward Carson and the Ulster Movement* (London, 1915), p. 47.
20. A. Jackson, 'Unionist Myths 1912–1985', *Past and Present*, no 138 (1992), pp. 164–80: M. Foy, 'The Ulster Volunteer Force: Its Domestic Development and Political Impact in the period 1913–20' (PhD thesis, Queen's University, Belfast, 1986).
21. A. Jackson, *Sir Edward Carson*, Historical Association of Ireland (1993); A. Gailey, 'King Carson: an Essay on the invention of Leadership', *IHS*, XXX, 117 (1996), 66–87.
22. A. Sykes, *Tariff Reform in British Politics 1903–1913* (Oxford, 1979); A. Sykes 'The Radical Right and the Crisis of Conservatism before the First World War', *HJ*, 28 (1983); G. Searle, 'The Revolt from the Right in Edwardian Britain', in P. Kennedy and A. Nichols (eds), *Nationalist and Racialist Movements in Britain and Germany before 1914* (London, 1981); F. Coetzee, *For Party and Country: Nationalism and the Dilemmas of Popular Conservatism in Edwardian England* (Oxford, 1990); M. Fforde, *Conservatism and Collectivism 1880–1914* (Edinburgh, 1991); D. Dutton, *His Majesty's Loyal Opposition* (Liverpool, 1992); E.H.H. Green, 'Radical Conservatism: the Electoral Genesis of Tariff Reform', *HJ*, 28 (1985); E.H.H. Green, 'The Strange Death of Tory England', *Twentieth Century British History*, 2 (1991); E.H.H. Green, *The Crisis of Conservatism: The politics, economics and ideology of the British Conservative party, 1880–1914* (Routledge, 1995).

23. E.H.H. Green, *The Crisis of Conservatism.*
24. Earl of Birkenhead, *F.E.: F.E. Smith First Earl of Birkenhead* (London, 1959), p. 156.
25. A. Sykes' three-way division is both instructive and relevant, in 'The Radical Right and the Crisis of Conservatism before the First World War', *HJ*, 26, 3 (1983); P. Norton and A. Aughey make a similar if larger 'ideological' division, in *Conservatives and Conservatism* (London, 1981) pp. 53–89.
26. D. Brett, *The Construction of Heritage* (Cork, 1996), p. 5.
27. A.J. Beattie, 'High Political History in the Twentieth Century', unpublished paper presented to the Institute of Historical Research, April 1992.
28. M. Cowling, *1867: Disraeli, Gladstone and Revolution: The passing of the Second Reform Bill* (London, 1967); *The Impact of Labour 1920–1924: the Beginnings of Modern British Politics* (London, 1971); *The Impact of Hitler: British Politics and British Policies 1933–1940* (London, 1975).
29. T. Guinnane, *The Vanishing Irish: Households, Migration, and the Rural Economy in Ireland, 1850–1914* (New Jersey, 1997).
30. P. Marsh, *The Discipline of Popular Government: Lord Salisbury's domestic statecraft 1881–1902* (London, 1978).
31. A. Jackson, *The Ulster Party: Irish Unionists in the House of Commons, 1884–1911* (Clarendon Press, 1989).
32. Ibid.
33. Ibid., pp. 22–52.
34. A. O'Day, *Irish Home Rule, 1867–1921* (Manchester, 1998), p. 100.
35. R.F. Foster, 'To the Northern Station: Lord Randolph Churchill and the prelude to the Orange Card', in F.S.L. Lyons and R.A.J. Hawkins (eds), *Ireland Under the Union: Varieties of Tension* (Oxford, 1980).
36. P. Buckland, 'The Southern Irish Unionists …'.
37. A. Gaily, *Ireland and the Death of Kindness: The Experience of Constructive Unionism 1890–1905* (Cork, 1986).
38. A. Gailey, 'The making of a New Unionism', in D.G. Boyce (ed.), *The Revolution in Ireland 1879–1923* (London, 1988).
39. G. Wyndham was Irish Chief Secretary from 1900 to 1905.
40. A. Gaily, *Ireland and the Death of Kindness: The Experience of Constructive Unionism 1890–1905* (Cork, 1986).
41. Jackson, *The Ulster Party* ..., p. 115.
42. P. Bull, 'The Significance of the Nationalist response to the Irish Land Act of 1903', *IHS*, XXVIII (1993), pp. 283–305.
43. J. Kendle, *Ireland and the Federal Solution: The Debate over the United Kingdom Constitution 1870–1921* (Toronto, 1989) chs 3 and 4.
44. A. Gailey, *Ireland and the Death* ..., pt 2; Jackson, *The Ulster Party* ..., ch. 6; F.S.L. Lyons, 'The Irish Unionist Party and the Devolution Crisis of 1904–1905', *IHS*, vi, 21 (March 1948).
45. J. Kendle, *Walter Long and Ireland* (Toronto, 1992).
46. Jackson, *The Ulster Party* …, pp. 235–40.

NOTES TO CHAPTER 1

1. R. McNeill, *Ulster's Stand for Union* (London, 1922), p. 19.
2. R. Scally, *The Origins of the Lloyd George Coalition: The Politics of Social Imperialism, 1900–1918* (Princeton, 1975), pp. 172–210.
3. N. Blewett, *The Peers, the Parties and the People: The General Elections of 1910* (Oxford, 1972).
4. J. Kendle, *Ireland and the Federal Solution: The debate over the United Kingdom Constitution, 1870–1921* (Toronto, 1989).
5. P. Jalland, 'United Kingdom Devolution, 1910–1914: Political Panacea or Tactical Diversion?', *English Historical Review*, 94, 373 (1979), 757–85.
6. J.E. Kendle, 'The Round Table movement and Home Rule all Round', *Historical Journal*, 11, 2 (1968).
7. Ibid., Garvin to Sandars, 14 Feb. 1910 (69–77); 9 April (80–1); 21 April (82–3).
8. J. Kendle, *Ireland and the Federal ...*, p. 118.
9. Bodleian Library (Bod.L.), Lord Milner Papers, Ms Dep 36, Milner to Balfour, 17 April 1910 (240–1).
10. The Second Earl of Birkenhead, *F.E., The Life of F.E. Smith, First Earl of Birkenhead* (London, 1959), p. 156.
11. B.B. Gilbert, *David Lloyd George: A Political Life: The Architect of Change, 1863–1912* (London, 1987) pp. 412–24.
12. R. Scally, *Origins of the Lloyd George Coalition ...*, p. 202.
13. T.M. Healy, *Letters and Leaders of My Day* (London, 1928). Healy refers to a conversation with Moreton Frewen, a friend of Balfour's, that 'Balfour will join Asquith with his forces if Redmond makes trouble', 5 Nov. 1910, p. 502.
14. B.B. Gilbert, *David Lloyd George ...*, p. 422.
15. D. Lloyd George, *War Memoirs* (London, 1934) p. 36.
16. M.V. Brett (ed.), *The Journals and Letters of Reginald Viscount Esher*, vol. 3 (London, 1934), p. 148.
17. A.M. Gollin, *The Observer and J.L. Garvin, 1908–1914: A Study in Great Editorship* (London, 1960), p. 209.
18. *The Times*, 20 Oct.–4 Nov. 1910.
19. *The Morning Post*, 17 Oct. 1910.
20. Bod.L., Sandars Papers, Mss Eng Hist C.761, Smith to Balfour, 30 Oct. 1910 (290–5).
21. A.M. Gollin, *The Observer and J.L. Garvin ...*, p. 229.
22. A. Chamberlain, *Politics from ...*, p. 286.
23. B.L., Balfour Papers, Add Mss 49767, Sandars to Short, 31 Oct. 1910 (19–20).
24. Ibid.
25. Birmingham University Library (B.U.L.), Austen Chamberlain Papers, AC/10/2/4, Lyttleton to Balfour, 16 Oct. 1910.
26. Ibid.
27. B.L., Balfour Papers, Add Mss 49767, Sandars to Balfour, 18 Oct. 1910 (7–10): also 24 Oct. 1910 (13–17).
28. Ibid.

29. B.U.L., Chamberlain Papers, AC 10/2/4, Balfour to Lyttleton, 20 Oct. 1910.
30. A. Chamberlain, *Politics From the Inside, An Epistolary Chronicle, 1906–1914* (London, 1936), p. 288.
31. *The Morning Post*, 18 Oct. 1910; Lloyd George City Temple speech.
32. B.U.P., Chamberlain Papers, AC 10/2/18, Garvin to Chamberlain, 20 Oct. 1910; and AC 10/2/19 22 Oct. 1910.
33. Second Earl of Birkenhead, *F.E. The Life of* ... pp. 156–7.
34. A. Chamberlain, *Politics from* ..., p. 281.
35. Bod.L., Sandars Papers, Mss Eng Hist C.761, Chamberlain to Balfour, 25 Oct. 1910 (259–62).
36. A.M. Gollin, *The Oberver and J.L. Garvin* ..., p. 229.
37. Ibid., p. 231.
38. *The Morning Post*, 20 Oct. 1910: McNeill letter.
39. *The Times*, 22 Oct. 1910: UUC resolution.
40. J. Vincent (ed.), T*he Crawford Papers: The Journals of David Lindsay, Twenty-seventh Earl of Crawford and Tenth Earl of Balcarres, 1871–1940* (Manchester, 1984), p. 166.
41. A.M. Gollin, *The Observer and J.L. Garvin* ..., p. 231.
42. Ibid.
43. A. Chamberlain, *Politics from* ..., p. 289.
44. B.B. Gilbert, *David Lloyd George* ..., pp. 424–30: Gilbert denies this and imparts rather noble intentions to Lloyd George, particularly his desire to see National Insurance enacted.
45. Bod.L., Sandars Papers, Mss Eng Hist C.761, Gwynne to Balfour, 28 Oct. 1910 (275–8).
46. Bod.L., Milner Papers, Dep 9, vol. I, Johnston to Milner, 17 Nov. 1911 (1–4).
47. House of Lords Record Office (HLRO), Bonar Law Papers, 24/5/142, Earl Grey to Bonar Law, 17 Dec. 1911.
48. Ibid.
49. HLRO, Bonar Law Papers, 26/2/2, Plunkett to Bonar Law, 1 April 1912.
50. Cambridge University Library (C.U.L.), Chandos Papers, MSS Section B, 2/12/30–5, Grey to Balcarres, 12 Dec. 1911.
51. Ibid., 2/12/40–1, Grey to Lyttleton, 20 Dec. 1911.
52. B.U.L., Chamberlain Papers, AC/60/84, Oliver to Chamberlain, 16 Oct. 1911.
53. National Library of Scotland (NLS), Oliver Papers, MSS Acc 7726, box 85, 6, Oliver to Robinson, 27 Sept. 1911.
54. NLS, Oliver Papers, MSS Acc 7726, box 85/6/14, Milner to Oliver, 13 Oct. 1911.
55. Ibid.
56. S.R.O., Steel-Maitland Papers, 154/5/51, Oliver to Steel-Maitland, 15 Oct. 1911.
57. Ibid., 85/6/72, Garvin to Oliver, 5 Jan. 1912.
58. B.U.L., Chamberlain Papers, AC 9/3/41, Wyndham to Chamberlain, 10 Oct. 1911.
59. *The Morning Post*, 15 July 1910.

60. *The Morning Post*, 4 July 1910.
61. Bod.L., Second Earl of Selborne Papers, Ms 6, Salisbury to Selborne, 2 Aug. 1910 (59–62).
62. House of Lords Record Office (HLRO), Lord Wargrave Papers, WAR/2/73, Maxse to Goulding, 29 Sept. 1910.
63. J. Vincent, *The Crawford Papers* ..., p. 164.
64. *The Times*, 21 Oct. 1910: Acland-Hood speech.
65. HLRO, J. St Loe Strachey Papers, S/17/1/27, A. Elliot to Strachey, 1 Nov. 1910.
66. Bod.L., Sandars Papers, Mss Eng Hist C.761, Chamberlain to Balfour, 25 Oct. 1910 (254–62).
67. Durham County Record Office, Lady Londonderry Papers, D/LO/C/671/53, Sandars to Londonderry, 31 Oct. 1910.
68. *The Times*, 10 Nov. 1910.
69. L. Witherell, *Rebel on the Right: Henry Page Croft and the Crisis of British conservatism, 1903–1914* (Newark, Delaware, 1997).
70. *The Morning Post*, 14 Oct. 1910.
71. *The Times*, 5 Oct. 1910; *The Morning Post*, 8 Oct. 1910.
72. Ibid., 5 Nov. 1910: Reveille Group Manifesto.
73. *The Morning Post*, 29 Oct. 1910: Lonsdale speech.
74. *The Morning Post*, 20 Oct. 1910: McNeill letter.
75. HLRO, Wargrave Papers, WAR 2/77, Moore to Goulding, 25 Oct. 1910.
76. H.M. Hyde, *Carson: The Life of Sir Edward Carson, Lord Carson of Duncairn* (London, 1953), p. 279.
77. N.I.R.O., Londonderry Papers, D.2846 1/1/55, Carson to Londonderry, 27 Oct. 1910.
78. A. Jackson, *The Ulster Party* ..., pp. 311–12.
79. Ibid.
80. N.I.R.O., Crawford Papers, D.1700/5/6/1, Craig to Crawford, 20 April 1911.
81. N.I.R.O., Ulster Unionist Council Papers, D.1327/1/1, Minute Book of UUC, 5 April 1912.
82. Ibid.
83. N.I.R.O., UUC Papers, Joint Committee of the U.A.I., D.1327/2/1a, 1 Dec. 1911.
84. D.R.O., Londonderry Papers, D/LO/C 686, minute book for the Ulster Unionist Women's Council.
85. Hatfield House, Quickswood Papers, QUI 14/161–8, Craig to Carson, 16 Sept. 1911.
86. Ibid., 11 Jan. 1911.
87. *The Morning Post*, 3 Jan. 1912.
88. N.I.R.O., UUC Papers, Joint Committee of U.A.I., D.1327/2/1a, 29 Jan. 1912.
89. A. Jackson, *The Ulster Party* ..., chp 5 and 6.
90. R. McNeill, *Ulster's stand* ..., p. 41.
91. A. Gailey, 'King Carson: An essay on the invention of leadership', *IHS*. vol.

XXX, 117 (May 1996), pp. 66–87.

92. A. Jackson, *Sir Edward Carson*, Historical Association of Ireland (1993), p. 29.
93. H.M. Hyde, *Carson*, p. 289.
94. Ibid.
95. Ibid.
96. *The Times*, 13 Oct. and 18 Oct. 1911.
97. W.S. Rodner, 'Lord Hugh Cecil', in J.A. Thompson and A. Mejia (eds), *Edwardian Conservatism: Five Studies in Adaptation* (London, 1988).
98. Hansard, Parl Debates XXXIX, 972–81, 8 Aug. 1911.
99. Hatfield House, Quickswood Papers, QUI 14/161–8, Craig to Carson, 16 Sept. 1911.
100. Carson speech, Dublin, 10 Oct. 1911 in *The Irish Times*, 11 Oct. 1911.
101. N.I.R.O., Londonderry Papers, D.2846/1/1/66, Carson to Lady Londonderry, 30 July 1911.
102. H.M. Hyde, *Carson*, pp. 286–7.
103. A. Jackson, *Sir Edward Carson*, pp. 30–1.
104. Hatfield House, Quickswood Papers, QUI 14/161–8, Craig to Carson, 16 Sept. 1911.
105. Hatfield House, Lord Quickswood Papers, QUI 14/161–8, Craig to Carson, 16 Sept. 1911.
106. A. Jackson, 'Unionist Myths, 1912–1985', *Past & Present*, 136, 1992; A. Gailey, 'King Carson: An essay on the invention of leadership', *IHS*, 117, 1996.
107. *The Times*, 11 Oct. 1911.
108. Hatfield House, Quickswood Papers, QUI 14/157, Carson to Cecil, 10 Sept. 1911.
109. *The Irish Times*, 6 Jan. 1912.
110. *The Irish Times*, 12 Oct. 1911.

NOTES TO CHAPTER 2

1. N.I.R.O., Lady Londonderry Papers, D.2846 1/1/71, Carson to Lady Londonderry, 7 Oct. 1911.
2. P. Williamson, *The Modernisation ...*, p. 53.
3. J. Vincent, *The Crawford Papers ...*, p. 247.
4. Ibid.
5. A. Clark (ed.), *A Good Innings: The Private Papers of Viscount Lee of Fareham* (London, 1974), p. 120.
6. *The Irish Times*, 11 Nov. 1911.
7. R. McNeill, *Ulster's Stand ...* (London, 1922), p. 60.
8. N.I.R.O., H.B. Armstrong Papers, D.3727 E/46, Lonsdale to Armstrong, 11 Nov. 1911.
9. Hatfield House, Salisbury Papers, 72/35-8, H. Cecil to Salisbury, 26 March 1912.

10. Blake, *The Unknown ...*, pp. 91–2.
11. *The Irish Times*, 11 Nov. 1911.
12. Hatfield House, Lord Robert Cecil Papers, CHE 112/105, Hugh to Robert, 11 Nov. 1911.
13. B. Lenman, *The Eclipse of Parliament: Appearance and Reality in British Politics since 1914* (London, 1992), chs 1 & 2.
14. D.G. Boyce (ed.)., *The Crisis of British Unionism: The Domestic political papers of the Second Earl of Selborne 1885–1922* (London, 1987) p. 79.
15. *The Times*, 9 Oct. 1911.
16. *The Times*, 28 January 1912: Albert Hall speech.
17. B. Girvin, 'The party in Comparative and International Context', in A. Seldon and S. Ball (eds), *Conservative Century: The Conservative Party since 1900* (Oxford, 1994), pp. 697–701.
18. The Earl of Oxford and Asquith, *Memories ...*, pp. 202–3.
19. L.S. Amery, *My Political Life: England before the Storm, 1899 to 1914* (London, 1953), p. 387.
20. V. Bonham-Carter, *Winston Churchill as I Knew him* (London, 1966), p. 292.
21. *The Times*, 8 Dec. 1911.
22. J. Vincent, *The Crawford Papers ...*, p. 264.
23. P. Jalland, *The Liberals and Ireland: The Ulster Question in British Politics to 1914* (London, 1980), p. 103.
24. J. Vincent, The Crawford Papers ..., p. 279.
25, Ibid., pp. 262–3.
26. HLRO, Bonar Law Papers, 25/1/65, Lord Camperdown to Bonar Law, 27 Jan. 1912.
27. R. Jenkins, *Asquith* (London, 1964), p. 275.
28. R. McNeill, *Ulster's Stand ...*, p. 21.
29. P. Marsh, *The Discipline of Popular Government: Lord Salisbury's Domestic Statecraft, 1881–1902* (London, 1978), pp. 35–47: C.C. Weston, 'Salisbury and the Lords, 1868–1895', *HJ*, xxv (1982), p. 106.
30. *The Times*, 26 July 1911.
31. Hansard, Parl Debates, XXIX, 1010–11, 8 Aug. 1911.
32. Bonar Law at St Andrews Hall, Glasgow, 21 May 1912 in *The Times*, 22 May 1912.
33. HLRO, Bonar Law Papers, 27/2/25, H. Cecil to Bonar Law, 30 Sept. 1912.
34. Hansard, Parl Debates, XXXVII, 296, 16 April 1912.
35. HLRO, Bonar Law Papers, 24/3/50, Strachey to Bonar Law, 17 Nov. 1911.
36. N. Blewett, *The Peers, the Parties, and the People: The General Elections of 1910* (London, 1972): E.H.H. Green, 'Radical Conservatism: The Electoral Genesis of Tariff Reform', *Historical Journal*, 28 (1985); F. Coetzee, *For Party or Country: Nationalism and the Dilemmas of Popular Conservatism in Edwardian England* (Oxford, 1990); E.H.H. Green, *The Crisis of Conservatism* (London, 1995).
37. D. Dutton, 'The Unionist Party and Social Policy 1906–1914', *HJ*, 24 (1981); J. Ridley, 'The Unionists' Social Reform Committee, 1911–1914: Wets

before the Deluge', *HJ*, 30 (1987); M. Fforde, *Conservatism and Collectivism, 1886–1914* (Edinburgh, 1990), ch. 3.

38. HLRO, Bonar Law Papers, 24/3/68, Sinclair to Bonar Law, 21 Nov. 1911.
39. A.T.Q. Stewart, *The Ulster Crisis* ..., p. 49.
40. Hansard, Parl Debates, XXXVII, 300–1, 16 April 1912.
41. R. McNeill, *Ulster's Stand* ..., p. 93.
42. HLRO, Bonar Law Papers, 24/5/142, Earl Grey to Bonar Law, 17 Dec. 1911.
43. *The Spectator*, 6 Jan. 1912.
44. *The Times*, 8 Dec. 1911.
45. Ibid., 27 Jan. 1912.

NOTES TO CHAPTER 3

1. J. Vincent, *The Crawford Papers* ..., p. 274.
2. A.J. Ward, *The Irish Constitutional Tradition: Responsible Government and Modern Ireland, 1782–1992* (Dublin, 1994), pp. 63–81: A. O'Day, *Irish Home Rule, 1867–1921* (Manchester, 1998), pp. 247–50.
3. Hansard, Parl Debates, XXXVI, 1401, 11 April 1912.
4. Ibid.
5. Ibid., 1433–4.
6. Ibid.
7. *The Times*, 14 June 1912.
8. Hansard, Parl Debates, XXXVII, 46-7, 15 April 1912.
9. Hansard, Parl Debates, XXXVII, 42, 15 April 1912.
10. N.I.R.O., Sir Edward Carson Papers, D.1507 A/3/19, Dunraven to Carson, 19 Dec. 1912.
11. P. Bew, *Ideology and the* ..., p. xiv.
12. *The Spectator*, 20 April 1912.
13. Hansard, Parl Debates, XXXVIII, 253, 7 May 1912.
14. Ibid., XXXVII, 252, 16 April 1912.
15. Ibid., 1781, 30 April 1912.
16. *The Spectator*, 13 April 1912.
17. D.G. Boyce, *The Crisis in British* ..., p. 81.
18. Hansard, Parl Debates, XXXVI, 1499, 11 April 1912.
19. Ibid., XXXVIII, 265, 7 May 1912.
20. *The Morning Post*, 22 May 1912.
21. *The Times*, 18 May 1912.
22. P. Jalland, *The Liberals* ..., pp. 84–5.
23. Hansard, Parl Debates, XXXVIII, 680, 9 May 1912.
24. *The Times*, 3 June 1912.
25. Ibid., 10 June 1912.
26. P. Jalland, *The Liberals* ..., p. 94.
27. *The Times*, 19 June 1912.
28. Ibid., 29 June 1912.

29. *The Times*, 10 June 1912.
30. Hansard, Parl Debates, XXXIX, 780, 11 June 1912.
31. R. McNeill, *Ulster's Stand ...*, p. 93.
32. Hansard, Parl Debates, XXXIX, 1078, 13 June 1912.
33. Ibid.
34. H. McNeill, *Ulster's Stand ...*, p. 93.
35. Ibid., p. 93.
36. Ibid., p. 90.
37. Hansard, Parl Debates, XXXIX, 1076–80, 13 June 1912.
38. *The Times*, 10 April 1912.
39. *The Morning Post*, 22 April 1912.
40. *The Belfast Newsletter*, 27 April 1912.
41. *The Times*, 21 Oct. 1912.
42. McNeill, *Ulster's Stand ...*, p. 129.
43. Earl of Midleton, *Records and Reactions: 1856–1939* (London, 1939), p. 226.
44. HLRO, Bonar Law Papers, 26/4/7, Long to Bonar Law, 4 June 1912.
45. Ibid., 26/4/12, 7 June 1912.
46. D.R.O., Londonderry Papers, D/LO/666/205i, Long to Lady Londonderry, 7 June 1912.
47. *The Times*, 15 June 1912.
48. Hansard, Parl Debates, XXXIX, 1068, 13 June 1912.
49. HLRO, Bonar Law Papers, 33/4/67, Bonar Law to Mackay-Wilson, 16 Nov. 1912.
50. *The Times*, 20 June 1912.
51. *The Times*, 15 June 1912.
52. T.M. Healy, *Letters and ...*, p. 507.
53. Hansard, Parl Debates, XXXIX, 1802, 19 June 1912.
54. J. Smith, 'Bluff, Bluster and Brinkmanship: Andrew Bonar Law and the Third Home Rule Bill', *HJ*, 36, 1 (1993), p. 170.
55. *The Morning Post*, 27 July 1912.
56. J. Ramsden, *Real Old ...*, p. 48.
57. *The Morning Post*, 8 Aug. 1912.
58. Ibid., 5 Oct. 1912.
59. Ibid.
60. Hansard, Parl Debates, XLV, 564, 10 Oct. 1912.
61. *The Times*, 10 Oct. 1912.
62. J. Ramsden, *Real Old ...*, p. 51.
63. P. Williamson, *The Modernisation ...*, p. 59.
64. J. Ramsden, *Real Old ...*, p. 48.
65. J. Vincent, *The Crawford Papers ...*, p. 279.
66. *The Times*, 10 Oct. 1912.
67. *The Times*, 26 Oct. 1912.
68. J. Vincent, *The Crawford Papers ...*, p 280.
69. Ibid., p. 283.
70. Ibid.

71. J. Ramsden, *Real Old ...*, p. 52.
72. Churchill College, Cambridge, Sir William Bull Papers, Bull Journal, 4/6 'Retrospect', Dec. 1912.
73. P. Williamson, *The Modernisation ...*, p. 63.
74. *The Morning Post*, 14 Nov. 1912.
75. HLRO, Bonar Law Papers, 33/4/65, Bonar Law to Stamfordham, 16 Nov. 1912.
76. *The Times*, 15 Nov. 1912.
77. Ibid., 14 Nov. 1912.
78. Ibid., 19 Nov. 1912.
79. *The Morning Post*, 29 July 1912.
80. E. Marjoribanks and I. Colvin, *Life of Lord Carson* (3 vols, London, 1932–36), p. 128.
81. *The Times*, 22 May 1912.
82. N.I.R.O., UUC Papers, D.1327/2/1a, Joint Committee of the U.A.I., minute books, June 1912.
83. P. Buckland, *Irish Unionism 1885–1923: A Documentary History* (Belfast, 1973), p. 216.
84. N.I.R.O., UUC Papers, D.1327/2/1a Joint committee of U.A.I., minute books, June 1912.
85. Sir J.G. Ervine, *Sir Edward Carson and the Ulster Movement* (London, 1915), p. 47.
86. N.I.R.O., Londonderry Papers, D.2846 1/6/11, R. Lucas to Londonderry, 25 Jan. 1914.
87. D.R.O., Londonderry Papers, D/LO/C/671/82, Sandars to Londonderry, 5 Oct. 1912.
88. R. McNeill, *Ulster's Stand ...*, p.81.
89. E. Marjoribanks and I. Colvin, *The Life of Lord Carson*, p. 111.
90. Gailey, 'King Carson ...', pp. 72–3.
91. *The Times*, 11 May 1912.
92. Ibid.
93. Ibid., 2 May 1912.
94. *The Morning Post*, 13 Nov. 1912.
95. J. Ramsden, *Real Old ...*, p. 46.
96. HLRO, Bonar Law Papers, 26/4/25, Amery to Bonar Law, 16 June 1912.
97. *The Times*, 9 May 1912.
98. J. Ramsden, *Real Old ...*, p. 46.
99. P. Jalland, *The Liberals ...*, p. 62: McNeill, *Ulster's Stand ...*, pp. 62–5.
100. J. Ramsden, *Real Old ...*, p. 46.
101. E. Marjoribanks and I. Colvin, *The Life of Lord Carson*, p. 132.
102. *The Times*, 11 July 1912.
103. Ibid., 13 July 1912.
104. Ibid., 29 July 1912.
105. Ibid., 29 July 1912.
106. N.I.R.O., Lady Craigavon Papers, D.1415/B/38/1–162, 28 July 1912.

107. R. Blake, *The Unknown* ..., p. 134.
108. *The Times*, 15 Aug. 1912.
109. *The Morning Post*, 23 Jan. 1912.
110. HLRO, Bonar Law Papers, 33/6/80, 'memorandum of the conversation with the Prime Minister', 15 Oct. 1913.
111. *The Morning Post*, 29 July 1912.
112. A.T.Q. Stewart, *The Ulster Crisis: Resistance to Home Rule, 1912–1914* (London, 1967), ch. 5.
113. *The Morning Post*, 17 Aug. 1912
114. Ibid., 12 Sept. 1912.
115. A.T.Q. Stewart, *The Ulster Crisis* ..., p. 62.
116. *The Times*, 30 Sept. 1912.
117. Ibid.
118. Ibid., 4 Oct. 1912.
119. Bod.L., H.A. Gwynne, Mss Dep 20, Bonar Law to Gwynne, 30 Sept. 1912.
120. *The Times*, 7 Oct. 1912.
121. D.R.O., Londonderry Papers, D/LO/C/684, St Aldwyn to Londonderry, 24 Oct. 1912.
122. Ibid., D/LO/C/671/83, Sandars to Londonderry, 3 Nov. 1912.
123. *The Times*, 29 July 1912.
124. J. Vincent, *The Crawford Papers* ..., p. 284.
125. HLRO, Bonar Law Papers, 27/3/6, Crichton-Stuart to Bonar Law, 4 Oct. 1912.
126. *The Morning Post*, 22 April 1912.
127. E. Marjoribanks and I. Colvin, *The Life of Lord Carson*, p. 129.
128. HLRO, Bonar Law Papers, 26/2/21, Earl of Mar to Bonar Law, 13 April 1912; 26/5/2, Duke of Sutherland to Bonar Law, 1 July 1912.
129. *The Times*, 12 June 1912.
130. HLRO, Bonar Law Papers, 27/1/32, Oliver to Bonar Law, 10 Aug. 1912.
131. Ibid., Bonar Law Papers, 27/1/47, Oliver to Bonar Law, 20 Aug. 1912.
132. S.R.O., Steel-Maitland Papers, 154/5/51, Oliver to Steel-Maitland, 15 Oct. 1912.
133. A.M. Gollin, *The Observer and J.L. Garvin* ..., pp. 394–5.
134. *The Morning Post*, 6 May 1912 and 8 May 1912.
135. *The Times*, 10 May 1912.
136. Ibid.
137. HLRO, Bonar Law Papers, 26/4/22, Frewen to Bonar Law, 14 June 1912.
138. T.M. Healy, *Letters and* ..., ch. XXXVIII.
139. HLRO, Bonar Law Papers, 26/4/27, Frewen to Bonar Law, 18 June 1912.
140. *The Times*, 15 Aug. 1912.
141. J. Kendle, *Ireland and the Federal* ..., p. 153.
142. Ibid., p. 154.
143. HLRO, Bonar Law Papers, 27/1/54, Frewen to Bonar Law, 24 Aug. 1912.
144. Ibid., 27/2/10, Dunraven to Bonar Law, 8 Sept. 1912.
145. Ibid.

146. Ibid., 27/3/27, Hythe to Bonar Law, 10 Oct. 1912.
147. *The Times*, 17 Oct. 1912.
148. *The Times*, 21 Oct. 1912.
149. A. Chamberlain, *Politics from* ..., pp. 289–91.
150. *The Morning Post*, 9 January 1913.
151. HLRO, Bonar Law Papers, 27/1/47, Oliver to Bonar Law, 20 Aug. 1912.
152. Ibid.
153. A. Sykes, *Tariff Reform in British Politics, 1903–1913* (Oxford, 1979), chp 12.

NOTES TO CHAPTER 4

1. A. Sykes, *Tariff Reform* ..., pp. 258–84: M. Fforde, *Conservatism and Collectivism* ..., pp. 126–59; I. Packer, 'Conservative Ideology ad Landownership', in M. Francis and I. Bargielowska (eds), *Conservatives and British Society, 1880–1980* (Cardiff, 1996).
2. J. Ramsden, *Real Old* ..., p. 63.
3. *The Times*, 9 June 1913.
4. Ibid., 11 April 1913: Hull speech.
5. HLRO, Bonar Law Papers, 29/6/32, Lansdowne to Stamfordham, 31 July 1913.
6. N.I.R.O., Lady Craigavon Papers, D.1415/B/38/1–162, 'Diary', 3 Jan. 1913.
7. *The Times*, 1 Feb. 1913.
8. Ibid., 17 May 1913.
9. P. Buckland, *Irish Unionism: A Documentary* ..., p. 225.
10. M. Foy, 'The Ulster Volunteer Force: It's Domestic Development and Political Consequences' (PhD Queen's University Belfast, 1986).
11. N.I.R.O., UUC Papers, D.1327/2/10, 'Sir Edward Carson Defence Fund', minute books, 19 Jan. 1913.
12. *The Times*, 26 March 1913.
13. Ibid., 4 June 1913.
14. Ibid., 20 June 1913.
15. Ibid., 6 July 1913.
16. A. Jackson, 'Unionist Myths, 1912–1985', *Past & Present*, 136 (1992), pp. 164–81.
17. HLRO, Bonar Law Papers, 28/2/31, de Broke to Bonar Law, 6 Jan. 1913.
18. *The Times*, 27 March 1913; see also, W.S. Rodner, 'Leaguers, Covenanters, Moderates: British support for Ulster, 1913–14', *Eire-Ireland*, 17, 3 (1982), pp. 68–85.
19. W.S. Rodner, 'Leaguers, Covenanters ..., pp. 68–75.
20. The Times, 9 May 1913.
21. A.T.Q. Stewart, *The Ulster Crisis* ..., pp. 73–4.
22. Churchill College, Cambridge William Bull Papers, 4/8, 'Journal', Report from Commissioner of Police, Scotland Yard, 4 June 1913.
23. HLRO, Bonar Law Papers, 28/2/31, de Broke to Bonar Law, 6 Jan. 1913.

24. *The Times*, 27 May 1913.
25. B.L., Cecil Papers, Add Mss 51161, de Broke to Cecil, 21 Sept. 1913 (24).
26. *The Morning Post*, 19 July 1913: Carson at Ballymena.
27. *The Times*, 14 July 1913.
28. J. Smith, 'Paralysing the Arm: Unionists and the Army Annual Act 1911–1914', *Parliamentary History*, 15, pt 2 (1996), pp. 191–207.
29. *The Times*, 26 July 1911: Bonar Law letter.
30. B.L., Cecil Papers, Add Mss 51075b, Hugh to Robert, 6 June 1913 (34–40).
31. Hansard, Lords Debates, XIII, 499–505, 27 Jan. 1913.
32. Ibid., 743.
33. Ibid., 461.
34. Ibid., 776.
35. Hatfield House, Salisbury Papers, 73/104, Salisbury to Bonar Law, 13 June 1913.
36. *The Times*, 2 June 1913.
37. *The Times*, 3 March 1913.
38. Ibid., 22 March 1913.
39. *The Times*, 12 Feb. 1913.
40. A. Chamberlain, *Politics from* ..., p. 291.
41. Ibid., p. 522.
42. J. Campbell, *F.E. Smith: First Earl of Birkenhead* (London, 1983), pp. 334–7.
43. Marjoribanks and I. Colvin, *The Life of Lord Carson*, p. 139.
44. J. Ramsden, *Real Old* ..., p. 64.
45. HLRO, Bonar Law Papers, 29/4/21, Younger to Bonar Law, 25 May 1913.
46. *The Times*, 13 June 1913.
47. Ibid., 17 June 1913.
48. E. Marjoribanks and I. Colvin, *The Life of Lord Carson*, p. 183.
49. A. Jackson, *Sir Edward Carson*, p. 20.
50. Ibid.
51. J. Campbell, *F.E. Smith* ..., p. 337.
52. P. Buckland, *Irish Unionism: A Documentary* ..., p. 172.
53. Hatfield House, Quickswood Papers, QUI 16/60, Midleton to H. Cecil, 18 April 1913.
54. HLRO, Bonar Law Papers, 29/2/10, G. Stewart to Bonar Law, 6 March 1913.
55. Ibid., 29/2/8, Stewart to Campbell, 5 March 1913.
56. Ibid., 29/2/19, 'Statement of Deputation of Irish Unionists to Mr Bonar Law', by G. Stewart, 14 March 1913.
57. B.L., Long Papers, Add Mss 62406, Dicey to Long, 18 May 1913 (181).
58. Hatfield House, Quickswood Papers, QUI 16/48–50, Midleton to Cecil, 12 April 1913.
59. N.I.R.O., UUC Papers, D.1327/1/1, Annual Meeting of the Council of Unionist Clubs of Ireland, 5 March 1913.
60. N.I.R.O., UUC Papers, D.1327/1/2, UUC Executive Committee, minute books, 19 Feb. 1913.
61. HLRO, Bonar Law Papers, 29/2/10, Carson to Bonar Law, 8 May 1913.

62. B.L., Long Papers, Add Mss 62406, Dicey to Long, 16 April 1913.
63. Ibid., 30 April 1913 (174–7).
64. HLRO, Bonar Law Papers, 33/5/35, Bonar Law to Dicey, 12 June 1913.
65. Ibid., 29/4/2, Midleton to Bonar Law, 2 May 1913.
66. Ibid., 29/4/3, Long to Bonar Law, 2 May 1913.
67. *The Times*, 11, 26, 31 March, 1913; 4, 8, 15 April 1913.
68. HLRO, Bonar Law Papers, 29/2/42, Dicey to Bonar Law, 25 March 1913.
69. *The Times*, 3 May 1913.
70. HLRO, Bonar Law Papers, 29/4/2, Midleton to Bonar Law, 2 May 1913.
71. B.L., Long Papers, Add Mss 62404, Long to Bonar Law, 27 June 1913 (33–4).
72. J. Ramsden, *Real Old ...*, pp. 50–1.
73. Hansard, Parl Debates, XLVI, 468, 1 Jan. 1913.
74. *The Times*, 11 June 1913: Carson on 2nd Reading.
75. Ibid., 16 July 1913.
76. Hansard, Parl Debates, XLVI, 2395, 16 Jan. 1913.
77. E. Marjoribanks and I. Colvin, *The Life of Lord Carson*, p. 192.
78. Hatfield House, Salisbury Papers, 73/104, Salisbury to Younger, 25 June 1913.
79. HLRO, Bonar Law Papers, 29/6/32–3, 'Memorandum on the King's ...'.
80. Ibid.
81. Ibid.
82. N.I.R.O., Londonderry Papers, D.2846 1/1/88, Carson to Londonderry, 13 Aug. 1912.
83. D.R.O., Londonderry Papers, D/LO/C/672/3, E. Saunderson to Londonderry, 10 Aug. 1913.
84. *The Times*, 21 Aug. 1913.
85. HLRO, Bonar Law Papers, 33/4/65, Bonar Law to Stamfordham, 16 Nov. 1912.
86. Ibid.
87. *The Times*, 25 Jan. 1913.
88. Ibid., 12 Feb. 1913.
89. *The Morning Post*, 27 Jan. 1913: Samuel at Redcar.
90. M. Brett (ed.), *The Journals and Letters of Reginald Viscount Esher* (4 vols, London, 1934–38), Vol. III, p. 117.
91. HLRO, Strachey Papers, S/5/6/8, Strachey to Dicey, 18 Feb. 1913.
92. Ibid., S/9/7/12, Strachey to Lansdowne, 24 June 1913.
93. Ibid., S/13/15/6, Stamfordham to Strachey, 11 Feb. 1913.
94. *The Times*, 16 May 1913.
95. B.L., Long Papers, Add Mss 62406, Long to Dicey, 19 April 1913 (164–5).
96. HLRO, Bonar Law Papers, 29/4/13, Steel-Maitland to Bonar Law, 21 May 1913.
97. Bod.L., Sandars Papers, Mss Eng Hist C.765, Talbort to Sandars, 12 Sept. 1913 (155–8).
98. Hatfield House, Salisbury Papers, 73/104, Salisbury to Younger, 25 June 1913.

99. HLRO, Strachey Papers, S/5/6/8, Strachey to Dicey, 18 Feb. 1913.
100. Ibid., S/5/6/8, Dicey to Strachey, 19 Feb. 1913.
101. Ibid.
102. HLRO, Bonar Law Papers, 33/5/20, Bonar Law to Dicey, 26 March 1913.
103. HLRO, Strachey Papers, S/9/7/2, Lansdowne to Strachey, 30 June 1913.
104. Jenkins, *Asquith*, p. 283.
105. HLRO, Bonar Law Papers, 29/6/32–3, 'Memorandum on the King's Position', 31 July 1913.
106. H. Nicholson, *King George The Fifth: His Life and Reign* (London, 1952), p. 223.
107. Ibid., p. 220.
108. Ibid.

NOTES TO CHAPTER 5

1. Bod.L., The Earl of Oxford and Asquith Papers, Mss 38, Crewe to Asquith, 8 Sept. 1913 (126–7).
2. P. Bew, *Ideology and the ...*, p. 98.
3. *The Times*, 11 Sept. 1913: Lord Loreburn letter.
4. R. Blake, *The Unknown Prime Minister ...*; J. Ramsden, *The Age of Balfour ...*; D. Dutton, *His Majesty's Loyal ....*
5. P. Jalland, *The Liberals ...*, pp. 58–65.
6. HLRO, Bonar Law Papers, 30/2/27, Hamilton to Lansdowne, 14 Sept. 1913.
7. Ibid., 33/5/57, Bonar Law to Lansdowne, 16 Sept. 1913.
8. Ibid.
9. Ibid.
10. Bod.L., Asquith Papers, Mss 38, Churchill to Asquith, 17 Sept. 1913 (192–5).
11. Ibid.
12. Ibid.
13. R. Williams, *Defending the Empire: The Conservative Party and British Defence Policy, 1899–1915* (Yale, 1991).
14. Bod.L., Asquith Papers, Mss 38, Churchill to Asquith, 21 Sept. 1913 (198–201).
15. A.T.Q. Stewart, *The Ulster Crisis ...*, pp. 94–6.
16. Ibid., p. 103.
17. HLRO, Bonar Law Papers, 33/5/68, Bonar Law to Lansdowne, 8 Oct. 1913.
18. Jackson, *Sir Edward ...*, p. 32.
19. HLRO, Bonar Law Papers, 30/2/15, Carson to Bonar Law, 20 Sept. 1913.
20. Ibid., 30/2/15, 'memorandum', Carson to Bonar Law, 20 Sept. 1913.
21. Ibid.
22. *The Morning Post*, 7 Jan. 1912, Carson speech at Omagh.
23. J. Campbell, *F.E. Smith ...*, pp. 340–1.

24. P. Jalland, *The Liberals …*, p. 150.
25. HLRO, Bonar Law Papers, 30/2/28, Stamfordham to Bonar Law, 26 Sept. 1913.
26. Ibid., 30/2/29, Lansdowne to Bonar Law, 27 Sept. 1913.
27. Ibid., 30/2/28, Stamfordham to Bonar Law, 26 Sept. 1913.
28. Ibid., 30/2/35, Harcourt-Kitchen to Bonar Law, 30 Sept. 1913.
29. Ibid.
30. Ibid., 30/3/3, Lansdowne to Bonar Law, 2 Oct. 1913.
31. Ibid., 30/3/1, Stamfordham to Bonar Law, 1 Oct. 1913.
32. Ibid., 30/3/10, Stamfordham to Bonar Law, 7 Oct. 1913.
33. Ibid., 33/5/67, Bonar Law to Lansdowne, 4 Oct. 1913.
34. Ibid., 33/5/68, Bonar Law to Lansdowne, 8 Oct. 1913.
35. Ibid.
36. Ibid.
37. A. Jackson, *Sir Edward Carson …*, p. 32.
38. HLRO, Bonar Law Papers, 30/3/11, Asquith to Bonar Law, 8 Oct. 1913.
39. *The Times*, 9 Oct. 1913.
40. HLRO, Bonar Law Papers, 30/3/13, Curzon to Bonar Law, 10 Oct. 1913.
41. Ibid., 30/3/23, Carson to Bonar Law, 11 Oct. 1913.
42. HLRO, Bonar Law Papers, 30/2/10, de Broke to Bonar Law, 11 Sept. 1913.
43. H. Nicholson, *King George V …*, p. 231.
44. HLRO, Bonar Law Papers, 30/2/21, Lansdowne to Bonar Law, 23 Sept. 1913.
45. Ibid., 30/2/17, Lansdowne to Bonar Law, 20 Sept. 1913.
46. Ibid., 30/2/21, Lansdowne to Bonar Law, 23 Sept. 1913.
47. Ibid.
48. Ibid., 30/2/27, Lansdowne to Bonar Law, 26 Sept. 1913.
49. Ibid.
50. Ibid., 30/2/37, Lansdowne to Bonar Law, 30 Sept. 1913.
51. Ibid., 30/2/29, Lansdowne to Bonar Law, 27 Sept. 1913.
52. HLRO, Bonar Law Papers, 30/3/17, Lansdowne to Bonar Law, 10 Oct. 1913.
53. B.L., Long Papers, Add Mss 62403, Lansdowne to Long, 3 Oct. 1913.
54. HLRO, Bonar Law Papers, 30/3/7, Long to Bonar Law, 5 Oct. 1913.
55. HLRO, Bonar Law Papers, 30/3/23, Carson to Lansdowne, 11 Oct. 1913.
56. Ibid., 30/3/20, Midleton to Bonar Law, 11 Oct. 1913.
57. Hatfield House, Salisbury Papers, 73/156–7, Midleton to Salisbury, 17 Sept. 1913.
58. Ibid., 30/3/26, Campbell to Bonar Law, 13 Oct. 1913.
59. HLRO, Lord Willoughby de Broke Papers, WB 6/5, Arran to de Broke, 4 Oct. 1913.
60. HLRO, Bonar Law Papers, 30/3/23, Lansdowne to Bonar Law, 11 Oct. 1913.
61. Ibid.

62. Ibid., 30/3/16, Lansdowne to Bonar Law, 10 Oct. 1913.
63. Ibid., 30/3/29, Lansdowne to Bonar Law, 13 Oct. 1913.
64. Ibid., 24/3/50, Strachey to Bonar Law, 15 Nov. 1911.
65. H.M. Hyde, *Carson* (London, 1953), p. 327.
66. HLRO, Bonar Law Papers, 33/5/57, Bonar Law to Carson, 18 Sept. 1913.
67. Ibid.
68. Ibid., 30/2/28, Stamfordham to Bonar Law, 26 Sept. 1913.
69. Ibid., 30/3/1, Stamfordham to Bonar Law, 1 Oct. 1913.
70. Ibid., 33/5/64, Bonar Law to Stamfordham, 1 Oct. 1913.
71. Ibid.
72. Ibid., 33/5/56, Bonar Law to Lansdowne, 18 Sept. 1913.
73. Ibid., 33/5/61, Bonar Law to Lansdowne, 27 Sept. 1913.
74. Ibid., 30/2/37, Lansdowne to Bonar Law, 30 Sept. 1913.
75. Ibid., 33/5/67, Bonar Law to Lansdowne, 4 Oct. 1913.
76. Ibid., 33/5/61, Bonar Law to Lansdowne, 27 Sept. 1913.
77. Ibid., 33/5/59, Bonar Law to Lansdowne, 24 Sept. 1913.
78. Ibid.
79. Ibid., 33/6/69, Bonar Law to Balfour, 9 Oct. 1913.
80. Ibid., 33/5/67, Bonar Law to Lansdowne, 4 Oct. 1913.
81. Ibid.
82. Ibid.
83. Ibid., 33/5/68, Bonar Law to Lansdowne, 8 Oct. 1913.
84. Ibid.
85. Ibid.
86. Ibid.
87. Ibid.
88. Ibid., 30/3/16, Lansdowne to Bonar Law, 10 Oct. 1913.
89. Ibid., 33/6/78, Bonar Law to Lansdowne, 11 Oct. 1913.
90. Ibid.
91. Ibid., 30/3/28, Balfour to Bonar Law, 13 Oct. 1913
92. Ibid., 33/5/68, Bonar Law to Lansdowne, 8 Oct. 1913.
93. HLRO, Bonar Law Papers, 33/6/80, Bonar Law to Lansdowne, 15 Oct. 1913.
94. Ibid.
95. Ibid.
96. Ibid.
97. Ibid., 30/3/31, Lansdowne to Bonar Law, 16 Oct. 1913.
98. Ibid.
99. Ibid., 33/6/80, Bonar Law to Lansdowne, 15 Oct. 1913.
100. Ibid.
101. Ibid.
102. Ibid.
103. Ibid., 33/6/84, Bonar Law to Croal, 18 Oct. 1913.
104. Ibid.
105. Ibid., 30/3/44, Croal to Bonar Law, 21 Oct. 1913.

NOTES TO CHAPTER 6

1. HLRO, Bonar Law Papers, 30/3/50, Milner to Bonar Law, 24 Oct. 1913.
2. Ibid., 33/6/116, Bonar Law to Selborne, 22 Dec. 1913.
3. NLS, Oliver Papers, 7726/86, Oliver to Robinson, 10 Oct. 1913 (19).
4. Ibid., 7726/86, Earl Grey to Oliver, 3 Oct. 1913 (34).
5. HLRO, Bonar Law Papers, 30/3/16, Lansdowne to Bonar Law, 10 Oct. 1913.
6. Ibid., 7726/86, Oliver to Robinson, 10 Oct. 1913 (19).
7. Kendle, *Ireland and the Federal* ..., p. 163.
8. Ibid.
9. NLS, 7726/86, Earl Grey to Oliver, 15 Oct. 1913 (36).
10. B.U.L., Austen Chamberlain Papers, 60/114, Oliver to Chamberlain, 17 Oct. 1913.
11. Bod.L., Milner Papers, Ms Dep 13, Oliver to Milner, 23 Oct. 1913 (38–41).
12. NLS, Oliver Papers, 7726/86, Oliver to Craik, 26 Oct. 1913 (99).
13. Ibid., 7726/86, Oliver to Craik, 27 Oct. 1913 (104). Earl Grey also argued against an election before a settlement, ibid., 7726/86, Grey to Oliver, 15 Oct. 1913 (36).
14. B.U.L., Austen Chamberlain, 60/114, Oliver to Earl Grey, 17 Oct. 1913.
15, Ibid.
16. HLRO, Bonar Law Papers, 30/4/16, Balfour to Bonar Law, 8 Nov. 1913.
17. NLS, Oliver Papers, 7726/86, Chamberlain to Oliver, 21 Oct. 1913 (24–6).
18. HLRO, Bonar Law Papers, 30/3/54, Frewen to Bonar Law, 27 Oct. 1913.
19. NLS, Oliver Papers, 7726/86, Oliver to Robinson, 27 Oct. 1913 (44).
20. Ibid., 7726/86, Oliver to M. Macdonald, 27 Oct. 1913 (107).
21. Ibid.
22. Ibid.
23. Ibid., 7726/86, Churchill to Oliver, 1 Nov. 1913 (40).
24. NLS, Oliver Papers, 7726/86, Oliver to Earl Grey, 24 Nov. 1913 (66–7).
25. B.U.L., Austen Chamberlain Papers, 60/104, Oliver to Chamberlain, 22 Oct. 1913.
26. Ibid., 60/105, Oliver to Chamberlain, 23 Oct. 1913, in A. Chamberlain, *Politics from* ..., p. 569.
27. Ibid., 60/107, Oliver to Chamberlain, 29 Oct. 1913.
28. B.U.L., Austen Chamberlain Papers, 60/108, Oliver to Chamberlain, 3 Nov. 1913.
29. NLS, Oliver Papers, 7726/86, Chamberlain to Oliver, 30 Oct. 1913 (28).
30. HLRO, Bonar Law Papers, 30/3/31, Lansdowne to Bonar Law, 16 Oct. 1913.
31. Ibid.
32. A. Sykes, *Tariff Reform* ..., pp. 262–84; I. Packer, 'The Conservatives and the Ideology of Landownership, 1910–1914', in *The Conservatives and British Society, 1880–1990*, M. Francis and I. Zweiniger-Bargielowska (eds) (University of Wales Press, 1996), 39–57.

33. HLRO, Bonar Law Papers, 30/3/47, Lansdowne to Bonar Law, 23 Oct. 1913.
34. A. Chamberlain, *Politics From ...*, p. 570.
35. Ibid.
36. Ibid.
37. Ibid., p. 570.
38. Ibid.
39. Ibid., p. 572.
40. HLRO, Bonar Law Papers, 30/3/56, Lansdowne to Bonar Law, 27 Oct. 1913.
41. Ibid.
42. Ibid.
43. A. Chamberlain, *Politics From ...*, p. 570.
44. Ibid.
45. NLS, Oliver Papers, 7726/86, Chamberlain to Oliver, 30 Oct. 1913 (28).
46. A. Chamberlain, *Politics From ...*, p. 571.
47. NLS, Oliver Papers, 7726/86, Chamberlain to Oliver, 6 Nov. 1913 (30).
48. B.U.L., Austen Chamberlain Papers, AC 11/1/20, Churchill to Chamberlain, 12 Nov. 1913.
49. NLS, Oliver Papers, 7726/86, Oliver to Earl Grey, 24 Nov. 1913 (66–7).
50. Ibid., Oliver to Northcliffe, 28 Nov. 1913 (158).
51. Ibid., Oliver to Earl Grey, 24 Nov. 1913 (66–7).
52. Ibid., Oliver to Churchill, 24 Nov. 1913 (138).
53. *The Times*, 19 Nov. 1913.
54. NLS, Oliver Papers, 7726/86, Oliver to Churchill, 24 Nov. 1913 (138).
55. Ibid., Chamberlain to Oliver, 24 Nov. 1913 (48–9).
56. B.U.L., Austen Chamberlain Papers, 11/1/4, Willoughby de Broke to Chamberlain, 21 Nov. 1913.
57. B.U.L., Austen Chamberlain Papers, 11/1/3, Avery to Chamberlain, 21 Nov. 1913.
58. A. Chamberlain, *Politics From ...*, pp. 572–7, 'Memorandum of conversation with Mr Churchill'.
59. Ibid.
60. Ibid.
61. Ibid.
62. Ibid.
63. Ibid.
64. Ibid.
65. NLS, Oliver Papers, 7726/86, Chamberlain to Oliver, 29 Nov. 1913 (34).
66. A. Chamberlain, *Politics From ...*, p. 579.
67. Ibid., p. 578.
68. *The Times*, 2 Dec. 1913.
69. A. Chamberlain, *Politics From ...*, p. 583.
70. Ibid.
71. Ibid., p. 579.
72. B.U.L., Austen Chamberlain Papers, 60/117, Oliver to Chamberlain, 2 Dec. 1913.

73. Ibid., 60/118, Oliver to Chamberlain, 4 Dec. 1913.
74. NLS, Oliver Papers, 7726/87, Carson to Oliver, 3 Dec. 1913.
75. B.U.L., Austen Chamberlain Papers, 60/118, Oliver to Chamberlain, 4 Dec. 1913.
76. J. Kendle, *Ireland and the Federal ...*, p. 167.
77. B.U.L., Austen Chamberlain Papers, 60/118, Oliver to Chamberlain, 4 Dec. 1913.
78. NLS, Oliver Papers, 7726/87, Garvin to Oliver, 'Friday' Dec. 1913.
79. A. Chamberlain, *Politics From ...*, p. 586.
80. NLS, Oliver Papers, 7726/87, Robinson to Oliver, 10 Dec. 1913 (57).
81. B.U.L., Austen Chamberlain Papers, 60/120 Oliver to Chamberlain 9 Dec. 1913.
82. NLS, Oliver Papers, 7726/86, Chamberlain to Oliver, 10 Dec. 1913.
83. B.U.L., Austen Chamberlain Papers, 60/121, Spender to Grigg, 11 Dec. 1913.
84. Ibid.
85. A. Chamberlain, *Politics From ...*, pp. 587–8.
86. Ibid.
87. Ibid., pp. 590–1.
88. Ibid.
89. Ibid., pp. 591–2.
90. HLRO, Bonar Law Papers, 33/6/117, Carson to Asquith (n.d.).
91. NLS, Oliver Papers, 7726/87, Maud Selborne to Oliver, 8 Dec. 1913 (201–2).
92. A. Chamberlain, *Politics From ...*, pp. 589–94.
93. Ibid.
94. NLS, Oliver Papers, 7726/87, Chamberlain to Oliver, 10 Dec. 1913 (36).
95. Ibid., Oliver to Chamberlain, 11 Dec. 1913 (122) and 12 Dec. (123).
96. A. Chamberlain, *Politics From ...*, pp. 589–94.
97. HLRO, Bonar Law Papers, 31/1/38, Lansdowne to Bonar Law, 16 Dec. 1913.
98. Ibid.
99. Ibid.
100. P. Bew, *Ideology and the Irish Question ...*, pp. 100–1.
101. HLRO, Bonar Law Papers, 31/1/47, Selborne to Bonar Law, 21 Dec. 1913.
102. Ibid., 31/1/41, Balfour to Bonar Law, 18 Dec. 1913.
103. NLS, Oliver Papers, 7726/87, Chamberlain to Oliver, 21 Dec. 1913 (40).
104. R. Blake, *The Unknown ...*, p. 161.
105. HLRO, Bonar Law Papers, 33/6/84, Bonar Law to Croal, 18 Oct. 1913.
106. Ibid., 30/3/50, Milner to Bonar Law, 24 Oct. 1913.
107. Ibid.
108. Ibid.
109. Bod.L., Milner Papers, MS Dep 40, Milner to Denison, 25 Oct. 1913 (160–3).
110. Ibid.
111. Bod.L., Milner Papers, Ms Dep 13, Milner to Oliver, 23 Oct. 1913 (42–3).
112. Ibid.

113. Ibid., Ms Dep 16, Milner to Roberts, 30 Oct. 1913 (211).
114. Ibid., Ms Dep 16, Roberts to Milner, 2 Nov. 1913 (212–13).
115. Ibid., Ms Dep, Milner to Roberts, 4 Nov. 1913 (214).
116. Hatfield House, Salisbury Papers, 73/187–9, Willoughby de Broke to Salisbury, 29 Oct. 1913.
117. Ibid.
118. HLRO, Willoughby de Broke Papers, Lord Arran to de Broke, 4 Oct. 1913.
119. Ibid.
120. HLRO, Bonar Law Papers, 30/3/61, Midleton to Bonar Law, 28 Oct. 1913.
121. Ibid., 30/3/80, Salisbury to Bonar Law, 31 Oct. 1913.
122. Ibid.
123. Viscount Long of Wraxell, *Memories* (London, 1923) p. 200.
124. HLRO, Bonar Law Papers, 30/4/20, Leslie Wilson to Bonar Law, 9 Nov. 1913.
125. Ibid., 30/4/18, Long to Bonar Law, 9 Nov. 1913.
126. Ibid., 30/4/16, Balfour to Bonar Law, 8 Nov. 1913.
127. Ibid., 31/1/14, Hugh Cecil to Bonar Law, 8 Dec. 1913.
128. J. Ramsden, *Real Old* ..., p. 66.
129. B.U.L., Austen Chamberlain Papers, 11/1/50, Lansdowne to Chamberlain, 24 Nov. 1913.
130. Ibid., 30/4/55, Gretton to Bonar Law, 26 Nov. 1913.
131. Ibid., 33/6/98, Bonar Law to Balfour, 18 Nov. 1913.
132. *The Morning Post*, 18 Nov. 1913.
133. Ibid.
134. Ibid.
135. NLS, Oliver Papers, 7726/87, Oliver to Craik, 24 Oct. 1913 (99).
136. Hatfield House Salisbury Papers, 73/187–9, Willoughby de Broke to Salisbury, 29 Oct. 1913.
137. HLRO., Bonar Law Papers, 30/3/77, Long to Bonar Law, 31 Oct. 1913.
138. Ibid., 30/4/11, Long to Bonar Law, 7 Nov. 1913.
139. Ibid., 30/4/18, Long to Bonar Law, 9 Nov. 1913.
140. Ibid., 30/4/11, Long to Bonar Law, 7 Nov. 1913.
141. Ibid., 30/4/46, Long to Bonar Law, 20 Nov. 1913.
142. Ibid.
143. Ibid.
144. Ibid., Long to Bonar Law, 20 Nov. 1913 (38).
145. Ibid., 31/1/32, Curzon to Bonar Law, 15 Dec. 1913.
146. HLRO, Bonar Law Papers, 31/1/25, Lansdowne to Bonar Law, 11 Dec. 1913.
147. Ibid., 31/1/38, Lansdowne to Bonar Law, 16 Dec. 1913.
148. Ibid.
149. Ibid., 31/1/46, Lansdowne to Bonar Law, 21 Dec. 1913.
150. Ibid., 31/1/47, Selborne to Bonar Law, 21 Dec. 1913.
151. A. Chamberlain, *Politics From* ..., p. 586.
152. HLRO, Bonar Law Papers, 33/6/111, 'Notes on conversation with Prime Minister', 10 Dec. 1913.

153. Ibid., 31/1/47, Selborne to Bonar Law, 21 Dec. 1913.
154. Ibid., 33/6/111, Memorandum 'Notes on ...,' 10 Dec. 1913.
155. Ibid., 31/1/38, Lansdowne to Bonar Law, 16 Dec. 1913.
156. Ibid., 31/1/47, Selborne to Bonar Law, 21 Dec. 1913.
157. Ibid., 31/1/54, R. Cecil to Bonar Law, 24 Dec. 1913.
158. Ibid.
159. Ibid., 31/1/38, Lansdowne to Bonar Law, 16 Dec. 1913.
160. Ibid.
161. Ibid., 31/1/31, Long to Bonar Law, 14 Dec. 1913.
162. Ibid., 31/1/25, Lansdowne to Bonar Law, 11 Dec. 1913.
163. Ibid., 31/1/54, R. Cecil to Bonar Law, 24 Dec. 1913.
164. Ibid., 31/1/14, H. Cecil to Bonar Law, 8 Dec. 1913.
165. Ibid., 31/1/54, R. Cecil to Bonar Law, 24 Dec. 1913.
166. Ibid., 33/6/115, Bonar Law to Lansdowne, 22 Dec. 1913.
167. Ibid., 31/1/52, Asquith to Carson, 23 Dec. 1913.
168. P. Jalland, *The Liberals ...*, p. 180.
169. HLRO, Bonar Law Papers, 33/6/117, Carson to Asquith, 27 Dec. 1913.
170. Ibid., 33/6/80, 'Conversations with ...,' 15 Oct. 1913.
171. Ibid., 33/6/84, Bonar Law to Croal, 18 Oct. 1913.
172. Ibid.
173. Bew, *Ideology and the Irish Question ...*, pp. 99–100.
174. HLRO, Bonar Law Papers, 30/3/33, Balfour to Bonar Law, 17 Oct. 1913.
175. Ibid., 30/3/46, Strachey to Bonar Law, 22 Oct. 1913.
176. Ibid., 30/3/37, Talbort to Bonar Law, 19 Oct. 1913.
177. Ibid.
178. M. Fforde, *Conservatism and Collectivism, 1886–1914* (Edinburgh, 1990), ch. 5.
179. Ibid., 33/6/84, Bonar Law to Croal, 18 Oct. 1913.
180. Bod.L., Milner Papers, Ms Dep 40, Milner to Glazebrook, 14 June 1913 (7–8).
181. A. Jackson, *Sir Edward Carson*, ch. 3.
182. R. Blake, *The Unknown ...*; J. Ramsden, *The Age of ...*; D. Dutton, His Majesty's ... .
183. HLRO, Bonar Law Papers, 30/3/57, Stamfordham to Bonar Law, 27 Oct. 1913.
184. *The Times*, 27 Oct. 1913.
185. Ibid.
186. HLRO, Bonar Law Papers, 30/3/80, Salisbury to Bonar Law, 31 Oct. 1913.
187. HLRO, Bonar Law Papers, 30/3/57, Stamfordham to Bonar Law, 27 Oct. 1913.
188. A. Chamberlain, *Politics From ...*, p. 570.
189. Ibid.
190. HLRO, Bonar Law Papers, 30/3/55, Steel-Maitland to Bonar Law, 27 Oct. 1913.
191. *The Times*, 30 Oct. 1913: speech at Newcastle.
192. Ibid.

193. Ibid.
194. Ibid.
195. Ibid.
196. A. Chamberlain, *Politics From ...*, p. 571.
197. HLRO, Bonar Law Papers, 30/3/73, Sir G. Younger to Bonar Law, 30 Oct. 1913.
198. Ibid., 30/3/80, Salisbury to Bonar Law, 31 Oct. 1913.
199. Ibid., 30/4/3, Ashtown to Bonar Law, 2 Nov. 1913.
200. Ibid., 30/3/75, Asquith to Bonar Law, 30 Oct. 1913.
201. Ibid., 33/6/93, 'Notes on a 2nd Conversation with the Prime Minister', 7 Nov. 1913.
202. Ibid.
203. Ibid., 30/3/58, Strachey to Bonar Law, 27 Oct. 1913.
204. Ibid., 33/6/93, 'Notes on a 2nd ...', 7 Nov. 1913.
205. Ibid.
206. Ibid.
207. Ibid., 30/4/18, Long to Bonar Law, 9 Nov. 1913.
208. Ibid., 33/6/93, 'Notes on a 2nd ...', 7 Nov. 1913.
209. Ibid.
210. P. Jalland, *The Liberals ...*, p. 157.
211. HLRO, Bonar Law Papers,, 33/6/97, Bonar Law to Balfour, 7 Nov. 1913.
212. Ibid., 33/6/94, Bonar Law to Long, 7 Nov. 1913.
213. Ibid., 33/6/98, Bonar Law to Balfour, 18 Nov. 1913.
214. Ibid., 33/6/99, Bonar Law to Long, 21 Nov. 1913.
215. Ibid., 33/6/111, Bonar Law to Landsdowne, 10 Dec. 1913.
216. Ibid., 33/6/103, Bonar Law to J.W. Hills, 1 Dec. 1913.
217. Ibid., 33/6/114, Bonar Law to Long, 15 Dec. 1913.
218. Ibid., 33/6/111, 'Notes on a Conversation with the Prime Minister', 10 Dec. 1913.
219. Ibid., 33/6/96, Bonar Law to Long, 8 Nov. 1913.
220. Ibid., 33/6/84, Bonar Law to J.P. Croal, 18 Oct. 1913.
221. Ibid., 30/4/18, Long to Bonar Law, 9 Nov. 1913.
222. Ibid., 33/6/99, Bonar Law to Long, 21 Nov. 1913.
223. Ibid., 31/1/31, Long to Bonar Law, 14 Dec. 1913.
224. Ibid., 33/6/114, Bonar Law to Long, 15 Dec. 1913.
225. Ibid., 31/1/37, Long to Bonar Law, 16 Dec. 1913.
226. B.Mus., Long Papers, Add Mss 62404, Long to Bonar Law, 31 Dec. 1913 (43–5).
227. P. Jalland, *The Liberals ...*, p. 178.

NOTES TO CHAPTER 7

1. Parl Debates, vol. XLIX, col. 933, 9 March 1914.
2. B.U.L., Austen Chamberlain Papers, 60/127, Oliver to Chamberlain, 7 Jan. 1914.

3. NLS, Oliver Papers, 7726/86, Garvin to Oliver, 31 Dec. 1913 (243–4).
4. NLS, Oliver Papers, 7726/87, Spender to Oliver, 6 Jan. 1914 (11–12).
5. *The Westminster*, 9 Jan. 1914, in Quickswood Papers, 17/12–3, Robert Cecil to Hugh, 15 Jan. 1914.
6. NLS, Oliver Papers, 7726/87, Hythe to Oliver, 22 Jan. 1914 (22–3).
7. Ibid., Chamberlain to Oliver, 24 Jan. 1914 (42).
8. A. Chamberlain, *Politics from* ..., p. 606.
9. P. Williamson, *The Modernisation* ..., p. 73.
10. Ibid.
11. *The Times*, 27 Jan. 1914.
12. A. Chamberlain, *Politics From* ..., p. 606.
13. J. Vincent, *The Crawford Papers* ..., pp. 324–5.
14. B.Mus., Cecil of Chelwood Papers, Add Mss 51085, Salisbury to Cecil, 6 Feb. 1914 (59–61).
15. P. Bew argues that Asquith was, at this point, 'following a policy of delay ... to keep the Opposition guessing as to his ultimate policy', in *Ideology and the Irish* ..., pp. 100–1.
16. A. Chamberlain, *Politics from* ..., p. 610.
17. Ibid.
18. Ibid., p. 611.
19. Ibid.
20. Ibid., pp. 612–13.
21. Ibid.
22. Ibid., p. 613.
23. Bod.L., Selborne Papers, Mss 77, Selborne to Charnwood, 7 Feb. 1914 (80–2).
24. A. Chamberlain, *Politics from* ..., p. 615.
25. NLS, Oliver Papers, 7726/87, Chamberlain to Oliver, 23 Feb. 1914 (46).
26. A. Chamberlain, *Politics from* ..., p. 615.
27. NLS, Oliver Papers, 7726/87, Chamberlain to Oliver, 18 Feb. 1914 (44).
28. A. Chamberlain, *Politics from* ..., p. 615.
29. P. Jalland, *The Liberals* ..., p. 194.
30. A. Chamberlain, *Politics from* ..., p. 614.
31. B.U.L., Austen Chamberlain Papers, 60/134, Oliver to Chamberlain, 4 March 1914.
32. B.U.L., Austen Chamberlain Papers, 60/130, Oliver to Chamberlain, 21 Feb. 1914.
33. Bod.L., Milner Papers, Add Mss Eng Hist C.689, 'Memorandum' by Oliver, 3 March 1914 (56–98).
34. B.U.L., Austen Chamberlain, 60/134, Oliver to Chamberlain, 4 March 1914.
35. A. Gollin, *The Observer* ..., p. 417.
36. P. Bew, *Ideology and the Irish* ..., p. 101.
37. NLS, Oliver Papers, 7726/87, Garvin to Oliver, 31 Dec. 1914 (243–4); Garvin to Oliver, 1 Jan. 1914 (1–2).
38. Ibid., Garvin to Oliver, 19 Jan. 1914 (21).

39. *The Times*, 20 Jan. 1914.
40. Sir Almeric Fitzroy, *Memoirs*, 2 vols (London, 1925), vol. ii, p. 536.
41. A. Chamberlain, *Politics from* ..., p. 613.
42. NLS, Oliver Papers, 7726/87, Stamfordham to Oliver, 13 Feb. 1914 (56).
43. Ibid., Carson to Oliver, 10 Feb. 1914 (3–4).
44. J. Kendle, *Ireland and the Federal* ..., p. 168.
45. NLS, Oliver Papers, 7726/87, Spender to Oliver, 17 Feb. 1914 (70).
46. J. Kendle, *Ireland and the Federal* ..., pp. 168–9.
47. NLS, Oliver Papers, 7726/87, Stamfordham to Oliver, 13 Feb. 1914 (56).
48. J. Ramsden, *Real Old Tory* ..., p. 73; Williamson, *The Modernisation* ..., p. 74.
49. A. Chamberlain, *Politics from* ..., p. 616.
50. J. Kendle, *Ireland and the Federal* ..., pp. 168–9.
51. NLS, Oliver Papers, 7726/87, Chamberlain to Oliver, 6 March 1914 (50).
52. Ramsden, *Real Old Tory* ..., p. 73.
53. *The Times*, 16 March 1914.
54. A. Chamberlain, *Politics from* ..., p. 621.
55. J. Ramsden, *Real Old Tory* ..., p. 73.
56. Ibid.
57. J. Kendle, *Ireland and the Federal* ..., p. 173.
58. J. Ramsden, *Real Old Tory* ..., p. 75.
59. HLRO, Bonar Law Papers, 32/2/1, Dicey to Bonar Law, 1 April 1914.
60. J. Kendle, *Ireland and the Federal* ..., p. 174. Also P. Jalland, 'UK Devolution, 1910–1914: Political Panacea or Tactical Diversion', *English Historical Review*, 1979, pp. 757–85.
61. A. Chamberlain, *Politics From* ..., pp. 636–7.
62. HLRO, Bonar Law Papers, 32/2/26, Chamberlain to Carson, 7 April 1914.
63. Bod.L., Selborne Papers, Mss 77, Selborne to Carson, 9 April 1914.
64. Ibid.
65. J. Kendle, *Ireland and the Federal* ..., p. 175.
66. HLRO, Bonar Law Papers, 32/2/26, Carson to Bonar Law, 7 April 1914.
67. A.T.Q. Stewart, *The Ulster Crisis* ..., chs 14–16; A. Jackson, 'The Larne Gun Running of 1914', *History Ireland*, vol. 1, no. 1 (1993), pp. 35–9.
68. A. Fitzroy, *Memoirs*, p. 547.
69. A. Chamberlain, *Politics from* ..., p. 640.
70. Sir Almeric Fitzroy, *Memoirs*, p. 547.
71. B.U.L., Austen Chamberlain Papers, 60/145, Oliver to Chamberlain, 26 April 1914.
72. Ibid., Oliver to Chamberlain, 27 April 1914.
73. A. Chamberlain, *Politics from* ..., p. 641.
74. J. Ramsden, *Real Old Tory* ..., p. 76.
75. A. Chamberlain, *Politics from* ..., p. 641.
76. B.U.L., Austen Chamberlain Papers, Amery to Chamberlain, 1 May 1914.
77. A. Chamberlain, *Politics from* ..., p. 642.
78. Ibid., p. 645.
79. Ibid., p. 642.

80. HLRO, Bonar Law Papers, 32/2/31, Midleton to Bonar Law, 13 April 1914.
81. Bonar Law Papers, 32/2/36, Lansdowne to Bonar Law, 16 April 1914.
82. *The Times*, 15 April 1914.
83. A. Chamberlain, *Politics from* ..., pp. 643–5.
84. Ibid.
85. Ibid.
86. B.U.L., Austen Chamberlain Papers, 60/147, Oliver to Chamberlain, 7 May 1914.
87. P. Jalland, 'UK Devolution 1910–1914 ...', pp. 776–83.
88. P. Bew, *Ideology and the Irish Question* ..., pp. 100–1.
89. P. Jalland, 'UK Devolution 1910–1914 ...', pp. 782–4.
90. A. Chamberlain, *Politics from* ..., p. 646.
91. HLRO, Willoughby de Broke Papers, 8/88, Arran to de Broke, Feb. 1914.
92. J. Vincent, *The Crawford Papers* ..., p. 326.
93. HLRO, Willoughby de Broke Papers, 7/6, Leconfield to de Broke, 12 Jan. 1914.
94. P.R.O.N.I., Carson Papers, A/5/3, Constance Williams to Carson, 4 Jan. 1914; A. Jackson, *Sir Edward Carson* ..., pp. 33–8; A. Jackson, 'Unionist Myths, 1912–1985', *Past and Present* (1992).
95. HLRO, Willoughby de Broke Papers, 7/8, Lord Peel to de Broke, 15 Jan. 1914.
96. Ibid., 7/2, Stanhope to de Broke, 5 Jan. 1914.
97. Ibid., 8/5, 'Letters to Peers', 4 Feb. 1914.
98. Ibid., 7/14, Bedford to de Broke, 28 Jan. 1914.
99. Ibid., 8/5, 'Letter ...', 4 Feb. 1914.
100. Ibid., 8/10, Lansdowne to de Broke, 5 Feb. 1914.
101. Ibid., 8/25, Selborne to de Broke, 7 Feb. 1914.
102. Ibid., 8/24, Lansdowne to de Broke, 7 Feb. 1914.
103. Ibid., 8/24a, Midleton to de Broke, 7 Feb. 1914.
104. Ibid., 8/2, Arran to de Broke, 4 Feb. 1914.
105. J. Vincent, *The Crawford Papers* ..., p. 323.
106. Bod.L., Milner Papers, Add Mss Eng Hist C.689, de Broke to Milner, 6 Jan. 1914 (2–4).
107. A. Gollin, *Proconsul in Power: A Study of Lord Milner in Opposition and in Power* (London, 1964), pp. 182–3.
108. W.S. Rodner, 'Leaguers, Covenanters, Moderates: British Support for Ulster, 1913–14', *Eire-Ireland*, vol. 17, 13 (1982), p. 75.
109. Bod.L., Milner Papers, Mss Dep 85, diary 11 January 1914.
110. W. Long, *Memories*, p. 201.
111. Bod.L., Milner Papers, Add Mss Eng Hist C.689, 'Memorandum' (178–85) n.d.
112. Ibid.
113. Ibid.
114. Bod.L., Milner Papers, Mss Dep 13, Milner to Oliver, 3 Feb. 1914 (71–4).
115. Ibid.

116. B.Mus., Cecil of Chelwood Papers, Add Mss 51072, Amery to Cecil, 16 Jan. 1914 (219–21).
117. Bod.L., Milner Papers, Add Mss Eng Hist C.689, Milner to Selborne, 18 Feb. 1914 (16–18).
118. Bod.L., Milner Papers, Mss Dep 41, Malcolm to Milner, March 1914 (16–17).
119. Bod.L., Milner Papers, Mss Dep 85, Diary entries for 3 and 4 Feb. 1914.
120. Ibid., Diary entry for 12 Jan. 1914.
121. B.Mus., Cecil of Chelwood Papers, Add Mss 51072, Amery to Cecil, 16 Jan. 1914 (219–21).
122. Ibid.
123. HLRO, Bonar Law Papers, 34/1/14, Bonar Law to Lansdowne, 17 Jan. 1914.
124. Ibid.
125. Bod.L., Milner Papers, Add Mss Eng Hist C.689. A copy of the *British Covenant*, with the signature of W. Cunningham, Archdeacon of Ely at the bottom, dated 1 March 1914 (113–15).
126. P. Rowland, *The Last Liberal governments: Unfinished business, 1911–1914* (London, 1971), pp. 339 and 370–1.
127. Bod.L., Milner Papers, Add Mss Eng Hist C.689, List of individuals who might be willing to contribute to the cause, 25 Feb. 1914 (42–4).
128. Ibid., Mss Dep 157, 'Balance sheet of Donations' (1–70).
129. *The Morning Post*, 27 Feb. 1914.
130. W. Long, *Memories*, p. 203.
131. Bod.L., Selborne Papers, Ms 12, Milner to Selborne, 6 March 1914 (242–5).
132. Ibid.
133. Bod.L., Milner Papers, Mss Dep 464, 'The Covenanter', 20 May 1914.
134. NLS, Oliver Papers, 7726/87, Milner to Oliver, 19 May 1914 (26–7).
135. W. Rodner, 'Leaguers, Covenanters ...', p. 81.
136. HLRO, Bonar Law Papers, 31/2/49, Lansdowne to Bonar Law, 18 Jan. 1914.
137. J. Vincent, *The Crawford Papers* ..., p. 323.
138. Bod.L., Milner Papers, Add Mss Eng Hist C.689, Chamberlain to Amery, 17 Jan. 1914 (5–6).
139. Ibid., R. Cecil to Amery, 18 Jan. 1914 (10–13).
140. Ibid., Mss Dep 41, Milner to Carson, 27 Feb. 1914 (14).
141. A. Gollin, *Proconsul in Politics* ..., p. 197.
142. G. Phillips, *The Diehards* ...; A. Sykes, 'The Radical Right and the Crisis of Conservatism ...'.
143. Hansard, Parl Debates., XXXVII, 296–7, 16 April 1912.
144. A.T.Q. Stewart, *The Ulster Crisis* ..., pp. 83–5.
145. HLRO, Bonar Law Papers, 34/2/39, Bonar Law to Craik, 16 March 1914.
146. C.C. Weston, 'Lord Selborne, Bonar Law and the "Tory Revolt"', in *The Lords of parliament: Studies, 1714–1914*, ed. R.W. Davies (Princeton, 1995); J. Smith, 'Paralysing the Arm: The Unionists and the Army Annual Act, 1911–1914', *Parliamentary History*, 15, 2 (1996).
147. A. Gollin, *The Observer* ..., pp. 336–7.
148. B.L., Cecil of Chelwood Papers, Add Mss 51075 (b), Hugh Cecil to Robert

Cecil, 6 June 1913 (34–40).

149. Bowood House, Fifth Marquis of Lansdowne Papers, Ireland 1914, LAB 4/1/5, Bonar Law to Lansdowne, 13 Jan. 1914.
150. HLRO, Bonar Law Papers, 34/1/25, Bonar Law to Lansdowne, 30 Jan. 1914.
151. Ibid.
152. Ibid., 34/1/20, Bonar Law to Finlay, 27 Jan. 1914.
153. Ibid., 34/1/31, Bonar Law to Balfour, 5 Feb. 1914.
154. J. Smith, 'Paralysing the Arm ...'.
155. Bowood House, Fifth Marquis of Lansdowne Papers, Ireland 1914, Lab 4/1/5, 'Memo on the Army Annual Act', 24 Feb. 1914.
156. HLRO, Bonar Law Papers, 34/2/39, Bonar Law to Craik, 16 March 1914.
157. NLS, Oliver Papers, 7726/87, Chamberlain to Oliver, 10 March 1914 (52–3).
158. J. Ramsden, *Real Old Tory* ..., p. 72.
159. B.U.L., Austen Chamberlain Papers, 60/138, Oliver to Chamberlain, 12 March 1914.
160. Bod.L., Milner Papers, Mss Dep 41, Dicey to Milner, 9 March 1914 (41–2).
161. NLS, Oliver Papers, 7726/87, Spender to Oliver, 9 March 1914 (101).
162. J. Vincent, *The Crawford Papers* ..., pp. 328–9.
163. Ibid.
164. Bod.L., Milner Papers, Mss Dep 41, Robinson to Milner, 18 March 1914 (58).
165. Ibid.
166. HLRO, Strachey Papers, S/4/17/17, Strachey to Curzon, 19 March 1914.
167. I. Beckett, *The Army and the Curragh Incident 1914* (London, 1986), p. 14.
168. N.I.R.O., Lady Craigavon Papers, Diary D.1415 B/38/1–162, 26 March 1914.
169. I. Beckett, *The Army and the Curragh* ..., pp. 1–29.
170. Ibid., p. 12.
171. P. Jalland, *The Liberals* ..., p. 230.
172. A.P. Ryan, *Mutiny at the Curragh* (London, 1956); J. Fergusson, *The Curragh Incident* (London, 1964); A.T.Q. Stewart, *The Ulster Crisis* ..., chs 12 and 13; I. Beckett, *The Army and the Curragh Incident* ....
173. I. Beckett, *The Army and the Curragh Incident* ..., p. 7.
174. *The Times*, 3 Jan. 1914.
175. Bod.L., Milner Papers, Add Mss Eng Hist C.689, Ridgeway to Milner, 2 Feb. 1914 (14–15).
176. Ibid.
177. N.I.R.O., Lady Craigavon Papers, Diary D.1415 B/38/1–162, 18 March 1914.
178. A.T.Q. Stewart, *The Ulster Crisis* ..., pp. 149–50.
179. M. Hyde, *Carson* ..., p. 351.
180. A. Gollin, *A Proconsul* ..., p. 196.
181. HLRO, Bonar Law Papers, 34/1/21, Bonar Law to Roberts, 27 Jan. 1914.
182. R. Blake, *The Unknown* ..., p. 178.
183. Bod.L., Milner Papers, Add Mss Eng Hist C.689, 'Memorandum' n.d. unsigned (178–85).

184. Imperial War Museum (I.W.Mus.), Sir Henry Wilson Papers, Diary Add Mss, 73/1/3 13, Nov. 1913.
185. Bod.L., Milner Papers, Mss Dep 41, Carson to Milner, 18 March 1914 (57); I. Beckett, *The Army and the Curragh Incident* ..., p. 5.
186. HLRO, Bonar Law Papers, 32/1/44, Long to Bonar Law, 22 March 1914.
187. I. Beckett, *The Army and the Curragh Incident* ..., p. 12.
188. I.W.Mus., Sir Henry Wilson Papers, Diary Add Mss 73/1/3, 20 March 1914.
189. Ibid., 21 and 22 March 1914.
190. A. Chamberlain, *Politics from* ..., p. 630.
191. HLRO, Bonar Law Papers, 32/1/66, Carson to Bonar Law, 26 March 1914.
192. A. Chamberlain, *Politics from* ..., p. 624.
193. Ibid., p. 625.
194. Ibid., p. 628.
195. P. Jalland, *The Liberals* ..., p. 233.
196. HLRO, Bonar Law Papers, 34/2/45, Bonar Law to Asquith, 22 March 1914.
197. Ibid., 32/1/51, Asquith to Bonar Law, 23 March 1914.
198. A.T.Q. Stewart, *The Ulster Crisis* ..., p. 172.
199. P. Williamson, *The Modernisation* ..., p. 76.
200. Parl Debates, vol. LX, cols 893–900, 30 March 1914.
201. J. Ramsden, *Real Old Tory* ..., p. 75.
202. Ibid.
203. A.T.Q. Stewart, *The Ulster Crisis* ..., pp. 150–1.
204. Ibid., chs 14, 15, 16, 17; A. Jackson, 'The Larne Gun Running of 1914 ...'; P. Buckland, *Irish Unionism, 1885–1923: A Documentary History* (Belfast, 1973), pp. 207–64.
205. A. Jackson, 'Ulster Myths ...', *Past and Present*; A. Jackson, 'Larne Gun Running', *Irish History*.
206. HLRO, Bonar Law Papers, 34/2/33, Bonar Law to Du Pre, 12 Feb. 1914.
207. Ibid., 34/1/8, Bonar Law to Balfour, 7 Jan. 1914.
208. *The Times*, 27 Jan. 1914.
209. Ibid., 29 Jan. 1914.
210. HLRO, Bonar Law Papers, 31/2/36, Balfour to Bonar Law, 13 Jan. 1914.
211. P. Bew, *Ideology and the Irish* ..., p. 101.
212. *The Times*, 16 Jan. 1914.
213. Ibid.
214. Ibid.
215. Ibid.
216. B.Mus., Cecil of Chelwood Papers, Add Mss 51072, Amery to Cecil, 16 Jan. 1914 (219–21).
217. HLRO, Bonar Law Papers, 31/2/52, Will de Broke to Bonar Law, 21 Jan. 1914.
218. D.G. Boyce, *The Irish Question in British Politics, 1868–1986* (London, 1988) p. 39.
219. J. Smith, 'Paralysing the Arm ...', *Parliamentary History*.
220. *The Times*, 26 July 1911.

221. Ibid., 16 Jan. 1914.
222. HLRO, Bonar Law Papers, 34/1/25, Bonar Law to Lansdowne, 30 Jan. 1914.
223. J. Ramsden, *The Age of Balfour ...*, p. 84.
224. HLRO, Bonar Law Papers, 34/1/25, Bonar Law to Lansdowne, 30 Jan. 1914.
225. Ibid.
226. Ibid., 34/2/39, Bonar Law to Craik, 16 March 1914.
227. A. Chamberlain, *Politics from Inside ...*, p. 611.
228. Bod.L., Milner Papers, Mss Dep 41, Dicey to Milner, 8 March 1914 (45).
229. J. Vincent, *The Crawford Papers ...*, p. 329.
230. HLRO, Bonar Law Papers, 31/4/27, Craik to Bonar Law, 14 March 1914.
231. Ibid., 34/2/44, Bonar Law to Croal, 20 March 1914.
232. Ibid., 34/2/56, Bonar Law to Selborne, 7 April 1914.
233. N. Mansergh, *The Unresolved Question: The Anglo-Irish Settlement and its Undoing, 1912–1972* (New Haven, 1991), p. 73.
234. B.Mus., Balfour Papers, Add Mss 49693, 'Memorandum of an interview with the prime minister' by Bonar Law, 5 May 1914 (165–8).
235. HLRO, Bonar Law Papers, 34/2/70, Bonar Law to Montgomery, 5 May 1914.
236. HLRO, Bonar Law Papers, 32/3/28, Midleton to Bonar Law, 4 May 1914.
237. Ibid.
238. Ibid.
239. *The Irish Times*, 25 May 1914.
240. HLRO, Bonar Law Papers, 32/2/68, Amery to Bonar Law, 30 April 1914.
241. Ibid., 33/1/10, Gwynne to Bonar Law, 3 July 1914.
242. HLRO, Willoughby de Broke Papers, WB 10/9, de Broke to Lansdowne, 13 May 1914.
243. HLRO, Bonar Law Papers, 32/3/55, Lansdowne to Bonar Law, 27 May 1914.
244. Ibid., 32/3/56, Long to Bonar Law, 28 May 1914.
245. Ibid., 32/4/31, Long to Bonar Law, 29 June 1914.
246. Ibid., 32/3/55, Lansdowne to Bonar Law, 27 May 1914.
247. B.Mus., Walter Long Papers, Add Mss 62405, Stamfordham to Long, 22 June 1914 (10–13); Add Mss 62417, Stamfordham to Armstrong, 17 June 1914.
248. Hatfield House, Salisbury Papers, 74/253–4, 'memorandum of conversation with the King', 31 May 1914.
249. HLRO, Willoughby de Broke Papers, WB 10/11, Milner to de Broke, 3 June 1914.
250. Hatfield House, Salisbury Papers, 74/244–46, Lansdowne to Salisbury 31 May 1914.
251. J. Vincent, *The Crawford Papers ...*, p. 335.
252. B.Mus., Walter Long Papers, Add Mss 62417, Long to Carson, 30 May 1914.
253. HLRO, Bonar Law Papers, 34/2/80, Bonar Law to Midleton, 17 June 1914.
254. B.Mus., Walter Long Papers, Add Mss 62417, Long to Midleton, 29 May 1914.
255. Ibid., 10 June 1914.

256. J. Vincent, *The Crawford Papers* ..., pp. 336–7.
257. HLRO, Bonar Law Papers, 32/4/29, Midleton to Bonar Law, 27 June 1914.
258. J. Charmley, *Churchill: The End of Glory* (London, 1993) p. 96.
259. P. Jalland, *The Liberals* ..., pp. 255–60.
260. De Tocqueville had written that 'the English Constitution does not really exist;. A.L. Lowell, *The Government of England* (London, 1908), vol. I, p. 1.
261. P. Pearse, *Political Writings and Speeches* (Dublin, 166), p. 185.

Bibliography

MANUSCRIPT COLLECTIONS

Birmingham University Library

Austen Chamberlain Papers
Joseph Chamberlain Papers
Neville Chamberlain Papers

Bodleian Library

Asquith Papers
Sanders Papers
Gwynne Papers
Hitchens Papers
Milner Papers
Lady Violet Milner Papers
Redmond Papers (microfilm)
Sandars Papers
Selborne Papers
Worthington-Evans Papers

Bowood House

Lansdowne Papers (Fifth Marquis)

British Library

Balfour Papers
Robert Cecil Papers
Cave Papers
Long Papers

Churchill College Cambridge

Bull Papers

Chandos Papers
Esher Papers
Page-Croft Papers

Durham County Record Office

Lady Londonderry Papers
Long Papers

Hatfield House

Salisbury Papers (Fourth Marquis)
Quickswood Papers

House of Lords Record Office

Beaverbrook Papers
Bonar Law Papers
Blumfield Papers
Lloyd George Papers
Strachey Papers
Wargrave Papers
Willoughby de Broke Papers

Imperial War Museum

Sir Henry Wilson Papers

India Office

Curzon Papers

Liverpool Central Library

Derby Papers

National Army Museum

Earl Roberts Papers

National Museum of Scotland

Oliver Papers

Northern Ireland Public Record Office

Armstrong Papers
Carson Papers
Lord Craigavon Papers
Lady Craigavon Papers
Crawford Papers
Cushenden Papers
Londonderry Papers
UUC files (D.1327)
U.A.I. files (D.989)

Public Record Office

Midleton Papers

Scottish Record Office

Lothian Papers
Steel-Maitland Papers

NEWSPAPERS AND PERIODICALS

Belfast News Letter
The Times
The Irish Times
Morning Post
National Gleanings and Memoranda
National Review

The Nineteenth Century
The Spectator

OFFICIAL

Hansard Parliamentary debates

CONTEMPORARY WORKS, AUTOBIOGRAPHIES, LETTERS AND DIARIES

L.S. Amery, *My Political Life* (3 vols, London, 1953–6).
H.H. Asquith, *Memories and Reflections, 1852–1927* (2 vols, London, 1928).
A.J. Balfour, *Opinions and Arguments* (London, 1927).
W.S. Blunt, *My diaries* (2 vols, London, 1919).

D.G. Boyce, *The Crisis of British Unionism: The Domestic Political Papers of the Second Earl of Selborne* (London, 1987).

M.V. Brett and Esher, Viscount (eds), *Journals and Letters of Reginald, Viscount Esher* (4 vols, London, 1934–8).

Callwell, Brigadier-General C.E., *Field Marshall, Sir Henry Wilson: His Life and Diaries* (2 vols, London, 1927).

Viscount Cecil of Chelwood, *All the Way* (London, 1949).

A. Chamberlain (ed.), *Politics from Inside: An Epistolary Chronicle, 1906–1914* (London, 1936).

A. Clark (ed.), *'A Good Innings': The Private Papers of Viscount Lee of Fareham* (London, 1974).

F.H. Crawford, *Guns for Ulster* (Belfast, 1947).

H. Page Croft, *My Life of Strife* (London, 1948).

A.V. Dicey, *A Leap in the Dark. A Criticism of the Principles of Home Rule as Illustrated by the Bill of 1893* (London, 1911).

A.V. Dicey, *A Fools Paradise: Being a Constitutionalist's Criticism on the Home Rule Bill of 1912* (London, 1913).

A.V. Dicey, *Law of the Constitution* (London, 1914).

Earl Dunraven, *Past Times and Pastimes* (London, 1922).

St John Ervine, *Sir Edward Carson and the Ulster Movement* (London, 1915).

Sir A. Fitzroy, *Memoirs* (2 vols, London, 1925).

A. Griffith-Boscawen, *Memories* (London, 1924).

T.H. Healy, *Letters and Leaders of My Day* (London, 1928).

K. Middlemas (ed.), *Thomas Jones, Whitehall Diary: Ireland 1918–1925* (London, 1971).

Viscount Long, *Memories* (London, 1923).

A.L. Lowell, *The Government of England* (2 vols, New York, 1908).

J.W. Mackail and G. Wyndham (eds), *The Life and Letters of George Wyndham* (2 vols, London, 1924).

R. McNeill, *Ulster's Stand for Union* (London, 1922).

Earl Midleton, *Records and Reactions, 1856–1939* (London, 1939).

Lord Newton, *Retrospection* (London, 1941).

Earl of Oxford and Asquith, *Fifty Years in Parliament* (2 vols, London, 1928).

P. Pearse, *Political Writings and Speeches* (Dublin, 1966).

G. Peel, *The Reign of Sir Edward Carson* (London, 1914).

Sir C. Petrie, *The Life and Letters of the Rt Hon Sir Austen Chamberlain* (2 vols, London, 1940).

'A Privy Councillor', *Studies of Yesterday* (London, 1928).

J. Ramsden (ed.), *Real Old Tory Politics: The Political Diaries of Robert Sanders, Lord Bayford, 1910–1935* (London, 1984).

Lord Riddell, *More Pages From My Diary 1908–1914* (London, 1934).

J. Ridley and C. Percy (eds), *The Letters of Arthur Balfour and Lady Elcho, 1885–1917* (London, 1992).

S. Rosenbaum (ed.), *Against Home Rule: The Case for the Union* (London, 1912).

J. Vincent (ed.), *The Crawford Papers: The Journals of David Lindsay, twenty-seventh*

Earl of Crawford and tenth Earl of Balcarres, during the years 1892 to 1940 (Manchester, 1984).

P. Williamson (ed.), *The Modernisation of Conservative Politics: the Diaries and Letters of William Bridgeman, 1904–1935* (London, 1988).

Lord Willoughby de Broke, *The Passing Years* (London, 1924).

T. Wilson, *The Political Diaries of C.P. Scott, 1911–1928* (London, 1970).

Earl Winterton, *Pre-War* (London, 1932).

Earl Winterton, *Orders of the Day* (London, 1953).

BIOGRAPHIES

P. Bew, *John Redmond* (Dublin, 1996).

J. Biggs-Davison, *George Wyndham: A Study in Toryism* (London, 1951).

Lord Birkenhead, *Frederick Edwin, Earl of Birkenhead* (2 vols, London, 1933).

R. Blake, *The Unknown Prime Minister: The Life and Times of Andrew Bonar Law, 1858–1923* (London, 1955).

P. Buckland, *James Craig* (Dublin, 1980).

J. Campbell, *F.E. Smith: First Earl of Birkenhead* (London, 1983).

R.S. Churchill, *Lord Derby: King of Lancashire* (London, 1959).

B. Dugdale, *Arthur James Balfour* (2 vols, London, 1936).

D. Dutton, *Austen Chamberlain: Gentleman in Politics* (Bolton, 1985).

M. Egremont, *Balfour* (London, 1980).

Sir J. Ervine, *Craigavon, Ulsterman* (London, 1949).

A. Gollin, *The Observer and J.L. Garvin 1908–1914* (Oxford, 1960).

A. Gollin, *Proconsul in Politics: A Study of Lord Milner in Opposition and in Power* (London, 1964).

J. Grigg, *Lloyd George: from Peace to War, 1912–1916* (Berkley, 1985).

H.M. Hyde, *Carson: The Life of Sir Edward Carson, Lord Carson of Duncairn* (London, 1953).

A. Jackson, *Sir Edward Carson* (Dublin, 1993).

R. Jenkins, *Asquith* (London, 1964).

J. Kendle, *Walter Long, Ireland and the Union* (Toronto, 1992).

S. Koss, *Asquith* (London, 1976).

E. Lyttelton, *Alfred Lyttelton: An Account of his Life* (London, 1917).

R. Mackay, *Balfour: Intellectual Statesman* (Oxford, 1985).

E. Marjoribanks and I. Colvin, *Life of Lord Carson* (3 vols, London, 1932–6).

Lord Newton, *Lord Lansdowne: A Biography* (London, 1929).

H. Nicholson, *King George V* (London, 1952).

Sir C. Petrie, *Walter Long and his Times* (London, 1936).

S. Salvidge, *Salvidge of Liverpool: Behind the Political Scenes* (London, 1934).

A.T.Q. Stewart, *Edward Carson* (Dublin, 1981).

A.J.P. Taylor, *Beaverbrook* (London, 1972).

K. Young, *Arthur James Balfour* (London, 1963).

S. Zebel, *Balfour* (London, 1973).

SECONDARY

J.C. Beckett, *The Making of Modern Ireland, 1603–1923* (London, 1981).
I. Beckett (ed.), *The Army and the Curragh Incident* (London, 1986).
P. Bew, *Ideology and the Irish Question* (Oxford, 1996).
R. Blake, *The Conservative Party from Peel to Churchill* (London, 1970).
N. Blewett, *The Peers, the Parties and the People: The General Elections of 1910* (Oxford, 1972).
D.G. Boyce, *Englishmen and Irish Troubles: British Public Opinion and the Making of Irish Policy* (London, 1972).
D.G. Boyce, *Nationalism in Ireland* (London, 1982).
D.G. Boyce (ed.), *The Revolution in Ireland, 1879–1923* (London, 1988).
P. Buckland, *Irish Unionism: The Anglo-Irish and the New Ireland, 1885–1922* (Dublin, 1972).
P. Buckland, *Irish Unionism: Ulster Unionism and the Origins of Northern Ireland* (Dublin, 1972).
Lord Butler (ed.), *The Conservatives* (London, 1977).
J. Charmley, *A History of Conservative Politics, 1900–1996* (London, 1996).
F. Coetzee, *For Party and Country: Nationalism and the Dilemmas of Popular Conservatism in Edwardian England* (Oxford, 1990).
P. Collins (ed.), *Nationalism and Unionism: Conflict in Ireland, 1885–1921* (Belfast, 1994).
R. Colls and P. Dodd (eds), *Englishness: Politics and Culture, 1880–1920* (London, 1986).
A. Cooke and J. Vincent, *The Governing Passion: Cabinet Government and Party Politics in Britain, 1885–6* (Brighton, 1974).
M. Cowling, *The Impact of Labour, 1920–24* (Cambridge, 1971).
L. Curtis, *Coercion and Conciliation in Ireland, 1880–1892* (Oxford, 1963).
A.J. Davies, *We, the Nation; The Conservative Party and the Pursuit of Power* (London, 1995).
D. Dutton, *'His Majesty's Loyal Opposition': The Unionist Party in Opposition, 1905–1915* (Liverpool, 1992).
B. Evans and A. Taylor, *From Salisbury to Major: Continuity and Change in Conservative Politics* (Manchester, 1996).
J.D. Fair, *British Inter-party Conferences* (Oxford, 1980).
J. Fergusson, *The Curragh Incident* (London, 1964).
M. Fforde, *Conservatism and Collectivism, 1880–1914* (Edinburgh, 1990).
D. Fitzpatrick, *The Two Irelands, 1912–1939* (Oxford, 1998).
R.F. Foster, *Modern Ireland, 1600–1972* (London, 1988).
R.F. Foster, *Paddy and Mr Punch: Connections in Irish and English History* (London, 1993).
M. Francis and I. Zweiniger-Bargielowska (eds), *The Conservatives in British Society, 1880–1980* (Cardiff, 1996).
A. Gailey, *Ireland and the Death of Kindness: The Experience of Constructive Unionism, 1890–1905* (Cork, 1987).

T. Garvin, *Nationalist Revolutionaries in Ireland, 1858–1928* (Oxford, 1987).

P. Gibbon, *The Origins of Ulster Unionism: The Formation of Popular Protestant Politics and Ideology in Nineteenth Century Ireland* (Manchester, 1975).

I. Gilmour, *Inside Right: A Study of Conservatism* (London, 1977).

W.H. Greenleaf, *The British Political Tradition*, 4 vols (1983)

E.H.H. Green, *The Crisis of Conservatism: The Politics, Economics and Ideology of the British Conservative Party, 1880–1914* (London, 1995).

C. Hazelhurst, *Politicians at War, July 1914 to May 1915* (London, 1971).

T. Hennesey, *Dividing Ireland: World War One and Partition* (London, 1998).

K.T. Hoppen, *Ireland since 1800: Conflict and Conformity* (London, 1989).

A. Jackson, *The Ulster Party: Irish Unionists in the House of Commons, 1884–1911* (Oxford, 1989).

P. Jalland, *The Liberals and Ireland: The Ulster Question in British Politics to 1914* (Brighton, 1980).

R. Jenkins, *Mr Balfour's Poodle: Peers versus the People* (London, 1954).

R. Kee, *The Green Flag: The Bold Fenian Men* (London, 1972).

J. Kendle, *Ireland and the Federal solution: The Debate over the United Kingdom constitution, 1870–1921* (Montreal, 1989)

L. Kennedy, *Colonialism, Religion and Nationalism in Ireland* (Belfast, 1996)

P. Kennedy and A. Nicholls (eds), *Nationalist and Racialist Movements in Britain and Germany before 1914* (London, 1981).

D. Kiberd, *Inventing Ireland* (London, 1995).

S. Koss, *The Rise and Fall of the Political Press in Britain: The Twentieth Century* (London, 1984).

M. Laffan, *The Partition of Ireland, 1911–1925* (Dundalk, 1983).

M. Langan and M. Schwarz (eds), *Crisis in the British State, 1880–1930* (London, 1985).

S. Lawlor, *Britain and Ireland, 1914–1923* (Dublin, 1983).

J.J. Lee, *Ireland, 1912–85* (Cambridge, 1989).

G. Le May, *The Victorian Constitution: Conventions, Usages and Contingencies* (London, 1979).

B. Lenman, *The Eclipse of Parliament: Appearance and Reality in British Politics since 1914* (London, 1992).

J. Loughlin, *Gladstone, Home Rule and the Ulster Question, 1882–1893* (Dublin, 1986).

F.S.L. Lyons, *John Dillion: A Biography* (London, 1968).

F.S.L. Lyons, *Ireland Since the Famine* (London, 1971).

F.S.L. Lyons, *Culture and Anarchy in Ireland, 1890–1939* (Oxford, 1979).

R.B. McDowell, *British Conservatism, 1832–1914* (London, 1959).

N. Mansergh, *The Unresolved Question: The Anglo-Irish Settlement and its Undoing, 1912–1972* (London, 1991).

K.O. Morgan, *Consensus and Disunity: The Lloyd George Coalition Government, 1918–22* (Oxford, 1979).

B. Murray, *The Peoples Budget: Lloyd George and Liberal Politics* (Oxford, 1980).

R. Nisbet, *Conservatism* (Milton Keynes, 1986).

P. Norton and A. Aughey, *Conservatives and Conservatism* (London, 1981).

C.C. O'Brien, *States of Ireland* (London, 1972).
C.C. O'Brien, *Ancestral Voices: Religion and Nationalism in Ireland* (Dublin, 1994).
M. O'Callaghan, *British High Politics and a Nationalist Ireland: Criminality, Land and the Law under Forster and Balfour* (Cork, 1994).
A. O'Day (ed.), *The Edwardian Age* (London, 1979).
A. O'Day (ed.), *Reactions to Irish Nationalism* (London, 1987).
A. O'Day, *Irish Home Rule, 1867–1921* (Manchester, 1998).
F. O'Gorman, *British Conservatism: Conservative Thought from Burke to Thatcher* (London, 1986).
E. O'Halpin, *The Decline of the Union: British Government in Ireland, 1892–1920* (Dublin, 1987).
H. Pelling, *Social Geography of British Elections, 1885–1910* (London, 1967).
G. Phillips, *The Diehards: Aristocratic Society and Politics in Edwardian England* (Harvard, 1979).
M. Pugh, *The Tories and the People* (Oxford, 1985).
J. Ramsden, *The Age of Balfour and Baldwin* (London, 1978).
D. Read (ed.), *Edwardian England* (London, 1982).
R. Rempel, *Unionists Divided* (Newton Abbott, 1972).
P. Rowland, *The Last Liberal Government: Unfinished Business, 1911–1914* (London, 1971).
A.P. Ryan, *Mutiny at the Curragh* (London, 1956).
R.J. Scally, *The Origins of the Lloyd George Coalition: The Politics of Social Imperialism* (Princeton, 1975).
G.R. Searle, *The Quest for National Efficiency* (London, 1971).
G.R. Searle, *Corruption in British Politics, 1895–1930* (Oxford, 1987).
B. Semmel, *Imperialism and Social Reform: English Social-Imperial Thought 1895–1914* (Harvard, 1960).
C. Shannon, *Arthur Balfour and Ireland, 1874–1922* (Washington, 1988).
R. Shannon, *The Age of Salisbury, 1881–1902* (London, 1996).
D. Southgate (ed.), *The Conservative Leadership, 1832–1932* (London, 1974).
J. Smith, *The Taming of Democracy: The Conservative Party, 1880–1924* (Cardiff, 1997).
A.T.Q. Stewart, *The Ulster Crisis: Resistance to Home Rule, 1912–14* (London, 1967).
A.T.Q. Stewart, *The Narrow Ground: Aspects of Ulster, 1609–1969* (London, 1977).
A. Sykes, *Tariff Reform in British Politics, 1903–1913* (Oxford, 1979).
A. Sykes, *The Rise and Fall of British Liberalism* (London, 1997).
D. Tanner, *Political Change and the Labour Party, 1900–1918* (Cambridge, 1990).
J.A. Thompson and A. Mejia, *Edwardian Conservatism: Five Studies in Adaptation* (New York, 1988).
C. Townshend, *Political Violence in Ireland: Government and Resistance since 1848* (Oxford, 1983).
J. Turner, *British Politics and the Great War: Coalition and Conflict, 1915–1918* (Yale, 1992).
W.E. Vaughan (ed.), *A New History of Ireland, VI: Ireland Under the Union, 1870–1921* (Oxford, 1996).

B. Walker, *Dancing to History's Tune: History, Myth and Politics in Ireland* (Belfast, 1996).

P.J. Waller, *Democracy and Sectarianism: A Political and Social History of Liverpool* (Liverpool, 1981).

ARTICLES

N. Blewett, 'The Franchise in the United Kingdom, 1885–1918', *Past & Present*, xxxii (1965).

D.G. Boyce, 'British Conservative Opinion, the Ulster Question and the Partition of Ireland, 1912–1921', *Irish Historical Studies*, xi (1970).

P. Buckland, 'The Southern Irish Unionists, the Irish Question and British Politics, 1906–1914', *Irish Historical Studies*, xv (1967).

F. Coetzee, 'Pressure Groups, Tory Businessmen and the Aura of Political Corruption before the First World War', *Historical Journal*, xxix (1986).

I. D'Alton, 'Southern Irish Unionism: A Study of Cork Unionists, 1884–1914', *Transactions of the Royal Historical Society*, xxiii (1973).

T. Denman, '"The Red Livery of Shame": The Campaign against Army Recruitment in Ireland, 1899–1914', *Irish Historical Studies*, xxix (1994).

D. Dutton, 'The Unionist Party and Social Reform, 1906–1914', *Historical Journal*, xxiv (1981).

R. Fanning, 'The Unionist Party and Ireland, 1906–1910', *Irish Historical Studies*, xv (1966).

M. Foy, 'Ulster Unionist Propaganda against Home Rule, 1912–1914', *History-Ireland*, iv, 1 (1996).

A. Gailey, 'King Carson: An Essay on the Invention of Leadership', *Irish Historical Studies*, xxx (1996).

H. Glickman, 'The Toryness of English Conservatism', *Journal of British Studies*, I (1961).

E.H.H. Green, 'Radical Conservatism: The Electoral Genesis of Tariff Reform', *Historical Journal*, xxviii (1985).

E.H.H. Green, 'The Strange Death of Tory England', *Twentieth Century British History*, ii (1991).

A. Jackson, 'Unionist Myths, 1912–1985', *Past and Present*, cxxxiv (1992).

P. Jalland, 'United Kingdom Devolution 1910–14: Political Panacea or Tactical Diversion', *English Historical Review*, xivc (1979).

P. Jalland and J. Stubbs, 'The Irish Question after the outbreak of war in 1914: some unfinished business', *English Historical Review*, xvic (1981).

J. Kendle, 'The Round Table Movement and "Home Rule all Round"', *Historical Journal*, xi (1968).

R. Murphy, 'Faction and the Conservative Party and the Home Rule Bill', *History*, lxxi (1986).

G. Phillips, 'The "Diehards" and the Myth of the "Backwoodsmen"', *Journal of British Studies*, xvi (1977).

G. Phillips, 'Lord Willoughby de Broke and the Politics of Radical Toryism', *Journal of British Studics*, xx (1980).

R. Rempel, 'Lord Hugh Cecil's Parliamentary Career 1900–1914: Promise Unfulfilled', *Journal of British Studies*, xi (1972).

J. Ridley, 'The Unionist Social Reform Committee, 1911–1914: Wets before the Deluge', *Historical Journal*, xxx (1987).

J. Ridley, 'The Unionist Opposition and the House of Lords', *Parliamentary History*, xi (1992).

W. Rodner, 'Leaguers, Covenanters, Moderates: British Support for Ulster, 1913–14', *Eire-Ireland*, xvii (1982).

J. Smith, 'Bluff, Bluster and Brinkmanship: Andrew Bonar Law and the Third Home Rule Bill', *Historical Journal*, xxxvi (1993).

J. Smith, '"Paralysing the Arm": The Unionists and the Army Annual Act, 1911–1914', *Parliamentary History*, xv, 2 (1996).

D. Southern, 'Lord Newton, the Conservative Peers and the Parliament Act of 1911', *English Historical Review*, xivc (1981).

J. Stubbs, 'The Unionists and Ireland, 1914–1918', *Historical Journal*, xxxiii (1990).

A. Sykes, 'The Radical Right and the Crisis of Conservatism before the First World War', *Historical Journal*, xxvi (1983).

C.C. Weston, 'The Liberal Leadership and the Lords Veto, 1907–1910', *Historical Journal*, xi (1977).

C.C. Weston, 'Salisbury and the Lords, 1868–1895', *Historical Journal*, xxv (1982).

C.C. Weston, 'Lord Selborne, Bonar Law and the "Tory Revolt"', in R. Davies (ed.), *The Lords of Parliament: Studies, 1714–1914* (1995).

THESES

W.R. Brockington, 'The Unionist Party and the Third Home Rule Bill, 1912–1914', PhD (South Carolina, 1972).

M. Foy, 'The Ulster Volunteer Force: Its Domestic Development and Political Importance in the period 1913–1920', PhD (Belfast, 1986).

R. Murphy, 'Walter Long and the Conservative Party in Parliament; 1905–1921', PhD (Bristol, 1984).

J. Ridley, 'Leadership and Management in the Conservative Party in Parliament, 1906–1914', DPhil (Oxford, 1985).

W. Rodner, 'Lord Hugh Cecil and the Unionist Opposition to the Third Irish Home Rule Bill', PhD (Penn State, 1977).

Index